FREE

Free Study Tips DVD

In addition to the tips and content in this guide, we have created a FREE DVD with helpful study tips to further assist your exam preparation. **This FREE Study Tips DVD provides you with top-notch tips to conquer your exam and reach your goals.**

Our simple request in exchange for the strategy-packed DVD is that you email us your feedback about our study guide. We would love to hear what you thought about the guide, and we welcome any and all feedback—positive, negative, or neutral. It is our #1 goal to provide you with top-quality products and customer service.

To receive your **FREE Study Tips DVD**, email freedvd@apexprep.com. Please put "FREE DVD" in the subject line and put the following in the email:

a. The name of the study guide you purchased.

b. Your rating of the study guide on a scale of 1-5, with 5 being the highest score.

c. Any thoughts or feedback about your study guide.

d. Your first and last name and your mailing address, so we know where to send your free DVD!

Thank you!

CBEST Prep Book 2019 & 2020

CBEST Test Preparation 2019 & 2020 and Practice Book for the California Basic Educational Skills Test [Includes Detailed Answer Explanations]

APEX Test Prep

Table of Contents

Test Taking Strategies

1. Reading the Whole Question

A popular assumption in Western culture is the idea that we don't have enough time for anything. We speed while driving to work, we want to read an assignment for class as quickly as possible, or we want the line in the supermarket to dwindle faster. However, speeding through such events robs us from being able to thoroughly appreciate and understand what's happening around us. While taking a timed test, the feeling one might have while reading a question is to find the correct answer as quickly as possible. Although pace is important, don't let it deter you from reading the whole question. Test writers know how to subtly change a test question toward the end in various ways, such as adding a negative or changing focus. If the question has a passage, carefully read the whole passage as well before moving on to the questions. This will help you process the information in the passage rather than worrying about the questions you've just read and where to find them. A thorough understanding of the passage or question is an important way for test takers to be able to succeed on an exam.

2. Examining Every Answer Choice

Let's say we're at the market buying apples. The first apple we see on top of the heap may *look* like the best apple, but if we turn it over we can see bruising on the skin. We must examine several apples before deciding which apple is the best. Finding the correct answer choice is like finding the best apple. Although it's tempting to choose an answer that seems correct at first without reading the others, it's important to read each answer choice thoroughly before making a final decision on the answer. The aim of a test writer might be to get as close as possible to the correct answer, so watch out for subtle words that may indicate an answer is incorrect. Once the correct answer choice is selected, read the question again and the answer in response to make sure all your bases are covered.

3. Eliminating Wrong Answer Choices

Sometimes we become paralyzed when we are confronted with too many choices. Which frozen yogurt flavor is the tastiest? Which pair of shoes look the best with this outfit? What type of car will fill my needs as a consumer? If you are unsure of which answer would be the best to choose, it may help to use process of elimination. We use "filtering" all the time on sites such as eBay® or Craigslist® to eliminate the ads that are not right for us. We can do the same thing on an exam. Process of elimination is crossing out the answer choices we know for sure are wrong and leaving the ones that might be correct. It may help to cover up the incorrect answer choice. Covering incorrect choices is a psychological act that alleviates stress due to the brain being exposed to a smaller amount of information. Choosing between two answer choices is much easier than choosing between all of them, and you have a better chance of selecting the correct answer if you have less to focus on.

4. Sticking to the World of the Question

When we are attempting to answer questions, our minds will often wander away from the question and what it is asking. We begin to see answer choices that are true in the real world instead of true in the world of the question. It may be helpful to think of each test question as its own little world. This world may be different from ours. This world may know as a truth that the chicken came before the egg or may assert that two plus two equals five. Remember that, no matter what hypothetical nonsense may be in the question, assume it to be true. If the question states that the chicken came before the egg, then choose your answer based on that truth. Sticking to the world of the question means placing all of our biases and assumptions aside and relying on the question to guide us to the correct answer. If we are simply looking for answers that are correct based on our own judgment, then we may choose incorrectly. Remember an answer that is true does not necessarily answer the question.

5. Key Words

If you come across a complex test question that you have to read over and over again, try pulling out some key words from the question in order to understand what exactly it is asking. Key words may be words that surround the question, such as *main idea, analogous, parallel, resembles, structured,* or *defines*. The question may be asking for the main idea, or it may be asking you to define something. Deconstructing the sentence may also be helpful in making the question simpler before trying to answer it. This means taking the sentence apart and obtaining meaning in pieces, or separating the question from the foundation of the question. For example, let's look at this question:

> Given the author's description of the content of paleontology in the first paragraph, which of the following is most parallel to what it taught?

The question asks which one of the answers most *parallels* the following information: The *description* of paleontology in the first paragraph. The first step would be to see *how* paleontology is described in the first paragraph. Then, we would find an answer choice that parallels that description. The question seems complex at first, but after we deconstruct it, the answer becomes much more attainable.

6. Subtle Negatives

Negative words in question stems will be words such as *not, but, neither,* or *except*. Test writers often use these words in order to trick unsuspecting test takers into selecting the wrong answer—or, at least, to test their reading comprehension of the question. Many exams will feature the negative words in all caps (*which of the following is NOT an example*), but some questions will add the negative word seamlessly into the sentence. The following is an example of a subtle negative used in a question stem:

> According to the passage, which of the following is *not* considered to be an example of paleontology?

If we rush through the exam, we might skip that tiny word, *not*, inside the question, and choose an answer that is opposite of the correct choice. Again, it's important to read the question fully, and double check for any words that may negate the statement in any way.

7. Spotting the Hedges

The word "hedging" refers to language that remains vague or avoids absolute terminology. Absolute terminology consists of words like *always, never, all, every, just, only, none,* and *must*. Hedging refers to words like *seem, tend, might, most, some, sometimes, perhaps, possibly, probability,* and *often*. In some cases, we want to choose answer choices that use hedging and avoid answer choices that use absolute terminology. It's important to pay attention to what subject you are on and adjust your response accordingly.

8. Restating to Understand

Every now and then we come across questions that we don't understand. The language may be too complex, or the question is structured in a way that is meant to confuse the test taker. When you come across a question like this, it may be worth your time to rewrite or restate the question in your own words in order to understand it better. For example, let's look at the following complicated question:

> Which of the following words, if substituted for the word *parochial* in the first paragraph, would LEAST change the meaning of the sentence?

Let's restate the question in order to understand it better. We know that they want the word *parochial* replaced. We also know that this new word would "least" or "not" change the meaning of the sentence. Now let's try the sentence again:

> Which word could we replace with *parochial,* and it would not change the meaning?

Restating it this way, we see that the question is asking for a synonym. Now, let's restate the question so we can answer it better:

> Which word is a synonym for the word *parochial*?

Before we even look at the answer choices, we have a simpler, restated version of a complicated question.

9. Predicting the Answer

After you read the question, try predicting the answer *before* reading the answer choices. By formulating an answer in your mind, you will be less likely to be distracted by any wrong answer choices. Using predictions will also help you feel more confident in the answer choice you select. Once you've chosen your answer, go back and reread the question and answer choices to make sure you have the best fit. If you have no idea what the answer may be for a particular question, forego using this strategy.

10. Avoiding Patterns

One popular myth in grade school relating to standardized testing is that test writers will often put multiple-choice answers in patterns. A runoff example of this kind of thinking is that the most common answer choice is "C," with "B" following close behind. Or, some will advocate certain made-up word patterns that simply do not exist. Test writers do not arrange their correct answer choices in any kind of pattern; their choices are randomized. There may even be times where the correct answer choice will be the same letter for two or three questions in a row, but we have no way of knowing when or if this might happen. Instead of trying to figure out what choice the test writer probably set as being correct, focus on what the *best answer choice* would be out of the answers you are presented with. Use the tips above, general knowledge, and reading comprehension skills in order to best answer the question, rather than looking for patterns that do not exist.

FREE DVD OFFER

Achieving a high score on your exam depends not only on understanding the content, but also on understanding how to apply your knowledge and your command of test taking strategies. **Because your success is our primary goal, we offer a FREE Study Tips DVD, which provides top-notch test taking strategies to help you optimize your testing experience.**

Our simple request in exchange for the strategy-packed DVD packed is that you email us your feedback about our study guide.

To receive your **FREE Study Tips DVD**, email freedvd@apexprep.com. Please put "FREE DVD" in the subject line and put the following in the email:

a. The name of the study guide you purchased.

b. Your rating of the study guide on a scale of 1-5, with 5 being the highest score.

c. Any thoughts or feedback about your study guide.

d. Your first and last name and your mailing address, so we know where to send your free DVD!

Introduction to the CBEST

Function of the Test

The California Basic Educational Skills Test™ (CBEST) is one of California's Educator Credentialing Assessments developed by California's government as a way for prospective educators to demonstrate their proficiency in reading, writing, and mathematics. The test is one of the established ways that candidates applying for their first California teaching credential or for admission to most teacher preparation and credentialing programs, or seeking employment in a school district in California can meet the California Basic Education Skills requirement. Nevada also uses the CBEST in their licensing and hiring process for educators. Rather than testing the candidate's ability to teach the various topics on the exam, the CBEST assesses the test taker's skills and knowledge in the three domains.

Test Administration

The computer-based version of the CBEST is administered at Pearson VUE testing centers year-round by appointment, Monday through Saturday, excluding some holidays. There is also a paper-based version, but the availability to take this version is much more limited. It is typically offered around five times per school year on specific dates. Test takers may register for one, two, or all three sections of the CBEST for any given testing appointment. Individuals who fail to pass the CBEST, or one of its sections, are required to wait 45 days to retake the computer-based exam, or they may retake the paper-based exam on any of the subsequent paper-administered test dates.

Alternative testing arrangements can be arranged with prior approval for test takers with documented disabilities and nursing mothers. Documentations must be submitted along with an Alternative Testing Arrangements Request Form prior to the candidate's testing date. There are also accommodations available to all test takers that do not require preapproval. For example, all CBEST test sites are wheelchair-accessible. Enlarged font is also available along with a variety of comfort aids. Test takers are also permitted to take breaks to use the restroom, have a snack, take medication, etc., although this time will be deducted from the allotted testing time.

Test Format

There are three separate sections of the CBEST exam: Reading, Mathematics, and Writing. At a given CBEST testing appointment, test takers may opt to take one, two, or all three sections of the test. Testing sessions are four hours regardless of how many sections are attempted. The Reading section contains passages, tables, and graphs along with 50 multiple-choice questions pertaining to the passages and graphics. The Mathematics section also contains 50 multiple-choice questions. The questions address a variety of math topics such as estimation, measurement, computations, algebra, problem solving, geometry, and data interpretation. A calculator is not permitted. The Writing section is composed of two essays. In one of the essays, candidates analyze and respond to a given situation or statement, while the other requires candidates to write about a personal experience.

The table below displays information about the three sections of the CBEST exam:

Section	Subsection	Approximate # of Questions
Reading	Critical Analysis and Evaluation	20
	Comprehension and Research Skills	30
Mathematics	Estimation, Measurement, and Statistical Principles	15
	Computation and Problem Solving	17
	Numerical and Graphic Relationships	17
Writing	Essays	2

Scoring

Upon completion of the computer-based exam, preliminary results for the Reading and Mathematics sections are reported on the screen. Official results—including results for the Writing section—are released within two weeks. They will be emailed to the test taker, if this option was selected, or available on the test taker's account. Score reports show test takers' passing status and their performance on the total test and each section, as well as their performance on the various skills areas for each section on the CBEST. The scores for the Reading and Mathematics sections are calculated from the number of correct responses given. There is no penalty for guesses or incorrect responses. These raw scores are then converted to a scaled score from 20-80. The two essays are reviewed by two trained educators, and scored independently on a scale from 1 to 4 by each of them. These scores are then summed and scaled from 20-80 as well. Essays that fail to meet the passing score are critiqued further and the test taker is provided written feedback.

There are two ways to pass the CBEST: either a scaled score of 41 or higher must be earned on each section, or a scaled score of at least 37 must be earned on each section with a total scaled score of at least 123. The total score for test takers who retake all or part of the exam is calculated from their highest earned scores. The passing rate for the CBEST is usually between 70-80%. Of the three sections, the Writing section has the lowest passing rate, hovering around 70%.

Reading

Critical Analysis and Evaluation

Comparing Ideas Presented in Different Sections of a Reading Selection

In order to better comprehend more complex texts, readers strive to draw connections between ideas or events in a text. Authors often have a main idea or argument that is supported by ideas, facts, or expert opinion. These relationships that are built into writing can take on several different forms.

Depending on the main argument of an informational text, authors may choose to employ a variety of relationship techniques. But before relationships can be developed in writing, the author needs to get organized. What is the main idea or argument? How does the author plan to support that idea? Once the author has a clear picture of what they would like to focus on, they need to build transitions from one idea to the next. Learning the importance of transitioning from one sentence to another, from one paragraph to another, and from one idea to another will not only strengthen the validity of the writing but will also enhance the reader's comprehension. In other words, by making writing more fluid and connected, authors facilitate a reader's understanding and enable a reader to follow the ideas presented in the text.

When transitioning from one sentence to another, authors employ specific connecting words that emphasize the relationships between sentences. Taking the time to consider these transitional words can make the difference between a choppy or confusing paragraph and a well-written one. Consider the following:

> When I was growing up, the neighborhood had kids at every turn. I lived in a townhouse then. In my adult years, I live in a quiet suburb with hardly any children.
>
> When I was growing up, I lived in a neighborhood where there were kids at every turn. In contrast to my younger years, my adult years are unfolding in a quiet suburb with hardly any children.

Notice how the first example, although written coherently, employs sentences that are somehow disjointed. The transition between the statements is far from smooth. However, in the second example, the simple addition of the phrase "in contrast" connects the two parts of the writer's life and allows the reader to fully comprehend the text.

Learning to transition from sentence to sentence, from paragraph to paragraph, and throughout any piece of writing is an essential skill that helps authors to demonstrate similarities, differences, and relationships, and it helps readers to strengthen comprehension.

The author's main idea should be supported by the details, examples, and thoughts provided by the author. These details demonstrate specific examples that support the main idea, and help the reader follow the logic intended by the author. For example, suppose a passage's main idea is "*Schools should be privatized.*" The passage supports this main idea with this detail: "*Students who attend private schools perform better.*" The main idea is further supported by this statistical detail: "*65% of students with the highest national GPAs are from private schools.*"

Like the connections between events, these relationships may be clearly stated, or they may be implied. The reader can infer these relationships by analyzing signal words and the stated or implied connections.

Below is a list of signal words or clues that can key readers into the nature of relationships between ideas and events in a text:

- **Time order,** or **temporal relationships,** can be inferred through words like *before* and *after,* or *next, then, first, lastly,* which signal that events occur one after the other.
- The words like *and, also, like* signal a **comparison** of the similarities between ideas
- Words like *but, however* signal a **contrast** of the differences between ideas.
- Words like *because, so, therefore* signal that one event or circumstance is the cause of another in **cause and effect relationships**.
- Ideas or objects are described by their location with respect to each other (called **spatial relationships**) by using words such as *behind* and *to the right.*

Identifying the Reasons, Examples, Details, or Facts That Support the Author's Main Idea

The **topic** of a text is the general subject matter. Text topics can usually be expressed in one word, or a few words at most. Additionally, readers should ask themselves what point the author is trying to make. This point is the **main idea** of the text—the one thing the author wants readers to know about the topic. Once the author has established the main idea, he or she will support the main idea with supporting details. **Supporting details** are evidence that support the main idea and include personal testimonies, examples, or statistics.

One analogy for these components and their relationships is that a text is like a well-designed house. The topic is the roof, covering all rooms. The main idea is the frame. The supporting details are the various rooms. To identify the topic of a text, readers can ask themselves what or who the author is writing about in the paragraph. To locate the main idea, readers can ask themselves what one idea the author wants readers to know about the topic. To identify supporting details, readers can put the main idea into question form and ask, "what does the author use to prove or explain their main idea?"

Let's look at an example. An author is writing an essay about the Amazon rainforest and trying to convince the audience that more funding should go into protecting the area from deforestation. The author makes the argument stronger by including evidence of the benefits of the rainforest: it provides habitats to a variety of species, it provides much of the earth's oxygen which in turn cleans the atmosphere, and it is the home to medicinal plants that useful against some of the world's deadliest diseases. Here is an outline of the essay looking at topic, main idea, and supporting details:

- Topic: Amazon rainforest
- Main Idea: The Amazon rainforest should receive more funding to protect it from deforestation.
- Supporting Details:
    - It provides habitats to a variety of species
    - It provides much of the earth's oxygen which in turn cleans the atmosphere
    - It is home to medicinal plants that are useful against some of the deadliest diseases.

Notice that the topic of the essay is listed in a few key words: "Amazon rainforest." The main idea tells us what about the topic is important: that the topic should be funded to prevent deforestation. Finally, the supporting details are what author relies on to convince the audience to act or to believe in the truth of the main idea.

Making Predictions and Inferences

One technique authors often use to make their fictional stories more interesting is not giving away too much information by providing hints and description. It is then up to the reader to draw a conclusion about the author's meaning by connecting textual clues with the reader's own pre-existing experiences and knowledge. Drawing conclusions is important as a reading strategy for understanding what is occurring in a text. Rather than directly stating who, what, where, when, or why, authors often describe story elements. Then, readers must draw conclusions to understand significant story components. As they go through a text, readers can think about the setting, characters, plot, problem, and solution; whether the author provided any clues for consideration; and combine any story clues with their existing knowledge and experiences to draw conclusions about what occurs in the text.

Making Predictions

Before and during reading, readers can apply the reading strategy of making predictions about what they think may happen next. For example, what plot and character developments will occur in fiction? What points will the author discuss in nonfiction? Making predictions about portions of text they have not yet read prepares readers mentally for reading, and also gives them a purpose for reading. To inform and make predictions about text, the reader can do the following:

- Consider the title of the text and what it implies
- Look at the cover of the book
- Look at any illustrations or diagrams for additional visual information
- Analyze the structure of the text
- Apply outside experience and knowledge to the text

Readers may adjust their predictions as they read. Reader predictions may or may not come true in text.

Making Inferences

Authors describe settings, characters, character emotions, and events. Readers must **infer** to understand text fully. Inferring enables readers to figure out meanings of unfamiliar words, make predictions about upcoming text, draw conclusions, and reflect on reading. Readers can infer about text before, during, and after reading. In everyday life, we use sensory information to infer. Readers can do the same with text. When authors do not answer all reader questions, readers must infer by saying "I think....This could be....This is because....Maybe....This means....I guess..." etc. Looking at illustrations, considering characters' behaviors, and asking questions during reading facilitate inference. Taking clues from text and connecting text to prior knowledge help to draw conclusions. Readers can infer word meanings, settings, reasons for occurrences, character emotions, pronoun referents, author messages, and answers to questions unstated in text. To practice inference, students can read sentences written/selected by the instructor, discuss the setting and character, draw conclusions, and make predictions.

Making inferences and drawing conclusions involve skills that are quite similar: both require readers to fill in information the author has omitted. Authors may omit information as a technique for inducing readers to discover the outcomes themselves; or they may consider certain information unimportant; or they may assume their reading audience already knows certain information. To make an inference or draw a conclusion about text, readers should observe all facts and arguments the author has presented and consider what they already know from their own personal experiences. Reading students taking multiple-choice tests that refer to text passages can determine correct and incorrect choices based on the information in the passage. For example, from a text passage describing an individual's signs of anxiety while unloading groceries and nervously clutching their wallet at a grocery store checkout, readers can infer or conclude that the individual may not have enough money to pay for everything.

Identifying the Author's Attitude or Viewpoint

The author's attitude toward a certain person or idea, or his or her purpose, may not always be stated. While it may seem impossible to know exactly what the author felt toward their subject, there are clues to indicate the emotion, or lack thereof, of the author. Clues like word choice or style will alert readers to the author's attitude. Some possible words that name the author's attitude are listed below:

- Admiring
- Angry
- Critical
- Defensive
- Enthusiastic
- Humorous
- Moralizing
- Neutral
- Objective
- Patriotic
- Persuasive
- Playful
- Sentimental
- Serious
- Supportive
- Sympathetic
- Unsupportive

An author's **tone** is the author's attitude toward their subject and is usually indicated by word choice. If an author's attitude toward their subject is one of disdain, the author will show the subject in a negative light, using deflating words or words that are negatively charged. If an author's attitude toward their subject is one of praise, the author will use agreeable words and show the subject in a positive light. If an author takes a neutral tone towards their subject, their words will be neutral as well, and they probably will show all sides of their subject, not just the negative or positive side.

Style is another indication of the author's attitude and includes aspects such as sentence structure, type of language, and formatting. Sentence structure is how a sentence is put together. Sometimes, short, choppy sentences will indicate a certain tone given the surrounding context, while longer sentences may serve to create a buffer to avoid being too harsh, or may be used to explain additional information. Style may also include formal or informal language. Using formal language to talk about a subject may indicate a level of respect. Using informal language may be used to create an atmosphere of friendliness or familiarity with a subject. Again, it depends on the surrounding context whether or not language is used in a negative or positive way. Style may also include formatting, such as determining the length of paragraphs or figuring out how to address the reader at the very beginning of the text.

The following is a passage from *The Florentine Painters of the Renaissance* by Bernhard Berenson. Following the passage is a question stem regarding the author's attitude toward their subject:

> Let us look now at an even greater triumph of movement than the Nudes, Pollaiuolo's "Hercules Strangling Antæus." As you realise the suction of Hercules' grip on the earth, the swelling of his calves with the pressure that falls on them, the violent throwing back of his chest, the stifling force of his embrace; as you realise the supreme effort of Antæus, with one hand crushing down upon the head and the other tearing at the arm of Hercules, you feel as if a fountain of energy had

sprung up under your feet and were playing through your veins. I cannot refrain from mentioning still another masterpiece, this time not only of movement, but of tactile values and personal beauty as well—Pollaiuolo's "David" at Berlin. The young warrior has sped his stone, cut off the giant's head, and now he strides over it, his graceful, slender figure still vibrating with the rapidity of his triumph, expectant, as if fearing the ease of it. What lightness, what buoyancy we feel as we realise the movement of this wonderful youth!

Which one of the following best captures the author's attitude toward the paintings depicted in the passage?

a. Neutrality towards the subject in this passage.
b. Disdain for the violence found in the paintings.
c. Excitement for the physical beauty found within the paintings.
d. Passion for the movement and energy of the paintings.
e. Disappointment in the quality of the paintings.

Choice *D* is the best answer. We know that the author feels positively about the subject because of the word choice. Berenson uses words and phrases like "supreme," "fountain of energy," "graceful," "figure still vibrating," "lightness," "buoyancy," and "wonderful youth." Notice also the exclamation mark at the end of the paragraph. These words and style depict an author full of passion, especially for the movement and energy found within the paintings.

Choice *A* is incorrect because the author is biased towards the subject due to the energy he writes with—he calls the movement in the paintings "wonderful" and by the other word choices and phrases, readers can tell that this is not an objective analysis of these paintings. For this reason, Choice *E* is clearly wrong; the author is impressed with the paintings, not disappointed. Choice *B* is incorrect because, although the author does mention the "violence" in the stance of Hercules, he does not exude disdain towards this. Choice *C* is incorrect. There is excitement in the author's tone, and some of this excitement is directed towards the paintings' physical beauty. However, this is not the *best* answer choice. Choice *D* is more accurate when stating the passion is for the movement and energy of the paintings, of which physical beauty is included.

Determining Whether Facts or Ideas are Relevant to an Argument

Evidence used in arguments must be credible and valid, such as that from peer-reviewed scholarly journals. Peer-reviewed sources are sources that have been reviewed by other experts in the field. must also be relevant by pertaining to the argument posed and being up-to-date, especially those within the science or technology fields.

For example, let's consider a passage that discusses pesticides and the collapse of bees. An argument without relevant examples would look like this:

> With the use of the world's most popular pesticides, bees are becoming extinct. This is also causing ecological devastation. We must do something soon about the bee population, or else we will chase bees to extinction and lose valuable resources as a result.

Here is the same argument with examples. The added examples are in italics:

> With the use of the world's most popular pesticides, bees are becoming extinct. *Beekeepers have reported losing 55 to 95 percent of their colony in just two short years due to toxic poisoning.* This is also causing ecological devastation. *Bees are known for pollinating more than two-thirds of the world's most essential crops.* We must do something soon about the bee population, or else we will chase bees to extinction and lose valuable resources as a result.

Adding examples to the above argument brings life to the bees—they are living, dying, pollinating—and readers feel more compelled to act as a result of adding relevant examples to the argument.

When authors want to strengthen the support for an argument, evidence-based data in the form of statistics or concrete examples can be used. Statistics and examples are often accompanied by detailed explanations to help increase the audience's understanding and shape their ideas. Expert opinions are another way to strengthen an argument. But all this effort toward supporting a given argument does not necessarily make the argument absolute. After all, the word "argument" implies that there is more than one way to think about the subject. Arguments are meant to be challenged, questioned, and analyzed.

Authors will generally use one of two argument models: deductive or inductive. **Deductive arguments** require two general statements to support the argument. **Inductive arguments** employ specific data, examples, or facts to support the argument.

Deductive	**Inductive**
All fruits contain seeds. Tomatoes contain seeds. Therefore, tomatoes are fruits.	9 out of 10 dentists prefer soft-bristled toothbrushes. Therefore, soft-bristled toothbrushes are the best type of toothbrush for optimal dental health.

No matter what evidence is presented, readers should still challenge the argument. In any text, readers are encouraged to ask specific questions to evaluate the overall validity of the argument. Some important points to consider include:

- Has the author employed logic in the argument?
- Is the argument clearly explained?
- Is the argument sufficiently supported?
- Do the examples and statistics used actually pertain to the author's opinion or argument?
- Who conducted the research, and for what purpose?
- Is the supporting data qualitative, quantitative, or a mixture of both?
- Is the presented data representative of the typical cross-section of society or of the phenomenon being discussed?
- Does the author present any bias?
- Has the author overlooked anything that should be explored to form a well-rounded argument?

Although informational writing should be written objectively, such writing still constitutes the author's particular point of view or belief about a given subject. The author's main idea will likely be backed up with reasons, evidence, and supporting details, but it is important for the audience to question the main idea and evaluate the presented evidence. Although the author's ideas and shared details drive the overall argument, readers should feel compelled to explore the topic further, assess the evidence, and determine whether they agree with the overall message. Authors present the argument in order to convince their readers, but readers must strive to evaluate and assess the information to arrive at an informed opinion of the subject matter.

Recognizing Statements That Strengthen or Weaken Arguments

In the CBEST Reading Section, there will likely be questions that ask the test taker about evidence or principles expressed in the selection that pertain to the argument. Test takers may need to determine if the ideas or statements strengthen or weaken the argument, and if they support the claims or conclusions. Some of the questions on the exam will require that test takers use new information from the question stem and apply to a claim in the passage. These questions typically ask which of the statements in the answer choices best strengthens or weakens a given claim. It's important to read the passage a few times first in order to understand the original claim's stance. Below is a list of questions that might fall under the these strengthening and weakening question stems:

- Which of the following, if true, best strengthens the author's claim?
- Which of the following, if true, most weakens the author's claim?
- Which of the following, if true, best supports the author's argument that says . . .?
- Which of the following, if true, most undermines the author's claim that says . . .?

The questions of this type will contain a synonym of the word "strengthens" or "weakens," such as "bolsters," "supports," or "undermines," and will also display the statement "if true." The latter is to make sure the test taker does not question the validity of the information in a real-world context. Everything in the passage or in the question stem will be assumed to be true unless otherwise stated or put into question by the stem. The following is an example of a strengthening question:

For elementary-age students, the biggest sports-related injuries are concussions incurred while playing soccer. The popular assumption is that football is more prone to causing concussions, but this is not the case for this age group. I think it would greatly benefit our school if we required our soccer players to wear helmets.

Which of the following, if true, best strengthens the author's claim above?

a. Concussions are not life-threatening, so students should not be required to wear helmets during soccer games.
b. Major concussions can limit a student's ability to read, write, and focus on schoolwork or any other work that demands mental attention.
c. The school board will give a monetary incentive to any school sports program that adopts helmets.
d. Forcing soccer players to wear helmets would be humiliating if they were playing a team that wasn't required to wear helmets.
e. We should get rid of soccer altogether since it causes elementary-age students the most concussions out of any sport.

Choice *C* is the best answer because it strengthens the author's claim by presenting an even stronger reason for requiring soccer players to wear helmets. If we as readers know that there is another advantage to accepting the author's claim that players should wear helmets besides preventing concussions, then the claim is strengthened.

Choice *A* is incorrect because it states that concussions are not life-threatening. This logic does not help the argument in question, that the school would benefit from requiring students to wear helmets.

Choice *B* is tricky because it builds upon a premise in the argument. However, the author's claim is not convincing us that concussions are dangerous. The author's claim is that the school would greatly benefit from requiring players to wear helmets during soccer. This choice is close, but it is not the best choice.

Choice *D* also goes against the argument in question—the argument is that requiring soccer players to wear helmets would benefit the school, and Choice *D* gives reason *not* to require soccer players to wear helmets. This choice weakens the claim.

Choice *E* goes beyond the argument. This choice doesn't strengthen the claim; it provides another claim altogether. This choice is incorrect.

In the above example of a strengthening question, we see which new information (answer choices) strengthens the claim presented in the passage. Let's take a look at a weakening question:

Last Sunday at the Lincolnville picnic, the town ate every single one of my mom's chocolate brownies. My mom makes the best dessert in Lincolnville.

Which of the following, if true, most undermines the author's claim above?

a. My mom went to cooking school and has her own television show dedicated to dessert recipes.
b. My mom also brought potato salad to the picnic, but no one ate it.
c. There were 250 people at the town picnic.
d. My mom won the town award for "tastiest treats."
e. Chocolate brownies were the only dessert brought to the picnic.

This is a basic form of a weakening question. The question stem has a premise (the town ate every single one of my mom's chocolate brownies) and a conclusion (my mom makes the best dessert in Lincolnville). In strengthening and weakening questions, it's important to look for a bridge between the premise and conclusion that will either hurt or help the conclusion. Choice *E* is the best answer choice because it most undermines, or weakens, the author's conclusion that the mom makes the best dessert in Lincolnville. If the speaker's only proof that the mom makes the best dessert in Lincolnville is that the town ate all the brownies, then the fact that brownies were the *only* dessert makes us think the town ate the brownies because that was the only option, not because they were the best dessert.

Choices *A* and *D* serve to strengthen the claim, not to weaken it. Choice *B* does not weaken or strengthen the claim, because the claim has to do with desserts, and this answer choice is about potato salad. Choice *C* is incorrect because we don't know how big the town is to make a judgment on whether 250 people is an adequate representation of the community.

Again, most strengthening and weakening questions will provide some sort of gap between its premise and conclusion. The new information will make that gap stronger, weaken the gap, or be irrelevant to the claim altogether. Try not to get lost in the wording of the new information; rather, plug the new information in the passage and see how the new information works—that is, does it strengthen the claim or weaken the claim?

Persuasive Techniques Used By an Author

When authors write text for the purpose of persuading others to agree with them, they assume a position with the subject matter about which they are writing. Rather than presenting information objectively, the author treats the subject matter subjectively so that the information presented supports his or her position. In their argumentation, the author presents information that refutes or weakens opposing positions. Another technique authors use in persuasive writing is to anticipate arguments against the position. When students learn to read subjectively, they gain experience with the concept of persuasion in writing, and learn to identify positions taken by authors. This enhances their reading comprehension and develops their skills for identifying pro and con arguments and biases. Students should challenge the statements and opinions presented in a text by fully analyzing the argument or opinion stated and evaluating the evidence used by the author to support his or her stance.

There are five main parts of the classical argument that writers employ in a well-designed stance:

- Introduction: In the introduction to a classical argument, the author establishes goodwill and rapport with the reading audience, warms up the readers, and states the thesis or general theme of the argument.
- Narration: In the narration portion, the author gives a summary of pertinent background information, informs the readers of anything they need to know regarding the circumstances and environment surrounding and/or stimulating the argument, and establishes what is at risk or the stakes in the issue or topic. Literature reviews are common examples of narrations in academic writing.
- Confirmation: The confirmation states all claims supporting the thesis and furnishes evidence for each claim, arranging this material in logical order—e.g. from most obvious to most subtle or strongest to weakest.
- Refutation and Concession: The refutation and concession discuss opposing views and anticipate reader objections without weakening the thesis, yet permitting as many oppositions as possible.
- Summation: The summation strengthens the argument while summarizing it, supplying a strong conclusion and showing readers the superiority of the author's solution.

Introduction

A classical argument's introduction must pique reader interest, get readers to perceive the author as a writer, and establish the author's position. Shocking statistics, new ways of restating issues, or quotations or anecdotes focusing the text can pique reader interest. Personal statements, parallel instances, or analogies can also begin introductions—so can bold thesis statements if the author believes readers will agree. Word choice is also important for establishing author image with readers.

The introduction should typically narrow down to a clear, sound thesis statement. If readers cannot locate one sentence in the introduction explicitly stating the writer's position or the point they support, the writer probably has not refined the introduction sufficiently.

Narration and Confirmation

The narration part of a classical argument should create a context for the argument by explaining the issue to which the argument is responding, and by supplying any background information that influences the issue. Readers should understand the issues, alternatives, and stakes in the argument by the end of the narration to enable them to evaluate the author's claims equitably. The confirmation part of the classical argument enables the author to explain why they believe in the argument's thesis. The author builds a chain of reasoning by developing several individual supporting claims and explaining why that evidence supports each claim and also supports the overall thesis of the argument.

Refutation and Concession and Summation
The classical argument is the model for argumentative/persuasive writing, so authors often use it to establish, promote, and defend their positions. In the refutation aspect of the refutation and concession part of the argument, authors disarm reader opposition by anticipating and answering their possible objections, persuading them to accept the author's viewpoint. In the concession aspect, authors can concede those opposing viewpoints with which they agree. This can avoid weakening the author's thesis while establishing reader respect and goodwill for the author: all refutation and no concession can antagonize readers who disagree with the author's position. In the conclusion part of the classical argument, a less skilled writer might simply summarize or restate the thesis and related claims; however, this does not provide the argument with either momentum or closure. More skilled authors revisit the issues and the narration part of the argument, reminding readers of what is at stake.

Distinguishing Between Facts and Opinions

A **fact** is a statement that is true empirically or an event that has actually occurred in reality, and can be proven or supported by evidence; it is generally objective. In contrast, an **opinion** is subjective, representing something that someone believes rather than something that exists in the absolute. People's individual understandings, feelings, and perspectives contribute to variations in opinion. Though facts are typically objective in nature, in some instances, a statement of fact may be both factual and yet also subjective. For example, emotions are individual subjective experiences. If an individual says that he or she feels happy or sad, the feeling is subjective, but the statement is factual; hence, it is a subjective fact. In contrast, if one person tells another that the other is feeling happy or sad—whether this is true or not—it is an assumption or an opinion.

Authors use arguments to persuade the reader to agree with their claim. When analyzing the strength of an argument, the reader should summarize the author's message and determine whether or not they agree or disagree with the claim and whether, overall, they believe the evidence the author presented to support it. Next the reader should identify each individual detail and examine it to determine if it supports the claim, fails to support the claim, or even distract from the author's goal.

As readers examine each piece of evidence, they should consider its type and its effectiveness in proving the author's claim both individually and in context. Readers should pay attention to details that contradict the evidence, and readers should question the way the author uses details.

Facts can often be interpreted in ways that mislead the reader, so they will believe a claim that is unproven or untrue. If the claim is supported by facts such as statistics or empirical evidence, the reader should examine them. The reader should question whether the facts are relevant or, if they were interpreted differently, they would lead to a different conclusion that would fail to support the argument or even contradict it. They should consider whether the scope of the data is appropriate, or if it is too broad or narrow, and they should question whether the source is credible, and whether a source has been cited at all.

If the author uses expert opinions, the reader should consider whether the expert is credible and appropriate. If a doctor offers an opinion about pediatric medicine, the reader should ask if the doctor is an expert in that field or if they practice a different form of medicine.

Finally, the reader should consider whether the author has anticipated and adequately responded to any potential counterarguments to the claim and decide if the argument overall is strong, or if the evidence fails to persuade them to accept the author's claim.

Determining the Logical Assumptions Upon Which an Argument or Conclusion is Based

In the structure of an argument, an **assumption** is an unstated premise. To identify the assumption within arguments, you must find something that the argument is relying on that the author is not stating explicitly. Many strengthening and weakening questions deal with unstated assumptions, as well as necessary and sufficient assumption questions. Let's take a look at what an unsated assumption looks like:

> All restaurants in the Seattle area serve vegan food. *Haile's Seafood* must serve vegan food.

Let's identify all parts of the argument, including the unstated assumption. The conclusion of this argument is the last sentence: *Haile's Seafood* must serve vegan food. The premise we are given is the first sentence: All restaurants in the Seattle area serve vegan food. Now let's ask ourselves if there's a missing link. How did the author reach this conclusion? The author reached this conclusion with an unstated assumption, which might look like this: *Haile's Seafood* is in the Seattle area. Now we have the argument:

- Premise: All restaurants in the Seattle area serve vegan food.
- Unstated Assumption: *Haile's Seafood* is in the Seattle area.
- Conclusion: *Haile's Seafood* must serve vegan food

Another way to look at the missing link is like this: there is a connection between "Seattle area" and "vegan food," and one between *"Haile's Seafood"* and "vegan food", but there is no connection between "Seattle area" and *"Haile's Seafood."* The unstated assumption identifies this connection.

Challenging the Statements and Opinions Presented in a Text

Selecting the most relevant material to support a written text is a necessity in producing quality writing and for the credibility of an author. Arguments lacking in reasons or examples won't work in persuading the audience later on, because their hearts have not been pulled. Using examples to support ideas also gives the writing rhetorical effects such as **pathos** (emotion), **logos** (logic), or **ethos** (credibility), all three of which are necessary for a successful text.

Not all arguments are valid. Authors sometimes have one or more flaws in their argument's reasoning. Critical readers should always consider the validity and logic underlying the statements and opinions in a text. For example, texts wrought with bias or stereotypes should be read with caution and evaluated critically, rather than read complacently.

Biases usually occur when someone allows their personal preferences or ideologies to interfere with what should be an objective decision. In personal situations, someone is biased towards someone if they favor them in an unfair way. In academic writing, being biased in your sources means leaving out objective information that would turn the argument one way or the other. The evidence of bias in academic writing makes the text less credible, so be sure to present all viewpoints when writing, not just your own, so to avoid coming off as biased. Being objective when presenting information or dealing with people usually allows the person to gain more credibility.

Stereotypes are preconceived notions that place a particular rule or characteristics on an entire group of people. Stereotypes are usually offensive to the group they refer to or allies of that group, and often have negative connotations. The reinforcement of stereotypes isn't always obvious. Sometimes stereotypes can be very subtle and are still widely used in order for people to understand categories within the world. For example, saying that women are more emotional and intuitive than men is a stereotype, although this is still an assumption used by many in order to understand the differences between one another.

In addition, critical readers are able to identify flaws or holes in an argument's reasoning. Some CBEST questions may ask you to provide a description of that error. In order for you to be able to describe what flaw is occurring in the argument, it will help to know of various argumentative flaws, such as red herring, false choice, and correlation vs. causation.

Here are some examples of what this type of question looks like:

- The reasoning in the author's argument is flawed because the argument . . .
- The argument is most vulnerable to criticism on the grounds that it . . .
- Which one of the following is an error in the argument's reasoning?
- A flaw in the reasoning of the argument is that . . .
- Which one of the following most accurately describes X's criticism of the argument made by Y?

Bait/Switch

One common flaw that is good to know is called the "bait and switch." It occurs when the author will provide an argument that offers evidence about X, and ends the argument with a conclusion about Y. A "bait and switch" answer choice will look like this:

> The argument assumes that X does in fact address Y without providing justification.

Let's look at an example:

> Hannah will most likely always work out and maintain a healthy physique. After all, Hannah's IQ is extremely high.

The correct answer will look like this:

> The argument assumes that Hannah's high IQ addresses her likelihood of always working out without providing justification.

Ascriptive Error

The **ascriptive argument** will begin the argument with something a third party has claimed. Usually, it will be something very general, like "Some people say that . . ." or "Generally, it has been said . . ." Then, the arguer will follow up that claim with a refutation or opposing view. The problem here is that when the arguer phrases something in this general sense without a credible source, their refutation of that evidence doesn't really matter. Here's an example:

It has been said that peppermint oil has been proven to relieve stomach issues and, in some cases, prevent cancer. I can attest to the relief in stomach issues; however, there is just not enough evidence to prove whether or not peppermint oil has the ability to prevent any kind of cancerous cells from forming in the body.

The correct answer will look like this:

> The argument assumes that the refuting evidence matters to the position that is being challenged.
>
> We have no credible source in this argument, so the refutation is senseless.

Prescriptive Error

First, let's take a look at what "prescriptive" means. **Prescriptive** means to give directions, or to say something *ought to* or *should* do something else. Sometimes an argument will be a descriptive premise (simply describing) that leads to a prescriptive conclusion, which makes for a very weak argument. This is like saying "There is a hurricane coming; therefore, we should leave the state." Even though this seems like common sense, the logical soundness of this argument is missing. A valid argument is when the truth of the premise leads absolutely to the truth of the conclusion. It's when the conclusion *is* something, not when the conclusion *should* be or do something. The flaw here is the assumption that the conclusion is going to work out; something prescriptive is not ever guaranteed to work out in a logical argument.

False Choice

A **false choice**, or **false dilemma**, flaw is a statement that assumes only the object it lists in the statement is the solution, or the only options that exist, for that problem. Here is an example:

> I didn't get the grade I want in Chemistry class. I must either be really stupid, I didn't get enough sleep, or I didn't eat enough that day.

This is a false choice error. We are offered only three options for why the speaker did not get the grade he or she wanted in Chemistry class. However, there is potentially more options why the grade was not achieved other than the three listed. The speaker could have been fighting a cold, or the professor may not have taught the material in a comprehensive way. It is our job as test takers to recognize that there are more options other than the choices we are given, although it appears that the only three choices are listed in the example.

Red Herring

A **red herring** is a point offered in an argument that is only meant to distract or mislead. A red herring will throw something out after the argument that is unrelated to the argument, although it still commands attention, thus taking attention away from the relevant issue. The following is an example of a red herring fallacy:

> Kirby: It seems like therapy is moving toward a more holistic model rather than something prescriptive, where the space between a therapist and client is seen more organic rather than a controlled space. This helps empower the client to reach their own conclusions about what should be done rather than having someone tell them what to do.
>
> Barlock: What's the point of therapy anyway? It seems like "talking out" problems with a stranger is a waste of time and always has been. Is it even successful as a profession?

We see Kirby present an argument about the route therapy is taking toward the future. Instead of responding to the argument by presenting their own side regarding where therapy is headed, Barlock questions the overall point of therapy. Barlock throws out a red herring here: Kirby cannot proceed with the argument because now Kirby must defend the existence of therapy instead of its future.

Correlation Versus Causality

Readers should be careful when reviewing causal conclusions because the reasoning is often flawed, incorrectly classifying correlation as causality. Two events that may or may not be associated with one another are said to be linked such that one was the cause or reason for the other, which is considered the effect. To be a true "cause-and-effect" relationship, one factor or event must occur first (the cause) and be the sole reason (unless others are also listed) that the other occurred (the effect). The cause serves as the initiator of the relationship between the two events.

For example, consider the following argument:

> Last weekend, the local bakery ran out of blueberry muffins and some customers had to select something else instead. This week, the bakery's sales have fallen. Therefore, the blueberry muffin shortage last weekend resulted in fewer sales this week.

In this argument, the author states that the decline in sales this week (the effect) was caused by the shortage of blueberry muffins last weekend. However, there are other viable alternate causes for the decline in sales this week besides the blueberry muffin shortage. Perhaps it is summer and many normal patrons are away this week on vacation, or maybe another local bakery just opened or is running a special sale this week. There might be a large construction project or road work in town near the bakery, deterring customers from navigating the detours or busy roads. It is entirely possible that the decline this week is just a random coincidence and not attributable to any factor other than chance, and that next week, sales will return to normal or even exceed typical sales. Insufficient evidence exists to confidently assert that the blueberry muffin shortage was the sole reason for the decline in sales, thus mistaking correlation for causation.

Identifying Inconsistencies or Differences in Points of View Within One or More Texts

Words can be very powerful. When written words are used with the intent to make an argument or support a position, the words used—and the way in which they are arranged—can have a dramatic effect on the readers. Clichés, colloquialisms, run-on sentences, and misused words are all examples of ways that word choice can negatively affect writing quality. Unless the writer carefully considers word choice, a written work stands to lose credibility.

If a writer's overall intent is to provide a clear meaning on a subject with a consistent point of view, he or she must consider not only the exact words to use, but also their placement, repetition, and suitability. Academic writing should be intentional and clear, and it should be devoid of awkward or vague descriptions that can easily lead to misunderstandings. When readers find themselves reading and rereading just to gain a clear understanding of the writer's intent, there may be an issue with word choice. Although the words used in academic writing are different from those used in a casual conversation, they shouldn't necessarily be overly academic either. It may be relevant to employ key words that are associated with the subject, but struggling to inject these words into a paper just to sound academic may defeat the purpose. If the message cannot be clearly understood the first time, word choice may be the culprit.

Word choice also conveys the author's attitude and sets a tone. Although each word in a sentence carries a specific denotation, it might also carry positive or negative connotations—and it is the connotations that set the tone and convey the author's attitude. Consider the following similar sentences:

> It was the same old routine that happens every Saturday morning—eat, exercise, chores.
>
> The Saturday morning routine went off without a hitch—eat, exercise, chores.

The first sentence carries a negative connotation with the author's "same old routine" word choice. The feelings and attitudes associated with this phrase suggest that the author is bored or annoyed at the Saturday morning routine. Although the second sentence carries the same topic—explaining the Saturday morning routine—the choice to use the expression "without a hitch" conveys a positive or cheery attitude.

An author's writing style can likewise be greatly affected by word choice. When writing for an academic audience, for example, it is necessary for the author to consider how to convey the message by carefully considering word choice. If the author interchanges between third-person formal writing and second-person informal writing, the author's writing quality and credibility are at risk. Formal writing involves complex sentences, an objective viewpoint, and the use of full words as opposed to the use of a subjective viewpoint, contractions, and first- or second-person usage commonly found in informal writing.

Content validity, the author's ability to support the argument, and the audience's ability to comprehend the written work are all affected by the author's word choice and ability to maintain a consistent tone, opinion, main idea throughout the text.

Identifying the Audience for a Given Text

An author needs to think about the audience and tailor their language, argument, or narrative for that audience. For example, an opinion piece about the benefits of consuming a plant-based diet would highlight different reasons for a young child compared to an adult in a medical setting. The audience's education level, age, and position/opinion should be considered. Are they indifferent? An author might use a personal story or example in order stir empathy. Are they resistant? If so, an author might use logical reasoning based in factual evidence so they will be convinced. Personal stories or testimonials, statistics, or documentary evidence are various types of examples that one can use for their writing.

Language that Creates an Inappropriate or Inconsistent Tone

Tone conveys the author's attitude toward the topic and the audience. The tone also reveals their level of confidence on the subject, and whether they intend to bring humor, emotion, or seriousness to the writing. Setting the tone ultimately determines how readers will receive the overall message.

In professional writing, it is imperative that authors maintain an appropriate and professional tone that strengthens the writing quality. Framing the writing ahead of time, determining the purpose of the paper, and even considering the author's own bias on the subject will help to set the appropriate tone. Why is the paper being written? What message does the author want to convey, and to whom? Why would the intended audience find this paper interesting, and how does the author expect the audience to react? These are just some of the questions that can help to frame a piece of writing and develop an appropriate tone. To help develop the tone before writing, it sometimes helps to consider the intended audience's perspective.

When an author wishes to convey a clear message but does not want to compromise credibility by writing subjectively, using emphasis can be very effective. This is done by introducing and stressing the important points of the subject in the opening sentence or at the beginning of specific paragraphs. Consider the following:

> Music soothes the soul and captures our hearts. The following is a study on how music has affected North American society during the past five decades.
>
> The following is a study on how music has affected North American society during the past five decades. Music soothes the soul and captures our hearts.

Clearly, the author's attitude toward music is captured in the first sentence of the first example. When the sentences are rearranged in the second example, however, the emphasis is lost. With the subtle positioning of key words and phrases, an author can emphasize important points of the paper and set the tone.

Written tone can either capture readers' attention or turn them away. Considering the intended audience and how readers will perceive the message helps to develop the appropriate tone. In academic or professional writing, writers tend to employ a more serious tone, but serious does not mean dull or boring. Academic writing can engage readers by setting a tone that, although serious, also reveals a connection to readers. Authors who wish to connect with their audience on a more personal level might introduce their topic with a surprising or entertaining fact, or quote a famous individual who reinforces the paper's topic.

Comprehension and Context

Identifying the Relationships Between General and Specific Ideas in a Text

A paragraph is made up of a series of related sentences that support a single main idea or message. Whether the main idea is clearly stated or implied by the supporting details, the reader can be guided to the desired conclusion.

The **main idea** is what the passage is about. When this main idea is clearly stated, the reader can easily determine how the evidence or details that follow support this main idea. Suppose the author states, "*Because of their inexperience with predators, dodos went extinct in the 17th century.*" The subsequent sentences will support this claim with details. The author will describe the sequence of events, each one leading the reader to agree with the statement based on the evidence and reach the conclusion the author wants them to reach.

If the main idea is not directly stated, the author must imply the main idea through the use of strong supporting details. These details could be comparisons of like ideas or contrasts of different ideas, factual evidence in graphs and statistics, quotes from experts, or vivid descriptions that evoke the desired emotional response.

Determining the Sequence of Events or Steps in a Process

Sequence structure is the order of events in which a story or information is presented to the audience. Sometimes the text will be presented in chronological order, or sometimes it will be presented by displaying the most recent information first, then moving backwards in time. The sequence structure depends on the author, the context, and the audience. The structure of a text also depends on the genre in which the text is written. Is it literary fiction? Is it a magazine article? Is it instructions for how to complete a certain task? Different genres will have different purposes for switching up the sequence of their writing.

The structure presented in literary fiction is also known as **narrative structure**. Narrative structure is the foundation on which the text moves. The basic ways for moving the text along are in the plot and the setting. The plot is the sequence of events in the narrative that move the text forward through cause and effect. The setting of a story is the place or time period in which the story takes place. Narrative structure has two main categories: linear and nonlinear.

Linear Narrative
Linear narrative is a narrative told in chronological order. Traditional linear narratives will follow the plot diagram below depicting the narrative arc. The narrative arc consists of the exposition, conflict, rising action, climax, falling action, and resolution.

- **Exposition**: The exposition is in the beginning of a narrative and introduces the characters, setting, and background information of the story. The importance of the exposition lies in its framing of the upcoming narrative. Exposition literally means "a showing forth" in Latin.
- **Conflict**: The conflict, in a traditional narrative, is presented toward the beginning of the story after the audience becomes familiar with the characters and setting. The conflict is a single instance between characters, nature, or the self, in which the central character is forced to make a decision or move forward with some kind of action. The conflict presents something for the main character, or protagonist, to overcome.
- **Rising Action**: The rising action is the part of the story that leads into the climax. The rising action will feature the development of characters and plot, and creates the tension and suspense that eventually lead to the climax.

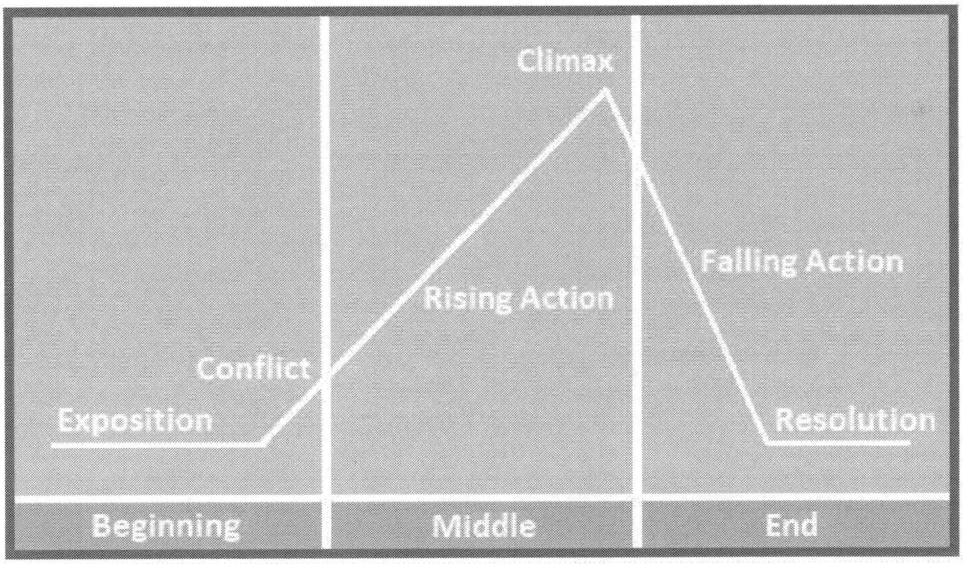

- **Climax**: The climax is the part of the story where the tension produced in the rising action comes to a culmination. The climax is the peak of the story. In a traditional structure, everything before the climax builds up to it, and everything after the climax falls from it. It is the height of the narrative, and is usually either the most exciting part of the story or is marked by some turning point in the character's journey.

- **Falling Action**: The falling action happens as a result of the climax. Characters continue to develop, although there is a wrapping up of loose ends here. The falling action leads to the resolution.

- **Resolution**: The resolution is where the story comes to an end and usually leaves the reader with the satisfaction of knowing what happened within the story and why. However, stories do not always end in this fashion. Sometimes readers can be confused or frustrated at the end from lack of information or the absence of a happy ending.

Nonlinear Narrative
A nonlinear narrative deviates from the traditional narrative in that it does not always follow the traditional plot structure of the narrative arc. Nonlinear narratives may include structures that are disjointed, circular, or disruptive, in the sense that they do not follow chronological order, but rather a nontraditional order of structure. ***In medias res*** is an example of a structure that predates the linear narrative. *In medias res* is Latin for "in the middle of things," which is how many ancient texts, especially epic poems, began their story, such as Homer's *Iliad*. Instead of having a clear exposition with a full development of characters, they would begin right in the middle of the action.

Modernist texts in the late nineteenth and early twentieth century are known for their experimentation with disjointed narratives, moving away from traditional linear narrative. Disjointed narratives are depicted in novels like *Catch 22*, where the author, Joseph Heller, structures the narrative based on free association of ideas rather than chronology. Another nonlinear narrative can be seen in the novel *Wuthering Heights*, written by Emily Bronte, which disrupts the chronological order by being told retrospectively after the first chapter. There seem to be two narratives in *Wuthering Heights* working at the same time: a present narrative as well as a past narrative. Authors employ disrupting narratives for various reasons; some use it for the purpose of creating situational irony for the readers, while some use it to create a certain effect in the reader, such as excitement, or even a feeling of discomfort or fear.

Sequence Structure in Technical Documents
The purpose of technical documents, such as instructions manuals, cookbooks, or "user-friendly" documents, is to provide information to users as clearly and efficiently as possible. In order to do this, the sequence structure in technical documents that should be used is one that is as straightforward as possible. This usually involves some kind of chronological order or a direct sequence of events. For example, someone who is reading an instruction manual on how to set up their Smart TV wants directions in a clear, simple, straightforward manner that does not leave the reader to guess at the proper sequence or lead to confusion.

Sequence Structure in Informational Texts
The structure in informational texts depends again on the genre. For example, a newspaper article may start by stating an exciting event that happened, and then move on to talk about that event in chronological order, known as sequence or order structure. Many informational texts also use cause and effect structure, which describes an event and then identifies reasons for why that event occurred. Some essays may write about their subjects by way of comparison and contrast, which is a structure that compares two things or contrasts them to highlight their differences. Other documents, such as proposals, will have a problem to solution structure, where the document highlights some kind of problem and then offers a solution toward the end. Finally, some informational texts are written with lush details and description in order to captivate the audience, allowing them to visualize the information presented to them. This type of structure is known as descriptive.

Arranging the Ideas in a Text Into an Outline

An **outline** is a system used to organize ideas. Outlines can be effectively used by readers and writers alike. Outlining, or using some other form of graphic organizers, can be a helpful tool because it enables readers to organize important information in a logical pattern using Roman numerals or numbers. In this way, it encourages readers to consider the author's main points and differentiate these from pieces of supporting evidence. It also allows readers to pair pieces of evidence with the specific concept or idea they support. For fictional pieces, outlining can help readers keep track of the plot, characters, or chronology of the story. Usually, outlines start out with the main ideas and then branch out into subgroups or subsidiary thoughts or subjects. Not only do outlines provide a visual tool for readers to reflect on how events, ideas, evidence, or other key parts of the argument relate to one another, but they can also lead readers to improved comprehension and understanding.

The sample below demonstrates what a general outline looks like:

I. Introduction
    1. Background
    2. Thesis statement
II. Body
    1. Point A
        a. Supporting evidence
        b. Supporting evidence
    2. Point B
        a. Supporting evidence
        b. Supporting evidence
    3. Point C
        a. Supporting evidence
        b. Supporting evidence
III. Conclusion
    1. Restate main points of the paper.
    2. End with something memorable.

Identifying the Author's Purpose in a Given Text

Authors may have many purposes for writing a specific text. Their purposes may be to try and convince readers to agree with their position on a subject, to impart information, or to entertain. Other writers are motivated to write from a desire to express their own feelings. Authors' purposes are their reasons for writing something. A single author may have one overriding purpose for writing or multiple reasons. An author may explicitly state their intention in the text, or the reader may need to infer that intention. Those who read reflectively benefit from identifying the purpose because it enables them to analyze information in the text. By knowing why the author wrote the text, readers can glean ideas for how to approach it.

The following is a list of questions readers can ask in order to discern an author's purpose for writing a text:

- From the title of the text, why do you think the author wrote it?
- Was the purpose of the text to give information to readers?
- Did the author want to describe an event, issue, or individual?
- Was it written to express emotions and thoughts?
- Did the author want to convince readers to consider a particular issue?

- Was the author primarily motivated to write the text to entertain?
- Why do you think the author wrote this text from a certain point of view?
- What is your response to the text as a reader?
- Did the author state their purpose for writing it?

Students should read to interpret information rather than simply content themselves with roles as text consumers. Being able to identify an author's purpose efficiently improves reading comprehension, develops critical thinking, and makes students more likely to consider issues in depth before accepting writer viewpoints. Authors of fiction frequently write to entertain readers. Another purpose for writing fiction is making a political statement; for example, Jonathan Swift wrote "A Modest Proposal" (1729) as a political satire. Another purpose for writing fiction as well as nonfiction is to persuade readers to take some action or further a particular cause. Fiction authors and poets both frequently write to evoke certain moods; for example, Edgar Allan Poe wrote novels, short stories, and poems that evoke moods of gloom, guilt, terror, and dread. Another purpose of poets is evoking certain emotions: love is popular, as in Shakespeare's sonnets and numerous others. In "The Waste Land" (1922), T.S. Eliot evokes society's alienation, disaffection, sterility, and fragmentation.

Authors seldom directly state their purposes in texts. Some students may be confronted with nonfiction texts such as biographies, histories, magazine and newspaper articles, and instruction manuals, among others. To identify the purpose in nonfiction texts, students can ask the following questions:

- Is the author trying to teach something?
- Is the author trying to persuade the reader?
- Is the author imparting factual information only?
- Is this a reliable source?
- Does the author have some kind of hidden agenda?

To apply author purpose in nonfictional passages, students can also analyze sentence structure, word choice, and transitions to answer the aforementioned questions and to make inferences. For example, authors wanting to convince readers to view a topic negatively often choose words with negative connotations.

Narrative Writing

Narrative writing tells a story. The most prominent examples of narrative writing are fictional novels. Here are some examples:

- Mark Twain's *The Adventures of Tom Sawyer* and *The Adventures of Huckleberry Finn*

- Victor Hugo's *Les Misérables*

- Charles Dickens' *Great Expectations, David Copperfield*, and *A Tale of Two Cities*

- Jane Austen's *Northanger Abbey, Mansfield Park, Pride and Prejudice, Sense and Sensibility,* and *Emma*

- Toni Morrison's *Beloved, The Bluest Eye*, and *Song of Solomon*

- Gabriel García Márquez's *One Hundred Years of Solitude* and *Love in the Time of Cholera*

Some nonfiction works are also written in narrative form. For example, some authors choose a narrative style to convey factual information about a topic, such as a specific animal, country, geographic region, and scientific or natural phenomenon.

Since narrative is the type of writing that tells a story, it must be told by someone, who is the narrator. The narrator may be a fictional character telling the story from their own viewpoint. This narrator uses the first person (*I, me, my, mine* and *we, us, our,* and *ours*). The narrator may simply be the author; for example, when Louisa May Alcott writes "Dear reader" in *Little Women*, she (the author) addresses us as readers. In this case, the novel is typically told in third person, referring to the characters as he, she, they, or them. Another more common technique is the omniscient narrator; i.e. the story is told by an unidentified individual who sees and knows everything about the events and characters—not only their externalized actions, but also their internalized feelings and thoughts. Second person, i.e. writing the story by addressing readers as "you" throughout, is less frequently used.

Expository Writing

Expository writing is also known as informational writing. Its purpose is not to tell a story as in narrative writing, to paint a picture as in descriptive writing, or to persuade readers to agree with something as in argumentative writing. Rather, its point is to communicate information to the reader. As such, the point of view of the author will necessarily be more objective. Whereas other types of writing appeal to the reader's emotions, appeal to the reader's reason by using logic, or use subjective descriptions to sway the reader's opinion or thinking, expository writing seeks to do none of these but simply to provide facts, evidence, observations, and objective descriptions of the subject matter. Some examples of expository writing include research reports, journal articles, articles and books about historical events or periods, academic subject textbooks, news articles and other factual journalistic reports, essays, how-to articles, and user instruction manuals.

Technical Writing

Technical writing is similar to expository writing in that it is factual, objective, and intended to provide information to the reader. Indeed, it may even be considered a subcategory of expository writing. However, technical writing differs from expository writing in that (1) it is specific to a particular field, discipline, or subject; and (2) it uses the specific technical terminology that belongs only to that area. Writing that uses technical terms is intended only for an audience familiar with those terms. A primary example of technical writing today is writing related to computer programming and use.

Persuasive Writing

Persuasive writing is intended to persuade the reader to agree with the author's position. It is also known as argumentative writing. Some writers may be responding to other writers' arguments, in which case they make reference to those authors or text and then disagree with them. However, another common technique is for the author to anticipate opposing viewpoints in general, both from other authors and from the author's own readers. The author brings up these opposing viewpoints, and then refutes them before they can even be raised, strengthening the author's argument. Writers persuade readers by appealing to their reason, which Aristotle called **logos;** appealing to emotion, which Aristotle called **pathos;** or appealing to readers based on the author's character and credibility, which Aristotle called **ethos.**

Summarizing and Paraphrasing

An important skill is the ability to read a complex text and then reduce its length and complexity by focusing on the key events and details. A **summary** is a shortened version of the original text, written by the reader in their own words. The summary should be shorter than the original text, and it must be thoughtfully formed to include critical points from the original text.

In order to effectively summarize a complex text, it's necessary to understand the original source and identify the major points covered. It may be helpful to outline the original text to get the big picture and avoid getting bogged down in the minor details. For example, a summary wouldn't include a statistic from the original source unless it was the major focus of the text. It's also important for readers to use their own words, yet retain the original meaning of the passage. The key to a good summary is emphasizing the main idea without changing the focus of the original information.

The more complex a text, the more difficult it can be to summarize. Readers must evaluate all points from the original source and then filter out what they feel are the less necessary details. Only the essential ideas should remain. The summary often mirrors the original text's organizational structure. For example, in a problem-solution text structure, the author typically presents readers with a problem and then develops solutions through the course of the text. An effective summary would likely retain this general structure, rephrasing the problem and then reporting the most useful or plausible solutions.

Paraphrasing is somewhat similar to summarizing. It calls for the reader to take a small part of the passage and list or describe its main points. Paraphrasing is more than rewording the original passage, though. Like a summary, a paraphrase should be written in the reader's own words, while still retaining the meaning of the original source. The main difference between summarizing and paraphrasing is that a summary would be appropriate for a much larger text, while a paraphrase might focus on just a few lines of text. Effective paraphrasing will indicate an understanding of the original source, yet still help the reader expand on their interpretation. A paraphrase should neither add new information nor remove essential facts that change the meaning of the source.

Identifying Facts and Details Presented in a Text

To determine whether details support the main idea of a passage, determine the relationships between ideas. For example, suppose the main idea of the passage is *"Due to inflation, the value of a dollar is different today than it was 100 years ago, and different than it will be 100 years from now."* This idea is then directly supported by the statements like this: *"In 1918, an item that cost a dollar would cost almost $17 today."* Another detail supporting it is this: *"Experts estimate that the expected rate of inflation over the next 10 years is about 2%."*

To determine whether a detail supports the main idea, a reader must determine whether there is a connection. Then, they must decide whether the detail directly supports the main idea, one of the supporting ideas, or none of the ideas. Suppose a supporting idea in a passage about inflation is *"In 1918, an item that cost a dollar would cost almost $17 today."* The reader then reads this detail: *"That means a coffee that costs $5 today would have cost about 30 cents back then."* The detail about the coffee price is an example of the supporting idea about prices in 1918. However, the statement *The value of an item is determined by how popular the item is* does not support the main idea ("*Due to inflation, the value of a dollar is different today than it was 100 years ago, and different than it will be 100 years from now.*") or any of the supporting ideas.

Drawing Conclusions or Generalizations from Material Presented in a Text

Readers form hypotheses about the main idea as they read a passage. Hypotheses are based on incomplete evidence, so as the reader gathers more the details from the passage, their hypothesis changes or is proven by the evidence. They start to form generalizations about the author's message.

Generalizations are broad conclusions based on the way the reader interprets the details. These generalizations might be correct, or the reader might have made inferences from the evidence that the author did not intend.

To determine if these generalizations were implied by the author, or if they are incorrect, the reader should examine the evidence they collected.

For example:

1. Humans cannot live without water.
2. People use thousands of gallons of water a year to keep their lawns green.

Based on these details, the reader concludes that *people who water their lawns are wasting water.*

The author has not offered evidence that watering lawns is wasteful, so the generalization is not supported. If the passage includes the detail *scientists say water will soon be dangerously scarce*, the generalization is supported. However, the following statement would contradict the reader's generalization: *"Lawns also need water to grow and sustain life."*

Making inferences and drawing conclusions involve skills that are quite similar: both require readers to fill in information the test writer has omitted. To make an inference or draw a conclusion about the text, test takers should observe all facts and arguments the test writer has presented. The best way to understand ways to drawing well-supported conclusions and generalizations is by practice. Let's take a look at the following example:

Nutritionist: More and more bodybuilders each year turn to whey protein as a source for their supplement intake to repair muscle tissue after working out. More and more studies are showing that using whey as a source of protein is linked to prostate cancer in men. Bodybuilders who use whey protein may consider switching to a plant-based protein source in order to avoid developing the negative effects that come with whey protein consumption.

Which of the following most accurately expresses the conclusion of the nutritionist's argument?

a. Whey protein is an excellent way to repair muscles after a workout.
b. Bodybuilders should switch from whey to a plant-based protein.
c. Whey protein causes every single instance of prostate cancer in men.
d. We still don't know the causes of prostate cancer in men.
e. Whey protein is not effective at repairing muscle tissue after working out.

The correct answer choice is *B*: bodybuilders should switch from whey to a plant-based protein. We can gather this from the entirety of the passage, as it begins with what kind of protein bodybuilders consume, the dangers of that protein, and what kind of protein to switch to. Choice *A* is incorrect; this is the opposite of what the passage states. When reading through answer choices, it's important to look for choices that include the words "every," "always," or "all." In many instances, absolute answer choices will not be the correct answer. This example is shown in Choice *C*; the passage does not state that whey protein causes "every single instance" of prostate cancer in men, only that it is *linked* to prostate cancer in men. Choice *D* is incorrect; although the nutritionist doesn't list all the causes of prostate cancer in men, the nutritionist does not conclude that we don't know the causes of prostate cancer in men either. Finally, Choice *E* is incorrect because the argument does not provide any evidence that whey protein isn't effective at repairing muscle tissue, rather it raises concerns about the potentially dangerous side effect.

The key to drawing well-supported conclusions is to read the question stem in its entirety a few times over and then paraphrase the passage in your own words. Once you do this, you will get an idea of the passage's conclusion before you are confused by all the different answer choices. Remember that drawing a conclusion is different than making an assumption. With drawing a conclusion, we are relying solely on the passage for facts to come to our conclusion. Making an assumption goes beyond the facts of the passage, so be careful of answer choices depicting assumptions instead of passage-based conclusions.

Making Inferences and Based on Information from a Text

Making an inference from a selection means to make an educated guess from the passage read. **Inferences** should be conclusions based off of sound evidence and reasoning. When multiple-choice test questions ask about the logical conclusion that can be drawn from reading text, the test taker must identify which choice will unavoidably lead to that conclusion. In order to eliminate the incorrect choices, the test taker should come up with a hypothetical situation wherein an answer choice is true, but the conclusion is not true.

For example, here is an example with three answer choices:

> Fred purchased the newest PC available on the market. Therefore, he purchased the most expensive PC in the computer store.
>
> What can one assume for this conclusion to follow logically?
>
> a. Fred enjoys purchasing expensive items.
> b. PCs are some of the most expensive personal technology products available.
> c. The newest PC is the most expensive one.

The premise of the text is the first sentence: *Fred purchased the newest PC.* The conclusion is the second sentence: *Fred purchased the most expensive PC.* Recent release and price are two different factors; the difference between them is the logical gap. To eliminate the gap, one must equate whatever new information the conclusion introduces with the pertinent information the premise has stated. This example simplifies the process by having only one of each: one must equate product recency with product price. Therefore, a possible bridge to the logical gap could be a sentence stating that the newest PCs always cost the most.

Analyzing Relationships within Passages, Including How People, Events, and Ideas are Connected

In a reading passage—whether on the test or in practice—the relationships between people, events, and ideas may be clearly stated, or the reader might have to infer the relationships based on clues in the passage. Again, to **infer** means to arrive at a conclusion based on evidence, clues, or facts.

People might be related through connections like family or friendship, or through events that link them directly or indirectly. In the passage, relationships may be described in background information or dialogue, or they may be implied through interactions between the characters.

Events and ideas in a passage can be related through sequence or through cause and effect. To relate events and ideas through sequence means to show what happened first and what happened next. Or a sequence could be ordered in another way, such as alphabetically, or geographically. Ideas and events can also be related through a comparison the author makes, showing the similarities and differences.

Sequence
When ideas are related through sequence, as in a series of events, the author typically uses signal words like *after, and then, while,* and *before.*

Cause and Effect
In cause and effect relationships, the cause is an event or circumstance that occurs before and is directly responsible for the effect. Signal words such as *because, due to,* and *as a result of* indicate a cause and effect relationship. When the relationship is implied, the reader must use clues in the passage to infer that the effect resulted from the cause.

Compare and Contrast
Ideas are often connected through comparisons of their similarities to one another using the signal words such as *like* or *and.* Ideas can also be connected through a contrast of their differences using signal words such as *but* or *however.*

Using Context Clues, Syntax, and Structural Analysis (e.g., affixes, prefixes, roots) to Determine the Meaning of Unknown Words

When readers encounter an unfamiliar word in text, they can use the surrounding **context**—the overall subject matter, specific chapter/section topic, and especially the immediate sentence context. Among others, one category of context clues is grammar. For example, the position of a word in a sentence and its relationship to the other words can help the reader establish whether the unfamiliar word is a verb, a noun, an adjective, an adverb, etc. This narrows down the possible meanings of the word to one part of speech. However, this may be insufficient. In a sentence that many birds *migrate* twice yearly, the reader can determine the word is a verb, and probably does not mean eat or drink; but it could mean travel, mate, lay eggs, hatch, molt, etc.

Another common context clue is a synonym or definition included in the sentence. Sometimes both exist in the same sentence. Here's an example:

> Scientists who study birds are *ornithologists.*

Many readers may not know the word *ornithologist.* However, the example contains a definition (scientists who study birds). The reader may also have the ability to analyze the suffix (*-logy,* meaning the study of) and root (*ornitho-,* meaning bird).

Another common context clue is a sentence that shows differences. Here's an example:

> Birds *incubate* their eggs outside of their bodies, unlike mammals.

Some readers may be unfamiliar with the word *incubate.* However, since we know that "unlike mammals," birds incubate their eggs outside of their bodies, we can infer that *incubate* has something to do with keeping eggs warm outside the body until they are hatched.

In addition to analyzing the etymology of a word's root and affixes and extrapolating word meaning from sentences that contrast an unknown word with an antonym, readers can also determine word meanings from sentence context clues based on logic. Here's an example:

> Birds are always looking out for predators that could attack their young.

The reader who is unfamiliar with the word *predator* could determine from the context of the sentence that predators usually prey upon baby birds and possibly other young animals. Readers might also use the context clue of etymology here, as *predator* and *prey* have the same root.

Analyzing Word Parts
By learning some of the etymologies of words and their parts, readers can break new words down into components and analyze their combined meanings. For example, the root word *soph* is Greek for wise or knowledge. Knowing this informs the meanings of English words including *sophomore, sophisticated,* and *philosophy.* Those who also know that *phil* is Greek for love will realize that *philosophy* means the love of knowledge. They can then extend this knowledge of *phil* to understand *philanthropist* (one who loves people), *bibliophile* (book lover), *philharmonic* (loving harmony), *hydrophilic* (water-loving), and so on. In addition, *phob-* derives from the Greek *phobos,* meaning fear. This informs all words ending with it as meaning fear of various things: *acrophobia* (fear of heights), *arachnophobia* (fear of spiders), *claustrophobia* (fear of enclosed spaces), *ergophobia* (fear of work), and *hydrophobia* (fear of water), among others.

Some English word origins from other languages, like ancient Greek, are found in large numbers and varieties of English words. An advantage of the shared ancestry of these words is that once readers recognize the meanings of some Greek words or word roots, they can determine or at least get an idea of what many different English words mean. As an example, the Greek word *métron* means to measure, a measure, or something used to measure; the English word meter derives from it. Knowing this informs many other English words, including *altimeter, barometer, diameter, hexameter, isometric,* and *metric.* While readers must know the meanings of the other parts of these words to decipher their meaning fully, they already have an idea that they are all related in some way to measures or measuring.

While all English words ultimately derive from a proto-language known as Indo-European, many of them historically came into the developing English vocabulary later, from sources like the ancient Greeks' language, the Latin used throughout Europe and much of the Middle East during the reign of the Roman Empire, and the Anglo-Saxon languages used by England's early tribes. In addition to classic revivals and native foundations, by the Renaissance era other influences included French, German, Italian, and Spanish. Today we can often discern English word meanings by knowing common roots and affixes, particularly from Greek and Latin.

The following is a list of common prefixes and their meanings:

Prefix	Definition	Examples
a-	without	atheist, agnostic
ad-	to, toward	advance
ante-	before	antecedent, antedate
anti-	opposing	antipathy, antidote
auto-	self	autonomy, autobiography
bene-	well, good	benefit, benefactor
bi-	two	bisect, biennial
bio-	life	biology, biosphere
chron-	time	chronometer, synchronize
circum-	around	circumspect, circumference
com-	with, together	commotion, complicate
contra-	against, opposing	contradict, contravene

Prefix	Definition	Examples
cred-	belief, trust	credible, credit
de-	from	depart
dem-	people	demographics, democracy
dis-	away, off, down, not	dissent, disappear
equi-	equal, equally	equivalent
ex-	former, out of	extract
for-	away, off, from	forget, forswear
fore-	before, previous	foretell, forefathers
homo-	same, equal	homogenized
hyper-	excessive, over	hypercritical, hypertension
in-	in, into	intrude, invade
inter-	among, between	intercede, interrupt
mal-	bad, poorly, not	malfunction
micr-	small	microbe, microscope
mis-	bad, poorly, not	misspell, misfire
mono-	one, single	monogamy, monologue
mor-	die, death	mortality, mortuary
neo-	new	neolithic, neoconservative
non-	not	nonentity, nonsense
omni-	all, everywhere	omniscient
over-	above	overbearing
pan-	all, entire	panorama, pandemonium
para-	beside, beyond	parallel, paradox
phil-	love, affection	philosophy, philanthropic
poly-	many	polymorphous, polygamous
pre-	before, previous	prevent, preclude
prim-	first, early	primitive, primary
pro-	forward, in place of	propel, pronoun
re-	back, backward, again	revoke, recur
sub-	under, beneath	subjugate, substitute
super-	above, extra	supersede, supernumerary
trans-	across, beyond, over	transact, transport
ultra-	beyond, excessively	ultramodern, ultrasonic, ultraviolet
un-	not, reverse of	unhappy, unlock
vis-	to see	visage, visible

The following is a list of common suffixes and their meanings:

Suffix	Definition	Examples
-able	likely, able to	capable, tolerable
-ance	act, condition	acceptance, vigilance
-ard	one that does excessively	drunkard, wizard
-ation	action, state	occupation, starvation
-cy	state, condition	accuracy, captaincy

Suffix	Definition	Examples
-er	one who does	teacher
-esce	become, grow, continue	convalesce, acquiesce
-esque	in the style of, like	picturesque, grotesque
-ess	feminine	waitress, lioness
-ful	full of, marked by	thankful, zestful
-ible	able, fit	edible, possible, divisible
-ion	action, result, state	union, fusion
-ish	suggesting, like	churlish, childish
-ism	act, manner, doctrine	barbarism, socialism
-ist	doer, believer	monopolist, socialist
-ition	action, result, state	sedition, expedition
-ity	quality, condition	acidity, civility
-ize	cause to be, treat with	sterilize, mechanize, criticize
-less	lacking, without	hopeless, countless
-like	like, similar	childlike, dreamlike
-ly	like, of the nature of	friendly, positively
-ment	means, result, action	refreshment, disappointment
-ness	quality, state	greatness, tallness
-or	doer, office, action	juror, elevator, honor
-ous	marked by, given to	religious, riotous
-some	apt to, showing	tiresome, lonesome
-th	act, state, quality	warmth, width
-ty	quality, state	enmity, activity

Figurative and Colloquial Language

Authors of a text use language with multiple levels of meaning for many different reasons. When the meaning of a text calls for directness, literal language should be used to provide clarity to the reader. Figurative language can be used when the author wants to produce an emotional effect in the reader or facilitate a deeper understanding of a word or passage. For example, if someone wanted to write a set of instructions on how to use a computer, they would write in literal language. However, if someone wanted to comment on the social implications of banning immigration, they might want to use a wide range of figurative language to highlight an empathetic response. It is important to keep in mind, too, that a single text can have a mixture of both literal and figurative language.

It's important to be able to recognize and interpret figurative, or non-literal, language. **Literal** statements rely directly on the denotations of words and express exactly what's happening in reality. **Figurative language** uses non-literal expressions to present information in a creative way. Consider the following sentences:

a. His pillow was very soft and he fell asleep quickly.

b. His pillow was a fluffy cloud and he floated away on it to the dream world.

Sentence *A* is literal, employing only the real meanings of each word. Sentence *B* is figurative. It employs a metaphor by stating that his pillow was a cloud. Of course, he isn't actually sleeping on a cloud, but the reader can draw on images of clouds as light, soft, fluffy, and relaxing to get a sense of how the character felt as he fell asleep. Also, in sentence *B*, the pillow becomes a vehicle that transports him to a magical dream world. The character isn't literally floating through the air—he's simply falling asleep! But by utilizing figurative language, the author creates a scene of peace, comfort, and relaxation that conveys stronger emotions and more creative imagery than the purely literal sentence. Not meant to be taken literally; figurative language is useful when the author of a text wants to produce an emotional effect in the reader or add a heightened complexity to the meaning of the text.

Figurative language is used more heavily in texts such as literary fiction, poetry, critical theory, and speeches. Figurative language goes beyond literal language, allowing readers to form associations they wouldn't normally form with literal language. Using language in a figurative sense appeals to the imagination of the reader. It is important to remember that words themselves are signifiers of objects and ideas, and not the objects and ideas themselves. Figurative language can highlight this detachment by creating multiple associations, but also points to the fact that language is fluid and capable of creating a world full of linguistic possibilities. Figurative language, it can be argued, is the heart of communication even outside of fiction and poetry. People connect through humor, metaphors, cultural allusions, puns, and symbolism in their everyday rhetoric. The following are terms associated with figurative language:

A **simile** is a comparison of two things using *like*, *than*, or *as*. A simile usually takes objects that have no apparent connection, such as a mind and an orchid, and compares them:

> His mind was as complex and rare as a field of ghost orchids.

Similes encourage a new, fresh perspective on objects or ideas that wouldn't otherwise occur. Similes are different than metaphors. Metaphors do not use *like*, *than*, or *as*. So, a metaphor from the above example would be:

> His mind was a field of ghost orchids.

Thus, similes highlight the comparison by focusing on the figurative side of the language, elucidating more the author's intent: a field of ghost orchids is something complex and rare, like the mind of a genius. With the metaphor, however, we get a beautiful yet somewhat equivocal comparison.

A popular use of figurative language, **metaphors** compare objects or ideas directly, asserting that something *is* a certain thing, even if it isn't. The following is an example of a metaphor used by writer Virginia Woolf:

> Books are the mirrors of the soul.

Metaphors have a vehicle and a tenor. The tenor is "books" and the vehicle is "mirrors of the soul." That is, the tenor is what is meant to be described, and the vehicle is that which carries the weight of the comparison. In this metaphor, perhaps the author means to say that written language (books) reflect a person's most inner thoughts and desires.

There are also **dead metaphors**, which means that the phrases have been so overused to the point where the figurative meaning becomes literal, like the phrase "What you're saying is crystal clear." The phrase compares "what's being said" to something "crystal clear." However, since the latter part of the phrase is in such popular use, the meaning seems literal ("I understand what you're saying") even when it's not.

Finally, an **extended metaphor** is a metaphor that goes on for several paragraphs, or even an entire text. John Keats' poem "On First Looking into Chapman's Homer" begins, "Much have I travell'd in the realms of gold," and goes on to explain the first time he hears Chapman's translation of Homer's writing. We see the extended metaphor begin in the first line. Keats is comparing travelling into "realms of gold" and exploration of new lands to the act of hearing a certain kind of literature for the first time. The extended metaphor goes on until the end of the poem where Keats stands "Silent, upon a peak in Darien," having heard the end of Chapman's translation. Keats has gained insight into new lands (new text) and is the richer for it.

The following are brief definitions and examples of popular figurative language:

- **Onomatopoeia**: A word that, when spoken, imitates the sound to which it refers. Example: "We heard a loud *boom* while driving to the beach yesterday."

- **Personification**: When human characteristics are given to animals, inanimate objects, or abstractions. An example would be in William Wordsworth's poem "Daffodils" where he sees a "crowd . . . / of golden daffodils . . . / Fluttering and dancing in the breeze." Dancing is usually a characteristic attributed solely to humans, but Wordsworth personifies the daffodils here as a crowd of people dancing.

- **Juxtaposition**: Juxtaposition is placing two objects side by side for comparison. In literature, this might look like placing two characters side by side for contrasting effect, like God and Satan in Milton's "Paradise Lost."

- **Paradox**: A paradox is a statement that is self-contradictory but will be found nonetheless true. One example of a paradoxical phrase is when Socrates said "I know one thing; that I know nothing." Seemingly, if Socrates knew nothing, he wouldn't know that he knew nothing. However, it is one thing he knows: that true wisdom begins with casting all presuppositions one has about the world aside.

- **Hyperbole**: A hyperbole is an exaggeration. Example: "I'm so tired I could sleep for centuries."

- **Allusion**: An allusion is a reference to a character or event that happened in the past. An example of a poem littered with allusions is T.S. Eliot's "The Waste Land." An example of a biblical allusion manifests when the poet says, "I will show you fear in a handful of dust," creating an ominous tone from Genesis 3:19 "For you are dust, and to dust you shall return."

- **Pun**: Puns are used in popular culture to invoke humor by exploiting the meanings of words. They can also be used in literature to give hints of meaning in unexpected places. One example of a pun is when Mercutio is giving his monologue after he is stabbed by Tybalt in "Romeo and Juliet" and says, "look for me tomorrow and you will find me a grave man."

- **Imagery**: This is a collection of images given to the reader by the author. If a text is rich in imagery, it is easier for the reader to imagine themselves in the author's world.

  One example of a poem that relies on *imagery* is William Carlos Williams' "The Red Wheelbarrow":

  > so much depends
  > upon
  >
  > a red wheel
  > barrow

glazed with rain
water

beside the white
chickens

The starkness of the imagery and the placement of the words in the poem, to some readers, throw the poem into a meditative state where, indeed, the world of this poem is made up solely of images of a purely simple life. This poem tells a story in sixteen words by using imagery.

- **Symbolism**: A symbol is used to represent an idea or belief system. For example, poets in Western civilization have been using the symbol of a rose for hundreds of years to represent love. In Japan, poets have used the firefly to symbolize passionate love, and sometimes even spirits of those who have died. Symbols can also express powerful political commentary and can be used in propaganda.

- **Irony**: There are three types of irony. Verbal irony is when a person states one thing and means the opposite. For example, a person is probably using irony when they say, "I can't wait to study for this exam next week." Dramatic irony occurs in a narrative and happens when the audience knows something that the characters do not. In the modern TV series *Hannibal*, we as an audience know that Hannibal Lecter is a serial killer, but most of the main characters do not. This is dramatic irony. Finally, situational irony is when one expects something to happen, and the opposite occurs. For example, we can say that a fire station burning down would be an instance of situational irony.

Lastly, **idiomatic expressions** are phrases or groups of words that have an established meaning when used together that's unrelated to the literal meanings of the individual words. For example, consider the following sentence that includes a common idiomatic phrase:

I know Phil is coming to visit this weekend because I heard it straight from the horse's mouth.

The speaker of this sentence did not consult a horse nor hear anything uttered from a horse in relation to Phil's visit. Instead, "straight from the horse's mouth" is an **idiom** that means it's the truth. As in the sentence in which it is used above, it often means whatever said should be taken as truth because it was spoken by a reliable source or by the person to which it pertains (in this case, Phil). The phrase is derived from the fact that sellers of horses at auctions would sometimes try to lie about the age of the horse. However, the size and shape of a horse's teeth can provide a fairly accurate estimate of the horse's true age. Therefore, essentially the truth regarding the horse's age come straight from their mouth. The idiomatic expression came to mean getting the truth in any situation.

Finding errors in idiomatic expressions can be difficult because it requires familiarity with the idiom. Because there are more than one thousand idioms in the English language, memorizing all of them is impractical. However, it is recommended to review the most common ones. There are many webpages dedicated to listing and explaining frequently used idioms.

Errors in the idiomatic expressions are typically one of two types. Either the idiomatic expression is stated improperly or it is used incorrectly. In the first type of issue, the prepositions used are often incorrect. Using the idiom from above, for example, it might say "straight *in* the horse's mouth" or "straight *with* the horse's mouth." In the second error type, the idiomatic expression is used improperly because the meaning it carries does not make sense in the context in which it is being used.

Consider the following:

> He was looking straight from the horse's mouth when he complained about the phone his father bought him.

Here, the writer has confused the idiom "straight from the horse's mouth" with "looking a gift horse in the mouth," which means to find fault in a gift or favor.

Either type of error can be difficult to detect and correct without prior knowledge of the idiomatic phrase. Practicing using idioms and discussing and studying their origins can help students remember the meanings and precise wordings, which will help them identify and correct errors in their usage.

Identifying Different Interpretations That Can Be Made of the Same Word or Phrase

Language can function differently in different contexts. The same words can convey meaning in nuanced ways depending on the surrounding context and the style and tone of the composition. Just as how people can speak with a variety of tones and inflections that can alter the meaning of the same sentence, so too can writers insert tone into written words. Punctuation choice is one example of how the same sentence can be interpreted slightly differently.

Consider the following three sentences:

> Camille hates dogs.
>
> Camille hates dogs!
>
> Camille hates dogs?

Although the wording is identical in these three simple sentences, the end punctuation choice provides slightly different interpretations because the tone is affected. The first is a statement. It lacks a significant overbearing tone. It's simply stating that Camille hates dogs, but readers aren't guided as to an emotional response to that fact. The second sentence ends in an exclamation point. This punctuation tends to evoke a feeling or surprise, exasperation, or urgency and alarm. Perhaps, for example, someone was about to introduce a large mastiff to Camille who had her back turned to the dog. One of Camille's friends who saw what was about to happen may have shouted that sentence in caution to prevent a terrified Camille. The last sentence is obviously a question, but that doesn't mean it's affectless. It may be said in an incredulous tone or one of surprise. The speaker may be a dog lover and find it hard to believe Camille is not. It might be uttered with doubt.

The writer could further display tone by italicizing one of the words to indicate emphasis. Taking just the question as an example, consider the difference between the following three examples:

> *Camille* hates dogs?
>
> Camille *hates* dogs?
>
> Camille hates *dogs*?

The first example places the emphasis on Camille. The speaker could be surprised or trying to clarify that it is Camille, not another person, who supposedly hates dogs. In the second example, the speaker's focus is on the word *hate.* He or she is seeking clarity or confirmation that Camille actually hates dogs (rather than loves them, likes them, is afraid of them, etc.). The italicized *dogs* in the last sentence indicates the speaker is verifying or shocked that it is dogs, in particular, that Camille hates (rather than cats, spiders, rats, etc.). Other punctuation marks, especially commas, can also shape the way a sentence is read and interpreted.

In addition to punctuation and emphasis indicators, the same words can be interpreted differently based on their context. **Denotation** refers to a word's explicit definition, like that found in the dictionary. Denotation is often set in comparison to connotation. **Connotation** is the emotional, cultural, social, or personal implication associated with a word. Denotation is more of an objective definition, whereas connotation can be more subjective, although many connotative meanings of words are similar for certain cultures. The denotative meanings of words are usually based on facts, and the connotative meanings of words are usually based on emotion. Here are some examples of words and their denotative and connotative meanings in Western culture:

Word	**Denotative Meaning**	**Connotative Meaning**
Home	A permanent place where one lives, usually as a member of a family.	A place of warmth; a place of familiarity; comforting; a place of safety and security. "Home" usually has a positive connotation.
Snake	A long reptile with no limbs and strong jaws that moves along the ground; some snakes have a poisonous bite.	An evil omen; a slithery creature (human or nonhuman) that is deceitful or unwelcome. "Snake" usually has a negative connotation.
Winter	A season of the year that is the coldest, usually from December to February in the northern hemisphere and from June to August in the southern hemisphere.	Circle of life, especially that of death and dying; cold or icy; dark and gloomy; hibernation, sleep, or rest. Winter can have a negative connotation, although many who have access to heat may enjoy the snowy season from their homes.

Recognizing How the Meaning of a Word is Affected by the Context in Which it Appears

Some words can have a number of different meanings depending on how they are used. For example, the word *fly* has a different meaning in each of the following sentences:

- "His trousers have a fly on them."
- "He swatted the fly on his trousers."
- "Those are some fly trousers."
- "They went fly fishing."
- "She hates to fly."
- "If humans were meant to fly, they would have wings."

As strategies, readers can try substituting a familiar word for an unfamiliar one and see whether it makes sense in the sentence. They can also identify other words in a sentence, offering clues to an unfamiliar word's meaning.

The Function of Transitional Words and Phrases

In connected writing, some sentences naturally lead to others, whereas in other cases, a new sentence expresses a new idea. We use transitional phrases to connect sentences and the ideas they convey. This makes the writing coherent. Transitional language also guides the reader from one thought to the next. For example, when pointing out an objection to the previous idea, starting a sentence with "However," "But," or "On the other hand" is transitional. When adding another idea or detail, writers use "Also," "In addition," "Furthermore," "Further," "Moreover," "Not only," etc. Readers have difficulty perceiving connections between ideas without such transitional wording.

Research and Reference Skills

Using the Table of Contents, Headings, and Index to Locate Information

Table of Contents and Index

When examining a book, a journal article, a monograph, or other publication, the table of contents is in the front. In books, it is typically found following the title page, publication information (often on the facing side of the title page), and dedication page, when one is included. In shorter publications, the table of contents may follow the title page, or the title on the same page. The table of contents in a book lists the number and title of each chapter and its beginning page number. An index, which is most common in books but may also be included in shorter works, is at the back of the publication. Books, especially academic texts, frequently have two: a subject index and an author index. Readers can look alphabetically for specific subjects in the subject index. Likewise, they can look up specific authors cited, quoted, discussed, or mentioned in the author index.

The index in a book offers particular advantages to students. For example, college course instructors typically assign certain textbooks, but do not expect students to read the entire book from cover to cover immediately. They usually assign specific chapters to read in preparation for specific lectures and/or discussions in certain upcoming classes. Reading portions at a time, some students may find references they either do not fully understand or want to know more about. They can look these topics up in the book's subject index to find them in later chapters. When a text author refers to another author, students can also look up the name in the book's author index to find all page numbers of all other references to that author. College students also typically are assigned research papers to write. A book's subject and author indexes can guide students to pages that may help inform them of other books to use for researching paper topics.

Headings

Headings and subheadings concisely inform readers what each section of a paper contains, as well as showing how its information is organized both visually and verbally. Headings are typically up to about five words long. They are not meant to give in-depth analytical information about the topic of their section, but rather an idea of its subject matter. Text authors should maintain consistent style across all headings. Readers should not expect headings if there is not material for more than one heading at each level, just as a list is unnecessary for a single item. Subheadings may be a bit longer than headings because they expand upon them. Readers should skim the subheadings in a paper to use them as a map of how content is arranged. Subheadings are in smaller fonts than headings to mirror relative importance. Subheadings are not necessary for every paragraph. They should enhance content, not substitute for topic sentences.

When a heading is brief, simple, and written in the form of a question, it can have the effect of further drawing readers into the text. An effective author will also answer the question in the heading soon in the following text. Question headings and their text answers are particularly helpful for engaging readers with average reading skills. Both headings and subheadings are most effective with more readers when they are obvious, simple, and get to their points immediately. Simple headings attract readers; simple subheadings allow readers a break, during which they also inform reader decisions whether to continue reading or not. Headings stand out from other text through boldface, but also italicizing and underlining them would be excessive. Uppercase-lowercase headings are easier for readers to comprehend than all capitals. More legible fonts are better. Some experts prefer serif fonts in text, but sans-serif fonts in headings. Brief subheadings that preview upcoming chunks of information reach more readers.

Text Features

Textbooks that are designed well employ varied text features for organizing their main ideas, illustrating central concepts, spotlighting significant details, and signaling evidence that supports the ideas and points conveyed. When a textbook uses these features in recurrent patterns that are predictable, it makes it easier for readers to locate information and come up with connections. When readers comprehend how to make use of text features, they will take less time and effort deciphering how the text is organized, leaving them more time and energy for focusing on the actual content in the text. Instructional activities can include not only previewing text through observing main text features, but moreover through examining and deconstructing the text and ascertaining how the text features can aid them in locating and applying text information for learning.

Included among various text features are a table of contents, headings, subheadings, an index, a glossary, a foreword, a preface, paragraphing spaces, bullet lists, footnotes, sidebars, diagrams, graphs, charts, pictures, illustrations, captions, italics, boldface, colors, and symbols. A **glossary** is a list of key vocabulary words and/or technical terminology and definitions. This helps readers recognize or learn specialized terms used in the text before reading it. A **foreword** is typically written by someone other than the text author and appears at the beginning to introduce, inform, recommend, and/or praise the work. A **preface** is often written by the author and also appears at the beginning, to introduce or explain something about the text, like new additions. A **sidebar** is a box with text and sometimes graphics at the left or right side of a page, typically focusing on a more specific issue, example, or aspect of the subject. **Footnotes** are additional comments/notes at the bottom of the page, signaled by superscript numbers in the text.

Text Features on Websites

On the Internet or in computer software programs, text features include URLs, home pages, pop-up menus, drop-down menus, bookmarks, buttons, links, navigation bars, text boxes, arrows, symbols, colors, graphics, logos, and abbreviations. URLs (Universal Resource Locators) indicate the internet "address" or location of a website or web page. They often start with www. (world wide web) or http:// (hypertext transfer protocol) or https:// (the "s" indicates a secure site) and appear in the Internet browser's top address bar. Clickable buttons are often links to specific pages on a website or other external sites. Users can click on some buttons to open pop-up or drop-down menus, which offer a list of actions or departments from which to select. Bookmarks are the electronic versions of physical bookmarks. When users bookmark a website/page, a link is established to the site URL and saved, enabling returning to the site in the future without having to remember its name or URL by clicking the bookmark.

Readers can more easily navigate websites and read their information by observing and utilizing their various text features. For example, most fully developed websites include search bars, where users can type in topics, questions, titles, or names to locate specific information within the large amounts stored on many sites. Navigation bars (software developers frequently use the abbreviation term "navbar") are graphical user interfaces (GUIs) that facilitate visiting different sections, departments, or pages within a website, which can be difficult or impossible to find without these. Typically, they appear as a series of links running horizontally across the top of each page. Navigation bars displayed vertically along the left side of the page are also called sidebars. Links, i.e. hyperlinks, enable hyperspeed browsing by allowing readers to jump to new pages/sites. They may be URLs, words, phrases, images, buttons, etc. They are often but not always underlined and/or blue, or other colors.

Locating the Place in a Text Where a Specific Kind of Information Can Be Found

When a student has an assignment to read a source and answer questions or research and write a paper, it's helpful to have the skills to locate a specific kind of information in the source being used. This will help save time and provide the necessary facts, points, or information. The following include descriptions of some common sources and features that can help direct a student to a desired place within that source:

Books as Resources
To evaluate the worth of the book for the research paper, the student first considers the book title to get an idea of its content. Then the student can scan the book's table of contents for chapter titles and topics to get further ideas of their applicability to the topic. The student may also turn to the end of the book to look for an alphabetized index. Most academic textbooks and scholarly works have these; students can look up key topic terms to see how many are included and how many pages are devoted to them.

Textbooks that are designed well employ varied text features for organizing their main ideas, illustrating central concepts, spotlighting significant details, and signaling evidence that supports the ideas and points conveyed. When a textbook uses these features in recurrent patterns that are predictable, it makes it easier for readers to locate information and come up with connections. When readers comprehend how to make use of text features, they will take less time and effort deciphering how the text is organized, leaving them more time and energy for focusing on the actual content in the text. Instructional activities can include not only previewing text through observing main text features, but moreover through examining and deconstructing the text and ascertaining how the text features can aid them in locating and applying text information for learning.

Included among various text features are a table of contents, headings, subheadings, an index, a glossary, a foreword, a preface, paragraphing spaces, bullet lists, footnotes, sidebars, diagrams, graphs, charts, pictures, illustrations, captions, italics, boldface, colors, and symbols. A glossary is a list of key vocabulary words and/or technical terminology and definitions. This helps readers recognize or learn specialized terms used in the text before reading it. A foreword is typically written by someone other than the text author and appears at the beginning to introduce, inform, recommend, and/or praise the work. A preface is often written by the author and also appears at the beginning, to introduce or explain something about the text, like new additions. A sidebar is a box with text and sometimes graphics at the left or right side of a page, typically focusing on a more specific issue, example, or aspect of the subject. Footnotes are additional comments/notes at the bottom of the page, signaled by superscript numbers in the text.

When examining a book, a journal article, a monograph, or other publication, the table of contents is in the front. In books, it is typically found following the title page, publication information (often on the facing side of the title page), and dedication page, when one is included. In shorter publications, the table of contents may follow the title page, or the title on the same page. The table of contents in a book lists the number and title of each chapter and its beginning page number. An index, which is most common in books but may also be included in shorter works, is at the back of the publication. Books, especially academic texts, frequently have two: a subject index and an author index. Readers can look alphabetically for specific subjects in the subject index. Likewise, they can look up specific authors cited, quoted, discussed, or mentioned in the author index.

The index in a book offers particular advantages to students. For example, college course instructors typically assign certain textbooks, but do not expect students to read the entire book from cover to cover immediately. They usually assign specific chapters to read in preparation for specific lectures and/or discussions in certain upcoming classes. Reading portions at a time, some students may find references they either do not fully understand or want to know more about. They can look these topics up in the book's subject index to find them in later chapters. When a text author refers to another author, students can also look up the name in the book's author index to find all page numbers of all other references to that author. College students also typically are assigned research papers to write. A book's subject and author indexes can guide students to pages that may help inform them of other books to use for researching paper topics.

Journal Articles

Like books, journal articles are primary or secondary sources the student may need to use for researching any topic. To assess whether a journal article will be a useful source for a particular paper topic, a student can first get some idea about the content of the article by reading its title and subtitle, if any exists. Many journal articles, particularly scientific ones, include abstracts. These are brief summaries of the content. The student should read the abstract to get a more specific idea of whether the experiment, literature review, or other work documented is applicable to the paper topic. Students should also check the references at the end of the article, which today often contain links to related works for exploring the topic further.

Headings and subheadings concisely inform readers what each section of a paper contains, as well as showing how its information is organized both visually and verbally. Headings are typically up to about five words long. They are not meant to give in-depth analytical information about the topic of their section, but rather an idea of its subject matter. Text authors should maintain consistent style across all headings. Readers should not expect headings if there is not material for more than one heading at each level, just as a list is unnecessary for a single item. Subheadings may be a bit longer than headings because they expand upon them. Readers should skim the subheadings in a paper to use them as a map of how content is arranged. Subheadings are in smaller fonts than headings to mirror relative importance. Subheadings are not necessary for every paragraph. They should enhance content, not substitute for topic sentences.

When a heading is brief, simple, and written in the form of a question, it can have the effect of further drawing readers into the text. An effective author will also answer the question in the heading soon in the following text. Question headings and their text answers are particularly helpful for engaging readers with average reading skills. Both headings and subheadings are most effective with more readers when they are obvious, simple, and get to their points immediately. Simple headings attract readers; simple subheadings allow readers a break, during which they also inform reader decisions whether to continue reading or not. Headings stand out from other text through boldface, but also italicizing and underlining them would be excessive. Uppercase-lowercase headings are easier for readers to comprehend than all capitals. More legible fonts are better. Some experts prefer serif fonts in text, but sans-serif fonts in headings. Brief subheadings that preview upcoming chunks of information reach more readers.

Encyclopedias and Dictionaries

Dictionaries and encyclopedias are both reference books for looking up information alphabetically. Dictionaries are more exclusively focused on vocabulary words. They include each word's correct spelling, pronunciation, variants, part(s) of speech, definitions of one or more meanings, and examples used in a sentence. Some dictionaries provide illustrations of certain words when these inform the meaning. Some dictionaries also offer synonyms, antonyms, and related words under a word's entry. Encyclopedias, like dictionaries, often provide word pronunciations and definitions. However, they have broader scopes: one can look up entire subjects in encyclopedias, not just words, and find comprehensive, detailed information about historical events, famous people, countries, disciplines of study, and many other things. Dictionaries are for finding word meanings, pronunciations, and spellings; encyclopedias are for finding breadth and depth of information on a variety of topics.

Card Catalogs

A card catalog is a means of organizing, classifying, and locating the large numbers of books found in libraries. Without being able to look up books in library card catalogs, it would be virtually impossible to find them on library shelves. Card catalogs may be on traditional paper cards filed in drawers, or electronic catalogs accessible online; some libraries combine both. Books are shelved by subject area; subjects are coded using formal classification systems—standardized sets of rules for identifying and labeling books by subject and author. These assign each book a call number: a code indicating the classification system, subject, author, and title. Call numbers also function as bookshelf "addresses" where books can be located. Most public libraries use the Dewey Decimal Classification System. Most university, college, and research libraries use the Library of Congress Classification. Nursing students will also encounter the National Institute of Health's National Library of Medicine Classification System, which major collections of health sciences publications utilize.

Databases

A database is a collection of digital information organized for easy access, updating, and management. Users can sort and search databases for information. One way of classifying databases is by content, i.e. full-text, numerical, bibliographical, or images. Another classification method used in computing is by organizational approach. The most common approach is a relational database, which is tabular and defines data so they can be accessed and reorganized in various ways. A distributed database can be reproduced or interspersed among different locations within a network. An object-oriented database is organized to be aligned with object classes and subclasses defining the data. Databases usually collect files like product inventories, catalogs, customer profiles, sales transactions, student bodies, and resources. An associated set of application programs is a database management system or database manager. It enables users to specify which reports to generate, control access to reading and writing data, and analyze database usage. Structured Query Language (SQL) is a standard computer language for updating, querying, and otherwise interfacing with databases.

Websites

On the Internet or in computer software programs, text features include URLs, home pages, pop-up menus, drop-down menus, bookmarks, buttons, links, navigation bars, text boxes, arrows, symbols, colors, graphics, logos, and abbreviations. URLs (Universal Resource Locators) indicate the internet "address" or location of a website or web page. They often start with www. (world wide web) or http:// (hypertext transfer protocol) or https:// (the "s" indicates a secure site) and appear in the Internet browser's top address bar. Clickable buttons are often links to specific pages on a website or other external sites. Users can click on some buttons to open pop-up or drop-down menus, which offer a list of actions or departments from which to select. Bookmarks are the electronic versions of physical bookmarks. When users bookmark a website/page, a link is established to the site URL and saved, enabling returning to the site in the future without having to remember its name or URL by clicking the bookmark.

Readers can more easily navigate websites and read their information by observing and utilizing their various text features. For example, most fully developed websites include search bars, where users can type in topics, questions, titles, or names to locate specific information within the large amounts stored on many sites. Navigation bars (software developers frequently use the abbreviation term "navbar") are graphical user interfaces (GUIs) that facilitate visiting different sections, departments, or pages within a website, which can be difficult or impossible to find without these. Typically, they appear as a series of links running horizontally across the top of each page. Navigation bars displayed vertically along the left side of the page are also called sidebars. Links, i.e. hyperlinks, enable hyperspeed browsing by allowing readers to jump to new pages/sites. They may be URLs, words, phrases, images, buttons, etc. They are often but not always underlined and/or blue, or other colors.

Business Memos

Whereas everyday office memos were traditionally typed on paper, photocopied, and distributed, today they are more often typed on computers and distributed via e-mail, both interoffice and externally. Technology has thus made these communications more immediate. It is also helpful for people to read carefully and be familiar with memo components. For example, e-mails automatically provide the same "To:, From:, and Re:" lines traditionally required in paper memos, and in corresponding places—the top of the page/screen. Readers should observe whether "To: names/positions" include all intended recipients in case of misdirection errors or omitted recipients. "From:" informs sender level, role, and who will receive responses when people click "Reply." Users must be careful not to click "Reply All" unintentionally. They should also observe the "CC:" line, typically below "Re:," showing additional recipients.

Classified Ads

Classified advertisements include "Help Wanted" ads informing readers of positions open for hiring, real estate listings, cars for sale, and home and business services available. Traditional ads in newspapers had to save space, and this necessity has largely transferred to online ads. Because of needing to save space, advertisers employ many abbreviations. For example, here are some examples of abbreviations:

- FT=full-time
- PT=part-time
- A/P=accounts payable
- A/R=accounts receivable
- Asst.=assistant
- Bkkg.=bookkeeping
- Comm.=commission
- Bet.=between
- EOE=equal opportunity employer
- G/L=general ledger
- Immed.=immediately
- Exc.=excellent
- Exp.=experience
- Eves.=evenings
- Secy.=secretary
- Temp=temporary
- Sal=salary
- Req=required
- Refs=references
- Wk=week or work
- WPM=words per minute

Classified ads frequently use abbreviations to take up less space, both on paper and digitally on websites. Those who read these ads will find it less confusing if they learn some common abbreviations used by businesses when advertising job positions. Here are some examples:

- Mgt.=management
- Mgr.=manager
- Mfg.=manufacturing
- Nat'l=national
- Dept.=department
- Min.=minimum
- Yrs.=years
- Nec=necessary
- Neg=negotiable
- Oppty=opportunity
- O/T=overtime
- K=1,000

Readers of classified ads may focus on certain features to the exclusion of others. For example, if a reader sees the job title or salary they are seeking, or notices the experience, education, degree, or other credentials required match their own qualifications perfectly, they may fail to notice other important information, like "No benefits." This is important because the employers are disclosing that they will not provide health insurance, retirement accounts, paid sick leave, paid maternity/paternity leave, paid vacation, etc. to any employee whom they hire. Someone expecting a traditional 9 to 5 job who fails to observe that an ad states "Evenings" or just the abbreviation "Eves" will be disappointed, as will the applicant who overlooks a line saying, "Some evenings and weekends reqd." Applicants overlooking information like "Apply in person" may e-mail or mail their resumes and receive no response. The job hopeful with no previous experience and one reference must attend to information like "Minimum 5 yrs. exp, 3 refs," meaning they likely will not qualify.

Employment Ads

Job applicants should pay attention to the information included in classified employment ads. On one hand, they do need to believe and accept certain statements, such as "Please, no phone calls," which is frequently used by employers posting ads on Craigslist and similar websites. New applicants just graduated from or still in college will be glad to see "No exp necessary" in some ads, indicating they need no previous work experience in that job category. "FT/PT" means the employer offers the options of working full-time or part-time, another plus for students. On the other hand, ad readers should also take into consideration the fact that many employers list all the attributes of their *ideal* employee, but they do not necessarily expect to find such a candidate. If a potential applicant's education, training, credentials, and experience are not exactly the same as what the employer lists as desired but are not radically different either, it can be productive to apply anyway, while honestly representing one's actual qualifications.

Atlases

A **road atlas** is a publication designed to assist travelers who are driving on road trips rather than taking airplanes, trains, ships, etc. Travelers use road atlases to determine which routes to take and places to stop; how to navigate specific cities, locate landmarks, estimate mileages and travel times; see photographs of places they plan to visit; and find other travel-related information. One familiar, reputable road atlas is published by the National Geographic Society. It includes detailed, accurate maps of the United States, Canada, and Mexico; historic sites, scenic routes, recreation information, and points of interest; and its Adventure Edition spotlights 100 top U.S. adventure destinations and most popular national parks. The best-selling road atlas in the United States, also probably the best-known and most trusted, is published annually by Rand McNally, which has published road atlases for many years. It includes maps, mileage charts, information on tourism and road construction, maps of individual city details, and the editor's favorite road trips (in the 2016 edition) including recommended points of interest en route.

Owners' Manuals

An **owner's manual** is typically a booklet, but may also be as short as a page or as long as a book, depending on the individual instance. The purpose of an owner's manual is to give the owner instructions, usually step-by-step, for how to use a specific product or a group or range of products. Manuals accompany consumer products as diverse as cars, computers, tablets, smartphones, printers, home appliances, shop machines, and many others. In addition to directions for operating products, they include important warnings of things *not* to do that pose safety or health hazards or can damage the product and void the manufacturer's product warranty, like immersion in water, exposure to high temperatures, operating something for too long, dropping fragile items, or rough handling. Manuals teach correct operating practices, sequences, precautions, and cautions, averting many costly and/or dangerous mishaps.

Food Labels

When reading the labels on food products, it is often necessary to interpret the nutrition facts and other product information. Without the consumer's being aware and informed of this, much of this information can be very misleading. For example, a popular brand name of corn chips lists the calories, fat, etc. per serving in the nutrition facts printed on the bag, but on closer inspection, it defines a serving size as six chips—far fewer than most people would consume at a time. Serving sizes and the number of servings per container can be unrealistic. For example, a jumbo muffin's wrapper indicates it contains three servings. Not only do most consumers not divide a muffin and eat only part; but it is moreover rather difficult to cut a muffin into equal thirds. A king-sized package of chili cheese-flavored corn chips says it contains 4.5 servings per container. This is not very useful information, since people cannot divide the package into equal servings and are unlikely to eat four servings and then ½ a serving.

Product Packaging

Consumers today cannot take product labels at face value. While many people do not read or even look at the information on packages before eating their contents, those who do must use more consideration and analysis than they might expect to understand it. For example, a well-known brand of strawberry-flavored breakfast toaster pastry displays a picture of four whole strawberries on the wrapper. While this looks appealing, encouraging consumers to infer the product contains wholesome fruit—and perhaps even believe it contains four whole strawberries—reading the ingredients list reveals it contains only 2 percent or less of dried strawberries. A consumer must be detail-oriented (and curious or motivated enough) to read the full ingredients list, which also reveals unhealthy corn syrup and high fructose corn syrup high on the list after enriched flour. Consumers must also educate themselves about euphemistically misleading terms: "enriched" flour has vitamins and minerals added, but it is refined flour without whole grain, bran, or fiber.

While manufacturers generally provide extensive information printed on their package labels, it is typically in very small print—many consumers do not read it—and even consumers who do read all the information must look for small details to discover that the information is often not realistic. For example, a box of brownie mix lists grams of fat, total calories, and calories from fat. However, by paying attention to small details like asterisks next to this information, and finding the additional information referenced by the asterisks, the consumer discovers that these amounts are for only the dry mix—not the added eggs, oil, or milk. Consumers typically do not eat dry cake mixes, and having to determine and add the fat and calories from the additional ingredients is inconvenient. In another example, a box of macaroni and cheese mix has an asterisk by the fat grams indicating this value is for the macaroni only without the cheese, butter, or milk required, which contributes 6.4 times more fat.

Ingredients' Lists
Consumers can realize the importance of reading drug labeling through an analogy: What might occur if they were to read only part of the directions on a standardized test? Reading only part of the directions on medications can have similar, even more serious consequences. Prescription drug packages typically contain inserts, which provide extremely extensive, thorough, detailed information, including results of clinical trials and statistics showing patient responses and adverse effects. Some over-the-counter medications include inserts, and some do not. "Active ingredients" are those ingredients making medication effective. "Inactive ingredients" including flavorings, preservatives, stabilizers, and emulsifiers have purposes, but not to treat symptoms. "Uses" indicates which symptoms a medication is meant to treat. "Directions" tell the dosage, frequency, maximum daily amount, and other requirements, like "Take with food," "Do not operate heavy machinery while using," etc. Drug labels also state how to store the product, like at what temperature or away from direct sunlight or humidity.

Many drugs which were previously available only by doctor prescription have recently become available over the counter without a prescription. While enough years of testing may have determined that these substances typically do not cause serious problems, consumers must nevertheless thoroughly read and understand all the information on the labels before taking them. If they do not, they could still suffer serious harm. For example, some individuals have allergies to specific substances. Both prescription and over-the-counter medication products list their ingredients, including warnings about allergies. Allergic reactions can include anaphylactic shock, which can be fatal if not treated immediately. Also, consumers must read and follow dosing directions: taking more than directed can cause harm, and taking less can be ineffective to treat symptoms. Some medication labels warn not to mix them with certain other drugs to avoid harmful drug interactions. Additionally, without reading ingredients, some consumers take multiple products including the same active ingredients, resulting in overdoses.

Understanding How a Text is Organized

The author's purpose determines the organization of a passage. The organization guides the connections between the ideas that support the main idea and establishes relationships between supporting ideas.

For example, suppose an author wants to explain why Henry VIII created the Church of England. This author might choose a sequential structure with time order relationships to describe the events. She would also include the cause and effect structure between the ideas to establish the relationship between the result and the circumstances that caused the result: "*Henry VIII created the Church of England because he was excommunicated from the Catholic church.*"

If the author's purpose is to convince someone to leave the Church of England to return to Catholicism, they might use comparison and contrast to describe the ideals of the two churches. The same series of events and cause and effect relationships contribute to the main idea, but the conclusion the author wants the reader to make is different: "*The foundation of the Church of England is sinful.*" The author could also use order of importance to provide a list of reasons why this event occurred, or the reasons the reader should leave the Church of England.

Text structure is the way in which the author organizes and presents textual information so readers can follow and comprehend it. One kind of text structure is **sequence**. This means the author arranges the text in a logical order from beginning to middle to end. There are three types of sequences:

- Chronological: ordering events in time from earliest to latest
- Spatial: describing objects, people, or spaces according to their relationships to one another in space
- Order of Importance: addressing topics, characters, or ideas according to how important they are, from either least important to most important

Chronological sequence is the most common sequential text structure. Readers can identify sequential structure by looking for words that signal it, like *first, earlier, meanwhile, next, then, later, finally;* and specific times and dates the author includes as chronological references.

Problem-Solution Text Structure

The **problem-solution** text structure organizes textual information by presenting readers with a problem and then developing its solution throughout the course of the text. The author may present a variety of alternatives as possible solutions, eliminating each as they are found unsuccessful, or gradually leading up to the ultimate solution. For example, in fiction, an author might write a murder mystery novel and have the character(s) solve it through investigating various clues or character alibis until the killer is identified. In nonfiction, an author writing an essay or book on a real-world problem might discuss various alternatives and explain their disadvantages or why they would not work before identifying the best solution. For scientific research, an author reporting and discussing scientific experiment results would explain why various alternatives failed or succeeded.

Comparison-Contrast Text Structure

Comparison identifies similarities between two or more things. **Contrast** identifies differences between two or more things. Authors typically employ both to illustrate relationships between things by highlighting their commonalities and deviations. For example, a writer might compare Windows and Linux as operating systems, and contrast Linux as free and open-source vs. Windows as proprietary. When writing an essay, sometimes it is useful to create an image of the two objects or events you are comparing or contrasting. Venn diagrams are useful because they show the differences as well as the similarities between two things. Once you've seen the similarities and differences on paper, it might be helpful to create an outline of the essay with both comparison and contrast. Every outline will look different, because every two or more things will have a different number of comparisons and contrasts. Say you are trying to compare and contrast carrots with sweet potatoes.

Here is an example of a compare/contrast outline using those topics:

- Introduction: Talk about why you are comparing and contrasting carrots and sweet potatoes. Give the thesis statement.
- Body paragraph 1: Sweet potatoes and carrots are both root vegetables (similarity)
- Body paragraph 2: Sweet potatoes and carrots are both orange (similarity)
- Body paragraph 3: Sweet potatoes and carrots have different nutritional components (difference)
- Conclusion: Restate the purpose of your comparison/contrast essay.

Of course, if there is only one similarity between your topics and two differences, you will want to rearrange your outline. Always tailor your essay to what works best with your topic.

Descriptive Text Structure

Description can be both a type of text structure and a type of text. Some texts are descriptive throughout entire books. For example, a book may describe the geography of a certain country, state, or region, or tell readers all about dolphins by describing many of their characteristics. Many other texts are not descriptive throughout, but use descriptive passages within the overall text. The following are a few examples of descriptive text:

- When the author describes a character in a novel
- When the author sets the scene for an event by describing the setting
- When a biographer describes the personality and behaviors of a real-life individual
- When a historian describes the details of a particular battle within a book about a specific war
- When a travel writer describes the climate, people, foods, and/or customs of a certain place

A hallmark of description is using sensory details, painting a vivid picture so readers can imagine it almost as if they were experiencing it personally.

Cause and Effect Text Structure

When using **cause and effect** to extrapolate meaning from text, readers must determine the cause when the author only communicates effects. For example, if a description of a child eating an ice cream cone includes details like beads of sweat forming on the child's face and the ice cream dripping down her hand faster than she can lick it off, the reader can infer or conclude it must be hot outside. A useful technique for making such decisions is wording them in "*If...then*" form, e.g. "*If* the child is perspiring and the ice cream melting, *then* it may be a hot day." Cause and effect text structures explain why certain events or actions resulted in particular outcomes. For example, an author might describe America's historical large flocks of dodo birds, the fact that gunshots did not startle/frighten dodos, and that because dodos did not flee, settlers killed whole flocks in one hunting session, explaining how the dodo was hunted into extinction.

Identifying Information in a Table or Graph

Line Graphs

Line graphs are useful for visually representing data that vary continuously over time, like an individual student's test scores. The horizontal or *x*-axis shows dates/times; the vertical or *y*-axis shows point values. A dot is plotted on the point where each horizontal date line intersects each vertical number line, and then these dots are connected, forming a line. Line graphs show whether changes in values over time exhibit trends like ascending, descending, flat, or more variable, like going up and down at different times. For example, suppose a student's scores on the same type of reading test were 75% in October, 80% in

November, 78% in December, 82% in January, 85% in February, 88% in March, and 90% in April. A line graph of these scores would look like this:

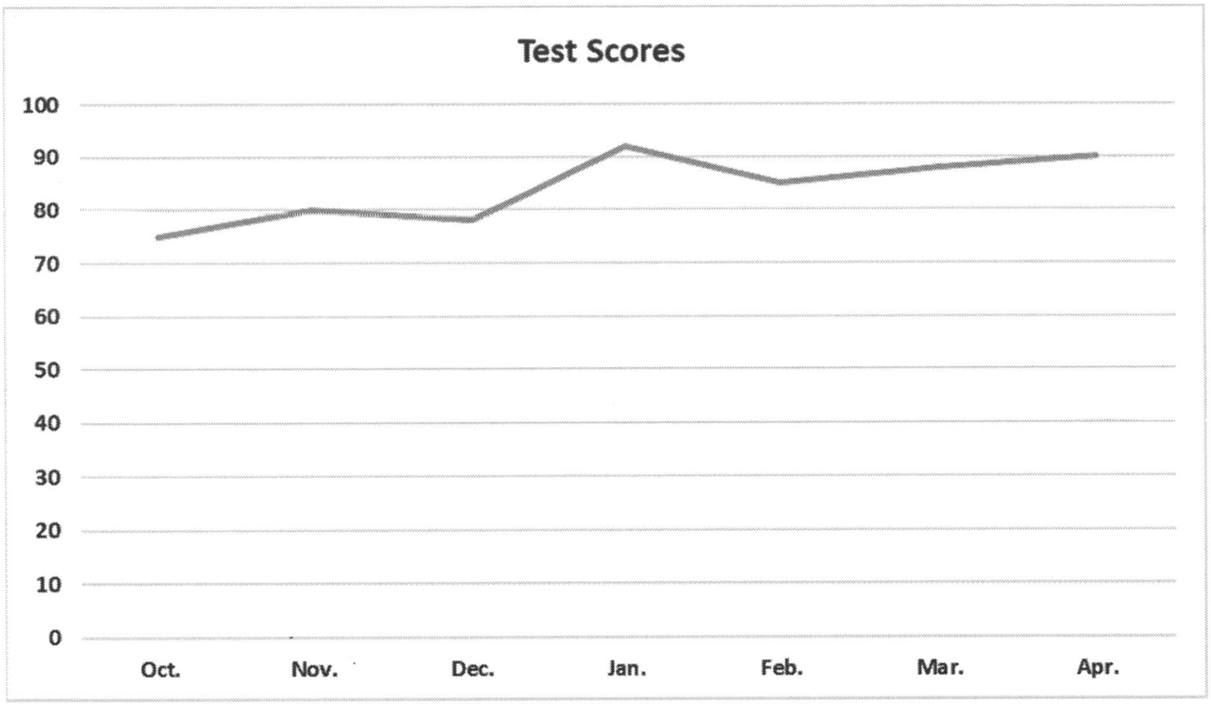

Bar Graphs

Bar graphs feature equally spaced, horizontal or vertical rectangular bars representing numerical values. They can show change over time as line graphs do, but unlike line graphs, bar graphs can also show differences and similarities among values at a single point in time. Bar graphs are also helpful for visually representing data from different categories, especially when the horizontal axis displays some value that is not numerical, like basketball players with their heights:

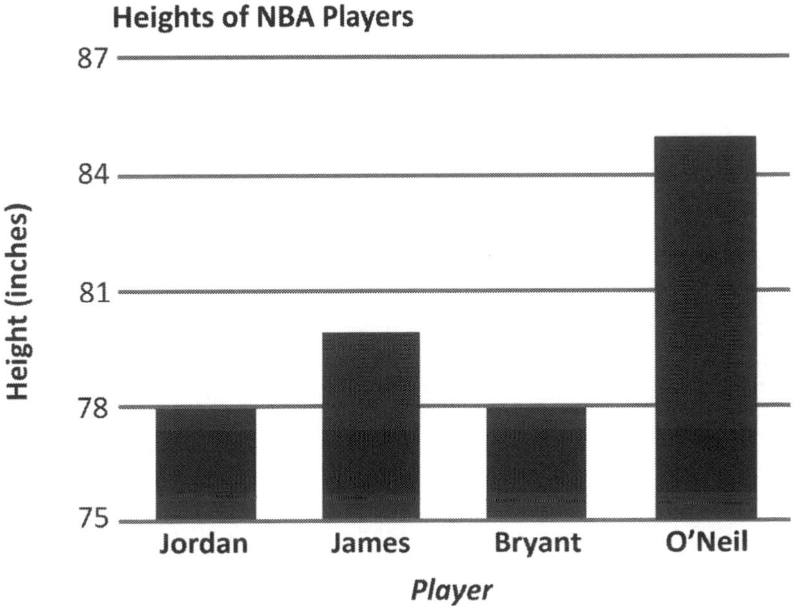

Pie Charts

Pie charts, also called **circle graphs**, are good for representing percentages or proportions of a whole quantity because they represent the whole as a circle or "pie", with the various proportion values shown as "slices" or wedges of the pie. This gives viewers a clear idea of how much of a total each item occupies. For example, biologists may have information that 62% of dogs have brown eyes, 20% have green eyes, and 18% have blue eyes. A pie chart of these distributions would look like this:

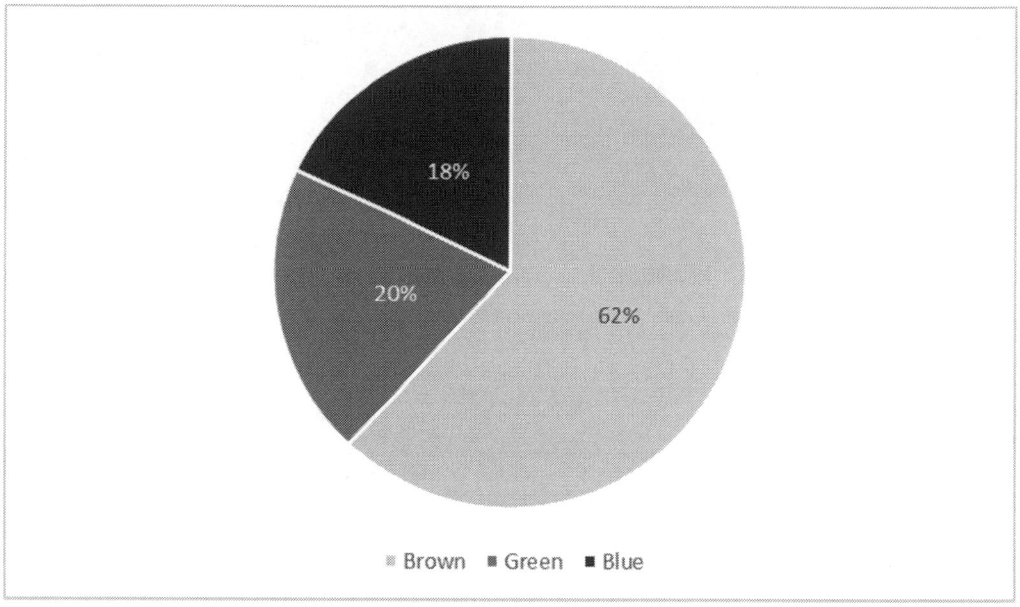

Pictograms

Magazines, newspapers, and other similar publications designed for consumption by the general public often use pictograms to represent data. **Pictograms** feature icons or symbols that look like whatever category of data is being counted, like little silhouettes shaped like human beings commonly used to represent people. If the data involve large numbers, like populations, one person symbol might represent one million people, or one thousand, etc. For smaller values, such as how many individuals out of ten fit a given description, one symbol might equal one person. Male and female silhouettes are used to differentiate gender, and child shapes for children. Little clock symbols are used to represent amounts of time, such as a given number of hours; calendar pages might depict months; suns and moons could show days and nights; hourglasses might represent minutes. While pictogram symbols are easily recognizable and appealing to general viewers, one disadvantage is that it is difficult to display partial symbols for in-between quantities.

Practice Questions

Questions 1-6 are based on the following passage from The Life, Crime, and Capture of John Wilkes Booth *by George Alfred Townsend:*

The box in which the President sat consisted of two boxes turned into one, the middle partition being removed, as on all occasions when a state party visited the theater. The box was on a level with the dress circle; about twelve feet above the stage. There were two entrances—the door nearest to the wall having been closed and locked; the door nearest the balustrades of the dress circle, and at right angles with it, being open and left open, after the visitors had entered. The interior was carpeted, lined with crimson paper, and furnished with a sofa covered with crimson velvet, three arm chairs similarly covered, and six cane-bottomed chairs. Festoons of flags hung before the front of the box against a background of lace.

President Lincoln took one of the arm-chairs and seated himself in the front of the box, in the angle nearest the audience, where, partially screened from observation, he had the best view of what was transpiring on the stage. Mrs. Lincoln sat next to him, and Miss Harris in the opposite angle nearest the stage. Major Rathbone sat just behind Mrs. Lincoln and Miss Harris. These four were the only persons in the box.

The play proceeded, although "Our American Cousin," without Mr. Sothern, has, since that gentleman's departure from this country, been justly esteemed a very dull affair. The audience at Ford's, including Mrs. Lincoln, seemed to enjoy it very much. The worthy wife of the President leaned forward, her hand upon her husband's knee, watching every scene in the drama with amused attention. Even across the President's face at intervals swept a smile, robbing it of its habitual sadness.

About the beginning of the second act, the mare, standing in the stable in the rear of the theater, was disturbed in the midst of her meal by the entrance of the young man who had quitted her in the afternoon. It is presumed that she was saddled and bridled with exquisite care.

Having completed these preparations, Mr. Booth entered the theater by the stage door; summoned one of the scene shifters, Mr. John Spangler, emerged through the same door with that individual, leaving the door open, and left the mare in his hands to be held until he (Booth) should return. Booth who was even more fashionably and richly dressed than usual, walked thence around to the front of the theater, and went in. Ascending to the dress circle, he stood for a little time gazing around upon the audience and occasionally upon the stage in his usual graceful manner. He was subsequently observed by Mr. Ford, the proprietor of the theater, to be slowly elbowing his way through the crowd that packed the rear of the dress circle toward the right side, at the extremity of which was the box where Mr. and Mrs. Lincoln and their companions were seated. Mr. Ford casually noticed this as a slightly extraordinary symptom of interest on the part of an actor so familiar with the routine of the theater and the play.

1. Which of the following best describes the author's attitude toward the events leading up to the assassination of President Lincoln?

   a. Excitement, due to the setting and its people
   b. Sadness, due to the death of a beloved president
   c. Anger, due to the impending violence
   d. Neutrality, due to the style of the report
   e. Apprehension, due to the crowd and their ignorance

2. What does the author mean by the last sentence in the passage?

   a. Mr. Ford was suspicious of Booth and assumed he was making his way to Mr. Lincoln's box.
   b. Mr. Ford assumed Booth's movement throughout the theater was due to being familiar with the theater.
   c. Mr. Ford thought that Booth was making his way to the theater lounge to find his companions.
   d. Mr. Ford thought that Booth was elbowing his way to the dressing room to get ready for the play.
   e. Mr. Ford thought that Booth was coming down with an illness due to the strange symptoms he displayed.

3. Given the author's description of the play "Our American Cousin," which one of the following is most analogous to Mr. Sothern's departure from the theater?

   a. A ballet dancer who leaves the New York City Ballet just before they go on to their final performance.
   b. A basketball player leaves an NBA team and the next year they make it to the championship but lose.
   c. A lead singer leaves their band to begin a solo career, and the band's sales on their next album drop by 50 percent.
   d. A movie actor who dies in the middle of making a movie and the movie is made anyway by actors who resemble the deceased.
   e. A professor who switches to the top-rated university for their department only to find the university they left behind has surpassed his new department's rating.

4. Which of the following texts most closely relates to the organizational structure of the passage?

   a. A chronological account in a fiction novel of a woman and a man meeting for the first time.
   b. A cause-and-effect text ruminating on the causes of global warming.
   c. An autobiography that begins with the subject's death and culminates in his birth.
   d. A text focusing on finding a solution to the problem of the Higgs boson particle.
   e. A text contrasting the realities of life on Mars versus life on Earth.

5. Which of the following words, if substituted for the word *festoons* in the first paragraph, would LEAST change the meaning of the sentence?

   a. Feathers
   b. Armies
   c. Adornments
   d. Buckets
   e. Boats

6. What is the primary purpose of the passage?
   a. To persuade the audience that John Wilkes Booth killed Abraham Lincoln
   b. To inform the audience of the setting wherein Lincoln was shot
   c. To narrate the bravery of Lincoln and his last days as President
   d. To recount in detail the events that led up to Abraham Lincoln's death
   e. To disprove the popular opinion that John Wilkes Booth is the person who killed Abraham Lincoln

Questions 7-13 are based on the following passage from The Story of Germ Life *by Herbert William Conn:*

The first and most universal change effected in milk is its souring. So universal is this phenomenon that it is generally regarded as an inevitable change that cannot be avoided, and, as already pointed out, has in the past been regarded as a normal property of milk. To-day, however, the phenomenon is well understood. It is due to the action of certain of the milk bacteria upon the milk sugar which converts it into lactic acid, and this acid gives the sour taste and curdles the milk. After this acid is produced in small quantity its presence proves deleterious to the growth of the bacteria, and further bacterial growth is checked. After souring, therefore, the milk for some time does not ordinarily undergo any further changes.

Milk souring has been commonly regarded as a single phenomenon, alike in all cases. When it was first studied by bacteriologists it was thought to be due in all cases to a single species of micro-organism which was discovered to be commonly present and named *Bacillus acidi lactici.* This bacterium has certainly the power of souring milk rapidly, and is found to be very common in dairies in Europe. As soon as bacteriologists turned their attention more closely to the subject it was found that the spontaneous souring of milk was not always caused by the same species of bacterium. Instead of finding this *Bacillus acidi lactici* always present, they found that quite a number of different species of bacteria have the power of souring milk, and are found in different specimens of soured milk.

The number of species of bacteria that have been found to sour milk has increased until something over a hundred are known to have this power. These different species do not affect the milk in the same way. All produce some acid, but they differ in the kind and the amount of acid, and especially in the other changes which are effected at the same time that the milk is soured, so that the resulting soured milk is quite variable. In spite of this variety, however, the most recent work tends to show that the majority of cases of spontaneous souring of milk are produced by bacteria which, though somewhat variable, probably constitute a single species, and are identical with the *Bacillus acidi lactici.* This species, found common in the dairies of Europe, according to recent investigations occurs in this country as well. We may say, then, that while there are many species of bacteria infesting the dairy which can sour the milk, there is one that is more common and more universally found than others, and this is the ordinary cause of milk souring.

When we study more carefully the effect upon the milk of the different species of bacteria found in the dairy, we find that there is a great variety of changes they produce when they are allowed to grow in milk. The dairyman experiences many troubles with his milk. It sometimes curdles without becoming acid. Sometimes it becomes bitter, or acquires an unpleasant "tainted" taste, or, again, a "soapy" taste. Occasionally, a dairyman finds his milk becoming slimy, instead of souring and curdling in the normal fashion. At such times, after a number of hours, the milk becomes so slimy that it can be drawn into long threads. Such an infection proves very troublesome, for many a time it persists in spite of all attempts made to remedy it. Again, in other cases the milk will turn blue, acquiring about the time it becomes sour a beautiful sky-blue colour.

Or it may become red, or occasionally yellow. All of these troubles the dairyman owes to the presence in his milk of unusual species of bacteria which grow there abundantly.

7. The word *deleterious* in the first paragraph can be best interpreted as meaning which one of the following?
   a. Amicable
   b. Smoldering
   c. Luminous
   d. Ruinous
   e. Virtuous

8. Which of the following best explains how the passage is organized?
   a. The author begins by presenting the effects of a phenomenon, then explains the process of this phenomenon, and then ends by giving the history of the study of this phenomenon.
   b. The author begins by explaining a process or phenomenon, then gives the history of the study of this phenomenon, this ends by presenting the effects of this phenomenon.
   c. The author begins by giving the history of the study of a certain phenomenon, then explains the process of this phenomenon, then ends by presenting the effects of this phenomenon.
   d. The author begins by giving a broad definition of a subject, then presents more specific cases of the subject, then ends by contrasting two different viewpoints on the subject.
   e. The author begins by contrasting two different viewpoints, then gives a short explanation of a subject, then ends by summarizing what was previously stated in the passage.

9. What is the primary purpose of the passage?
   a. To inform the reader of the phenomenon, investigation, and consequences of milk souring
   b. To persuade the reader that milk souring is due to *Bacillus acidi lactici*, which is commonly found in the dairies of Europe
   c. To describe the accounts and findings of researchers studying the phenomenon of milk souring
   d. To discount the former researchers' opinions on milk souring and bring light to new investigations
   e. To narrate the story of one researcher who discovered the phenomenon of milk souring and its subsequent effects

10. What does the author say about the ordinary cause of milk souring?
   a. Milk souring is caused mostly by a species of bacteria called *Bacillus acidi lactici*, although former research asserted that it was caused by a variety of bacteria.
   b. The ordinary cause of milk souring is unknown to current researchers, although former researchers thought it was due to a species of bacteria called *Bacillus acidi lactici*.
   c. Milk souring is caused mostly by a species of bacteria identical to that of *Bacillus acidi lactici*, although there are a variety of other bacteria that cause milk souring as well.
   d. The ordinary cause of milk souring will sometimes curdle without becoming acidic, though sometimes it will turn colors other than white, or have strange smells or tastes.
   e. The ordinary cause of milk souring is from bacteria with a strange, "soapy" smell, usually the color of sky blue.

11. The author of the passage would most likely agree most with which of the following?
   a. Milk researchers in the past have been incompetent and have sent us on a wild goose chase when determining what causes milk souring.
   b. Dairymen are considered more expert in the field of milk souring than milk researchers.
   c. The study of milk souring has improved throughout the years, as we now understand more of what causes milk souring and what happens afterward.
   d. Any type of bacteria will turn milk sour, so it's best to keep milk in an airtight container while it is being used.
   e. The effects of milk souring is a natural occurrence of milk, so it should not be dangerous to consume.

12. Given the author's account of the consequences of milk souring, which of the following is most closely analogous to the author's description of what happens after milk becomes slimy?
   a. The chemical change that occurs when a firework explodes.
   b. A rainstorm that overwaters a succulent plant.
   c. Mercury inside of a thermometer that leaks out.
   d. A child who swallows flea medication.
   e. A large block of ice that melts into a liquid.

13. What type of paragraph would most likely come after the third?
   a. A paragraph depicting the general effects of bacteria on milk.
   b. A paragraph explaining a broad history of what researchers have found in regard to milk souring.
   c. A paragraph outlining the properties of milk souring and the way in which it occurs.
   d. A paragraph showing the ways bacteria infiltrate milk and ways to avoid this infiltration.
   e. A paragraph naming all the bacteria in alphabetical order with a brief definition of what each does to milk.

Questions 14-20 are based on the following two passages, labeled "Passage A" and "Passage B":

Passage A

(from "Free Speech in War Time" by James Parker Hall, written in 1921, published in Columbia Law Review, Vol. 21 No. 6)

> In approaching this problem of interpretation, we may first put out of consideration certain obvious limitations upon the generality of all guaranties of free speech. An occasional unthinking malcontent may urge that the only meaning not fraught with danger to liberty is the literal one that no utterance may be forbidden, no matter what its intent or result; but in fact, it is nowhere seriously argued by anyone whose opinion is entitled to respect that direct and intentional incitations to crime may not be forbidden by the state. If a state may properly forbid murder or robbery or treason, it may also punish those who induce or counsel the commission of such crimes. Any other view makes a mockery of the state's power to declare and punish offences. And what the state may do to prevent the incitement of serious crimes that are universally condemned, it may also do to prevent the incitement of lesser crimes, or of those in regard to the bad tendency of which public opinion is divided. That is, if the state may punish John for burning straw in an alley, it may also constitutionally punish Frank for inciting John to do it, though Frank did so by speech or writing. And if, in 1857, the United States could punish John for helping a fugitive slave to escape, it could also punish Frank for inducing John to do this, even though a large section of public opinion might applaud John and condemn the Fugitive Slave Law.

Passage B

(from "Freedom of Speech in War Time" by Zechariah Chafee, Jr. written in 1919, published in Harvard Law Review Vol. 32 No. 8)

> The true boundary line of the First Amendment can be fixed only when Congress and the courts realize that the principle on which speech is classified as lawful or unlawful involves the balancing against each other of two very important social interests, in public safety and in the search for truth. Every reasonable attempt should be made to maintain both interests unimpaired, and the great interest in free speech should be sacrificed only when the interest in public safety is really imperiled, and not, as most men believe, when it is barely conceivable that it may be slightly affected. In war time, therefore, speech should be unrestricted by the censorship or by punishment, unless it is clearly liable to cause direct and dangerous interference with the conduct of the war.
>
> Thus our problem of locating the boundary line of free speech is solved. It is fixed close to the point where words will give rise to unlawful acts. We cannot define the right of free speech with the precision of the Rule against Perpetuities or the Rule in Shelley's Case, because it involves national policies which are much more flexible than private property, but we can establish a workable principle of classification in this method of balancing and this broad test of certain danger. There is a similar balancing in the determination of what is "due process of law." And we can with certitude declare that the First Amendment forbids the punishment of words merely for their injurious tendencies. The history of the Amendment and the political function of free speech corroborate each other and make this conclusion plain.

14. Which one of the following questions is central to both passages?
    a. Why is freedom of speech something to be protected in the first place?
    b. Do people want absolute liberty or do they only want liberty for a certain purpose?
    c. What is the true definition of freedom of speech in a democracy?
    d. How can we find an appropriate boundary of freedom of speech during wartime?
    e. What is the interpretation of the first amendment and its limitations?

15. The authors of the two passages would be most likely to disagree over which of the following?
    a. A man is thrown in jail due to his provocation of violence in Washington D.C. during a riot.
    b. A man is thrown in jail for stealing bread for his starving family, and the judge has mercy for him and lets him go.
    c. A man is thrown in jail for encouraging a riot against the U.S. government for the wartime tactics although no violence ensues.
    d. A man is thrown in jail because he has been caught as a German spy working within the U.S. army.
    e. A man is thrown in jail because he murdered a German-born citizen whom he thought was working for the Central Powers during World War I.

16. The relationship between Passage A and Passage B is most analogous to the relationship between the documents described in which of the following?

a. A research report that asserts water pollution in major cities in California has increased by thirty percent in the past five years; an article advocating the cessation of chicken farms in California near rivers to avoid pollution.

b. An article detailing the effects of radiation in Fukushima; a research report describing the deaths and birth defects as a result of the hazardous waste dumped on the Somali Coast.

c. An article that suggests that labor laws during times of war should be left up to the states; an article that showcases labor laws during the past that have been altered due to the current crisis of war.

d. A research report arguing that the leading cause of methane emissions in the world is from agriculture practices; an article citing that the leading cause of methane emissions in the world is from the transportation of coal, oil, and natural gas.

e. A journal article in the Netherlands about the law of euthanasia that cites evidence to support only the act of passive euthanasia as an appropriate way to die; a journal article in the Netherlands about the law of euthanasia that cites evidence to support voluntary euthanasia in any aspect.

17. The author uses the examples in the last lines of Passage A in order to do what?

a. To demonstrate different types of crimes for the purpose of comparing them to see by which one the principle of freedom of speech would become objectionable.

b. To demonstrate that anyone who incites a crime, despite the severity or magnitude of the crime, should be held accountable for that crime in some degree.

c. To prove that the definition of "freedom of speech" is altered depending on what kind of crime is being committed.

d. To show that some crimes are in the best interest of a nation and should not be punishable if they are proven to prevent harm to others.

e. To suggest that the crimes mentioned should be reopened in order to punish those who incited the crimes.

18. Which of the following, if true, would most seriously undermine the claim proposed by the author in Passage A that if the state can punish a crime, then it can punish the incitement of that crime?

a. The idea that human beings are able and likely to change their mind between the utterance and execution of an event that may harm others.

b. The idea that human beings will always choose what they think is right based on their cultural upbringing.

c. The idea that the limitation of free speech by the government during wartime will protect the country from any group that causes a threat to that country's freedom.

d. The idea that those who support freedom of speech probably have intentions of subverting the government.

e. The idea that if a man encourages a woman to commit a crime and she succeeds, the man is just as guilty as the woman.

19. What is the primary purpose of the second passage?
   a. To analyze the First Amendment in historical situations in order to make an analogy to the current war at hand in the nation.
   b. To demonstrate that the boundaries set during wartime are different from that when the country is at peace, and that we should change our laws accordingly.
   c. To offer the idea that during wartime, the principle of freedom of speech should be limited to that of even minor utterances in relation to a crime.
   d. To call upon the interpretation of freedom of speech to be already evident in the First Amendment and to offer a clear perimeter of the principle during war time.
   e. To assert that any limitation on freedom of speech is a violation of human rights and that the circumstances of war do not change this violation.

20. Which of the following words, if substituted for the word *malcontent* in Passage A, would LEAST change the meaning of the sentence?
   a. Regimen
   b. Cacophony
   c. Anecdote
   d. Residua
   e. Grievance

Questions 21-27 are based on the following passage from Rhetoric and Poetry in the Renaissance: A Study of Rhetorical Terms in English Renaissance Literary Criticism *by DL Clark:*

> To the Greeks and Romans, rhetoric meant the theory of oratory. As a pedagogical mechanism, it endeavored to teach students to persuade an audience. The content of rhetoric included all that the ancients had learned to be of value in persuasive public speech. It taught how to work up a case by drawing valid inferences from sound evidence, how to organize this material in the most persuasive order, and how to compose in clear and harmonious sentences. Thus, to the Greeks and Romans, rhetoric was defined by its function of discovering means to persuasion and was taught in the schools as something that every free-born man could and should learn.
>
> In both these respects the ancients felt that poetics, the theory of poetry, was different from rhetoric. As the critical theorists believed that the poets were inspired, they endeavored less to teach men to be poets than to point out the excellences which the poets had attained. Although these critics generally, with the exceptions of Aristotle and Eratosthenes, believed the greatest value of poetry to be in the teaching of morality, no one of them endeavored to define poetry, as they did rhetoric, by its purpose. To Aristotle, and centuries later to Plutarch, the distinguishing mark of poetry was imitation. Not until the renaissance did critics define poetry as an art of imitation endeavoring to inculcate morality . . .
>
> The same essential difference between classical rhetoric and poetics appears in the content of classical poetics. Whereas classical rhetoric deals with speeches which might be delivered to convict or acquit a defendant in the law court, or to secure a certain action by the deliberative assembly, or to adorn an occasion, classical poetic deals with lyric, epic, and drama. It is a commonplace that classical literary critics paid little attention to the lyric. It is less frequently realized that they devoted almost as little space to discussion of metrics. By far the greater bulk of classical treatises on poetics is devoted to characterization and to the technique of plot construction, involving as it does narrative and dramatic unity and movement as distinct from logical unity and movement.

21. What does the author say about one way in which the purpose of poetry changed for later philosophers?

a. The author says that at first, poetry was not defined by its purpose but was valued for its ability to be used to teach morality. Later, some philosophers would define poetry by its ability to instill morality. Finally, during the renaissance, poetry was believed to be an imitative art, but was not necessarily believed to instill morality in its readers.

b. The author says that the classical understanding of poetry dealt with its ability to be used to teach morality. Later, philosophers would define poetry by its ability to imitate life. Finally, during the renaissance, poetry was believed to be an imitative art that instilled morality in its readers.

c. The author says that at first, poetry was thought to be an imitation of reality, then later, philosophers valued poetry more for its ability to instill morality.

d. The author says that the classical understanding of poetry was that it dealt with the search for truth through its content; later, the purpose of poetry would be through its entertainment value.

e. The author says that the initial understanding of the purpose of poetry was its entertainment value. Then, as poetry evolved into a more religious era, the renaissance, it was valued for its ability to instill morality through its teaching.

22. What does the author of the passage say about classical literary critics in relation to poetics?

a. That rhetoric was valued more than poetry because rhetoric had a definitive purpose to persuade an audience, and poetry's wavering purpose made it harder for critics to teach.

b. That although most poetry was written as lyric, epic, or drama, the critics were most focused on the techniques of lyric and epic and their performance of musicality and structure.

c. That although most poetry was written as lyric, epic, or drama, the critics were most focused on the techniques of the epic and drama and their performance of structure and character.

d. That the study of poetics was more pleasurable than the study of rhetoric due to its ability to assuage its audience, and the critics, therefore, focused on what poets did to create that effect.

e. That since poetics was made by the elite in Greek and Roman society, literary critics resented poetics for its obsession of material things and its superfluous linguistics.

23. What is the primary purpose of this passage?

a. To alert the readers to Greek and Roman culture regarding poetic texts and the focus on characterization and plot construction rather than lyric and meter.

b. To inform the readers of the changes in poetic critical theory throughout the years and to contrast those changes to the solidity of rhetoric.

c. To educate the audience on rhetoric by explaining the historical implications of using rhetoric in the education system.

d. To convince the audience that poetics is a subset of rhetoric as viewed by the Greek and Roman culture.

e. To contemplate the differences between classical rhetoric and poetry and to consider their purposes in a particular culture.

24. The word *inculcate* in the second paragraph can be best interpreted as meaning which one of the following?

a. Imbibe

b. Instill

c. Implode

d. Inquire

e. Idolize

25. Which of the following most closely resembles the way in which the passage is structured?

a. The first paragraph presents an issue. The second paragraph offers a solution to the problem. The third paragraph summarizes the first two paragraphs.
b. The first paragraph presents definitions and examples of a particular subject. The second paragraph presents a second subject in the same way. The third paragraph offers a contrast of the two subjects.
c. The first paragraph presents an inquiry. The second paragraph explains the details of that inquiry. The last paragraph offers a solution.
d. The first paragraph presents two subjects alongside definitions and examples. The second paragraph presents us a comparison of the two subjects. The third paragraph presents a contrast of the two subjects.
e. The first paragraph offers a solution to a problem. The second paragraph questions the solution. The third paragraph offers a different solution.

26. Given the author's description of the content of rhetoric in the first paragraph, which one of the following is most analogous to what it taught? (The sentence is shown below.)

It taught how to work up a case by drawing valid inferences from sound evidence, how to organize this material in the most persuasive order, how to compose in clear and harmonious sentences.

a. As a musician, they taught me that the end product of the music is everything—what I did to get there was irrelevant, whether it was my ability to read music or the reliance on my intuition to compose.
b. As a detective, they taught me that time meant everything when dealing with a new case, that the simplest explanation is usually the right one, and that documentation is extremely important to credibility.
c. As a writer, they taught me the most important thing about writing was consistently showing up to the page every single day, no matter where my muse was.
d. As a football player, they taught me how to understand the logistics of the game, how my placement on the field affected the rest of the team, and how to run and throw with a mixture of finesse and strength.
e. As a doctor, they taught me how to show compassion towards patients and how to take care of my own physical and mental health while running my own practice.

27. Which of the following words, if substituted for the word *treatises* in paragraph two, would LEAST change the meaning of the sentence?

a. Thesauruses
b. Encyclopedias
c. Sermons
d. Anthems
e. Commentary

Questions 28–31 are based on the following passage. It is from Oregon, Washington, and Alaska. Sights and Scenes for the Tourist, *written by E.L. Lomax in 1890:*

> Portland is a very beautiful city of 60,000 inhabitants, and situated on the Willamette river twelve miles from its junction with the Columbia. It is perhaps true of many of the growing cities of the West, that they do not offer the same social advantages as the older cities of the East. But this is principally the case as to what may be called boom cities, where the larger part of the population is of that floating class which follows in the line of temporary growth for the purposes of speculation, and in no sense applies to those centers of trade whose prosperity is based on the

solid foundation of legitimate business. As the metropolis of a vast section of country, having broad agricultural valleys filled with improved farms, surrounded by mountains rich in mineral wealth, and boundless forests of as fine timber as the world produces, the cause of Portland's growth and prosperity is the trade which it has as the center of collection and distribution of this great wealth of natural resources, and it has attracted, not the boomer and speculator, who find their profits in the wild excitement of the boom, but the merchant, manufacturer, and investor, who seek the surer if slower channels of legitimate business and investment. These have come from the East, most of them within the last few years. They came as seeking a better and wider field to engage in the same occupations they had followed in their Eastern homes, and bringing with them all the love of polite life which they had acquired there, have established here a new society, equaling in all respects that which they left behind. Here are as fine churches, as complete a system of schools, as fine residences, as great a love of music and art, as can be found at any city of the East of equal size.

But while Portland may justly claim to be the peer of any city of its size in the United States in all that pertains to social life, in the attractions of beauty of location and surroundings it stands without its peer. The work of art is but the copy of nature. What the residents of other cities see but in the copy, or must travel half the world over to see in the original, the resident of Portland has at its very door.

The city is situated on a gently-sloping ground, with, on the one side, the river, and on the other a range of hills, which, within easy walking distance, rise to an elevation of a thousand feet above the river, affording a most picturesque building site. From the very streets of the thickly settled portion of the city, the Cascade Mountains, with the snow-capped peaks of Hood, Adams, St. Helens, and Rainier, are in plain view.

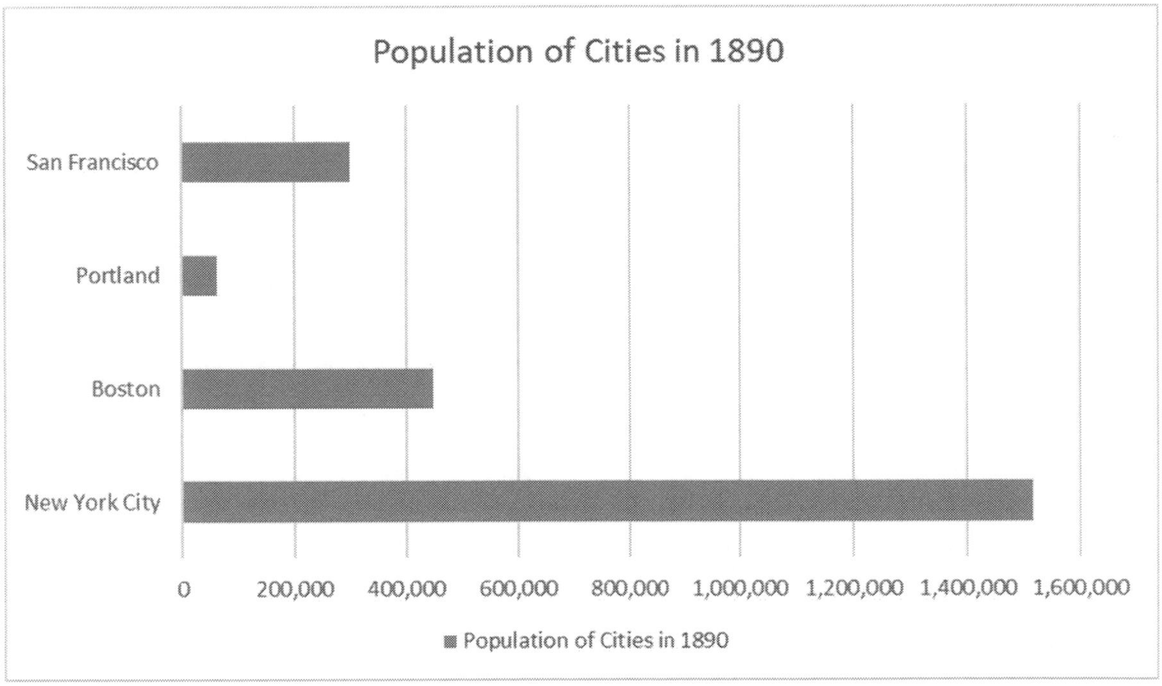

28. What is a characteristic of a "boom city," as indicated by the passage?
  a. A city that is built on a solid business foundation of mineral wealth and farming.
  b. An area of land on the west coast that quickly becomes populated by residents from the east coast.
  c. A city that, due to the hot weather and dry climate, catches fire frequently, resulting in a devastating population drop.
  d. A city whose population is made up of people who seek quick fortunes rather than building a solid business foundation.
  e. A city located on a river or river delta where the land is fertile and economic conditions are optimal.

29. By stating that "they do not offer the same social advantages as the older cities of the East" in the first paragraph, the author most likely intends to suggest which of the following?
  a. Inhabitants who reside in older cities in the East are much more social that inhabitants who reside in newer cities in the West because of background and experience.
  b. Cities in the West have no culture compared to the East because the culture in the East comes from European influence.
  c. Cities in the East are older than cities in the West, and older cities always have better culture than newer cities.
  d. Since cities in the West are newly established, it takes them a longer time to develop cultural roots and societal functions than those cities that are already established in the East.
  e. The culture in boom cities is likely to outpace previously-popular cities because they offer so much more.

30. Based on the information at the end of the first paragraph, what would the author say of Portland?
  a. It has twice as much culture as the cities in the East.
  b. It's amount of culture is dwindling as it becomes more business-oriented.
  c. It doesn't have as much culture as cities in the East.
  d. It doesn't have as much culture as cities in the West.
  e. It has as much culture as the cities in the East.

31. How many more citizens did San Francisco have than Portland in 1890?
  a. Approximately 110,000
  b. Approximately 240,000
  c. Approximately 500,000
  d. Approximately 1,000,000
  e. Approximately 1,500,000

Questions 32–34 are based on the excerpt from Variation of Animals and Plants *by Charles Darwin:*

> Peach (Amygdalus persica).—In the last chapter I gave two cases of a peach-almond and a double-flowered almond which suddenly produced fruit closely resembling true peaches. I have also given many cases of peach-trees producing buds, which, when developed into branches, have yielded nectarines. We have seen that no less than six named and several unnamed varieties of the peach have thus produced several varieties of nectarine. I have shown that it is highly improbable that all these peach-trees, some of which are old varieties, and have been propagated by the million, are hybrids from the peach and nectarine, and that it is opposed to all analogy to attribute the occasional production of nectarines on peach-trees to the direct action of pollen from some neighbouring nectarine-tree. Several of the cases are highly remarkable, because, firstly, the fruit thus produced has sometimes been in part a nectarine and in part a peach; secondly, because nectarines thus suddenly produced have reproduced themselves by seed; and

thirdly, because nectarines are produced from peach-trees from seed as well as from buds. The seed of the nectarine, on the other hand, occasionally produces peaches; and we have seen in one instance that a nectarine-tree yielded peaches by bud-variation. As the peach is certainly the oldest or primary variety, the production of peaches from nectarines, either by seeds or buds, may perhaps be considered as a case of reversion. Certain trees have also been described as indifferently bearing peaches or nectarines, and this may be considered as bud-variation carried to an extreme degree.

The grosse mignonne peach at Montreuil produced "from a sporting branch" the grosse mignonne tardive, "a most excellent variety," which ripens its fruit a fortnight later than the parent tree, and is equally good. (11/2. "Gardener's Chronicle" 1854 pg. 821.) This same peach has likewise produced by bud-variation the early grosse mignonne. Hunt's large tawny nectarine "originated from Hunt's small tawny nectarine, but not through seminal reproduction." (11/3. Lindley "Guide to Orchard" as quoted in "Gardener's Chronicle" 1852 pg. 821.)

Plums

Mr. Knight states that a tree of the yellow magnum bonum plum, forty years old, which had always borne ordinary fruit, produced a branch which yielded red magnum bonums. (11/4 "Transact. Hort. Soc." Volume 2 pg. 160.) Mr. Rivers, a Sawbridgeworth, informs me (January 1863) that a single tree out of 400 or 500 trees of the Early Prolific plum, which is a purple kind, descended from an old French variety bearing purple fruit, produced when about ten years old bright yellow plums; these differed in no respect except colour from those on the other trees, but were unlike any other known kind of yellow plum (11/5. See also "Gardener's Chronicle" 1863 pg. 27).

32. Which statement is NOT a detail from the passage?
   a. At least six named varieties of the peach have produced several varieties of nectarine.
   b. It is not probable that all of the peach-trees mentioned are hybrids from the peach and nectarine.
   c. An unremarkable case is the fact that nectarines are produced from peach-trees from seed as well as from buds.
   d. The production of peaches from nectarines might be considered a case of reversion.
   e. Some modern descendants of earlier plum trees now bear differently-colored fruit but are otherwise the same.

33. Which of the following most closely reveals the author's tone in this passage?
   a. Enthusiastic
   b. Objective
   c. Critical
   d. Desperate
   e. Anxious

34. Which of the following is an accurate paraphrasing of the following phrase?

Certain trees have also been described as indifferently bearing peaches or nectarines, and this may be considered as bud-variation carried to an extreme degree.

a. Some trees are described as bearing peaches and some trees have been described as bearing nectarines, but individually, the buds are extreme examples of variation.
b. One way in which bud-variation is said to be carried to an extreme degree is when specific trees have been shown to casually produce peaches or nectarines.
c. Certain trees are indifferent to bud-variation, as recently shown in the trees that produce both peaches and nectarines in the same season.
d. Nectarines and peaches are known to have cross-variation in their buds, which indifferently bears other sorts of fruit to an extreme degree.
e. Although possible, it's extremely uncommon in this day and age to find trees that can bear peaches or nectarines.

35. Which of the following is an acceptable heading to insert into the blank space?

Chapter 5: Literature and Language Usage
I. Figurative Speech
1. Alliteration
2. Metaphors
3. Onomatopoeia
4. _________

a. Nouns
b. Agreement
c. Personification
d. Syntax
e. Context

Questions 36–38 are based on the excerpt from A Christmas Carol *by Charles Dickens:*

Meanwhile the fog and darkness thickened so, that people ran about with flaring links, proffering their services to go before horses in carriages, and conduct them on their way. The ancient tower of a church, whose gruff old bell was always peeping slyly down at Scrooge out of a Gothic window in the wall, became invisible, and struck the hours and quarters in the clouds, with tremulous vibrations afterwards as if its teeth were chattering in its frozen head up there. The cold became intense. In the main street, at the corner of the court, some labourers were repairing the gas-pipes, and had lighted a great fire in a brazier, round which a party of ragged men and boys were gathered: warming their hands and winking their eyes before the blaze in rapture. The water-plug being left in solitude, its overflowings sullenly congealed, and turned to misanthropic ice. The brightness of the shops where holly sprigs and berries crackled in the lamp heat of the windows, made pale faces ruddy as they passed. Poulterers' and grocers' trades became a splendid joke; a glorious pageant, with which it was next to impossible to believe that such dull principles as bargain and sale had anything to do. The Lord Mayor, in the stronghold of the mighty Mansion House, gave orders to his fifty cooks and butlers to keep Christmas as a Lord Mayor's household should; and even the little tailor, whom he had fined five shillings on the previous Monday for being drunk and bloodthirsty in the streets, stirred up to-morrow's pudding in his garret, while his lean wife and the baby sallied out to buy the beef.

Foggier yet, and colder. Piercing, searching, biting cold. If the good Saint Dunstan had but nipped the Evil Spirit's nose with a touch of such weather as that, instead of using his familiar weapons, then indeed he would have roared to lusty purpose. The owner of one scant young nose, gnawed and mumbled by the hungry cold as bones are gnawed by dogs, stopped down at Scrooge's keyhole to regale him with a Christmas carol: but at the first sound of

"God bless you, merry gentleman! May nothing you dismay"

Scrooge seized the ruler with such energy of action, that the singer fled in terror, leaving the keyhole to the fog and even more congenial frost.

36. Which of the following can NOT be inferred from the passage?
    a. The season of this narrative is in the winter time.
    b. The majority of the narrative is located in a bustling city street.
    c. This passage takes place during the night time.
    d. The Lord Mayor is a wealthy person within the narrative.
    e. Scrooge was not kind and receptive to the caroler.

37. According to the passage, which of the following regarding the poulterers and grocers is true?
    a. They were so poor in the quality of their products that customers saw them as a joke.
    b. They put on a pageant in the streets every year for Christmas to entice their customers.
    c. They did not believe in Christmas, so they refused to participate in the town parade.
    d. They worked tirelessly to convert non-believers and spread the Christmas spirit.
    e. They set their shops up to be entertaining public spectacles rather than a dull trade exchange.

38. The author's depiction of the scene in the last few paragraphs does all EXCEPT which of the following?
    a. Offer an allusion to religious affiliation in England.
    b. Attempt to evoke empathy for the character of Scrooge.
    c. Provide a palpable experience through the use of imagery and diction.
    d. Depict Scrooge as an uncaring, terrifying character to his fellows.
    e. Help readers visualize the setting and the adverse personality of Scrooge.

Question 39 is based on the passage from Many Marriages *by Sherwood Anderson:*

There was a man named Webster lived in a town of twenty-five thousand people in the state of Wisconsin. He had a wife named Mary and a daughter named Jane and he was himself a fairly prosperous manufacturer of washing machines. When the thing happened of which I am about to write he was thirty-seven or thirty-eight years old and his one child, the daughter, was seventeen. Of the details of his life up to the time, a certain revolution happened within him it will be unnecessary to speak. He was however a rather quiet man inclined to have dreams which he tried to crush out of himself in order that he function as a washing machine manufacturer; and no doubt, at odd moments, when he was on a train going someplace or perhaps on Sunday afternoons in the summer when he went alone to the deserted office of the factory and sat several hours looking out at a window and along a railroad track, he gave way to dreams.

39. What does the author mean by the following sentence?

"Of the details of his life up to the time, a certain revolution happened within him it will be unnecessary to speak."

a. The details of his external life don't matter; only the details of his internal life matter.
b. Whatever happened in his life before he had a certain internal change is irrelevant.
c. He had a traumatic experience earlier in his life which rendered it impossible for him to speak.
d. Before the revolution, he was a lighthearted man who always wished to speak to others no matter who they were.
e. He cannot talk about the events he witnessed and experienced during the revolution.

Questions 40–43 are based on the book On the Trail *by Lina Beard and Adelia Belle Beard:*

For any journey, by rail or by boat, one has a general idea of the direction to be taken, the character of the land or water to be crossed, and of what one will find at the end. So it should be in striking the trail. Learn all you can about the path you are to follow. Whether it is plain or obscure, wet or dry; where it leads; and its length, measured more by time than by actual miles. A smooth, even trail of five miles will not consume the time and strength that must be expended upon a trail of half that length which leads over uneven ground, varied by bogs and obstructed by rocks and fallen trees, or a trail that is all up-hill climbing. If you are a novice and accustomed to walking only over smooth and level ground, you must allow more time for covering the distance than an experienced person would require and must count upon the expenditure of more strength, because your feet are not trained to the wilderness paths with their pitfalls and traps for the unwary, and every nerve and muscle will be strained to secure a safe foothold amid the tangled roots, on the slippery, moss-covered logs, over precipitous rocks that lie in your path. It will take time to pick your way over boggy places where the water oozes up through the thin, loamy soil as through a sponge; and experience alone will teach you which hummock of grass or moss will make a safe stepping-place and will not sink beneath your weight and soak your feet with hidden water. Do not scorn to learn all you can about the trail you are to take . . . It is not that you hesitate to encounter difficulties, but that you may prepare for them. In unknown regions take a responsible guide with you, unless the trail is short, easily followed, and a frequented one. Do not go alone through lonely places; and, being on the trail, keep it and try no explorations of your own, at least not until you are quite familiar with the country and the ways of the wild.

Blazing the Trail

A woodsman usually blazes his trail by chipping with his axe the trees he passes, leaving white scars on their trunks, and to follow such a trail you stand at your first tree until you see the blaze on the next, then go that and look for the one farther on; going in this way from tree to tree you keep the trail though it may, underfoot, be overgrown and indistinguishable.

If you must make a trail of your own, blaze it as you go by bending down and breaking branches of trees, underbrush, and bushes. Let the broken branches be on the side of bush or tree in the direction you are going, but bent down away from that side, or toward the bush, so that the lighter underside of the leaves will show and make a plain trail. Make these signs conspicuous and close together, for in returning, a dozen feet without the broken branch will sometimes confuse you, especially as everything has a different look when seen from the opposite side. By this same token it is a wise precaution to look back frequently as you go and impress the homeward-bound landmarks on your memory. If in your wanderings you have branched off and made ineffectual or blind trails which lead nowhere, and, in returning to camp, you are led astray by one of them, do not leave the false trail and strike out to make a new one, but turn back and follow the false trail to its beginning, for it must lead to the true trail again. Don't lose sight of your broken branches.

40. What part of the text is the girl most likely emulating in the image?
    a. Building a trap
    b. Setting up camp
    c. Blazing the trail
    d. Picking berries to eat
    e. Climbing an all uphill portion of a trail

41. According to the passage, what does the author say about unknown regions?
    a. You should try and explore unknown regions in order to learn the land better.
    b. Unless the trail is short or frequented, you should take a responsible guide with you.
    c. All unknown regions will contain pitfalls, traps, and boggy places.
    d. It's better to travel unknown regions by rail rather than by foot.
    e. It's wise to leave a false trail that you yourself know is false to deceive potential unwelcome people.

42. Which statement is NOT a detail from the passage?
    a. Learning about the trail beforehand is imperative.
    b. Time will differ depending on the land.
    c. Once you are familiar with the outdoors you can go places on your own.
    d. Be careful of wild animals on the trail you are on.
    e. Break branches on the side of bush or tree in the direction you are going.

43. In the last paragraph, which of the following does the author suggest when being led astray by a false trail?

a. Bend down and break the branches off trees, underbrush, and bushes.
b. Ignore the false trail and strike out to make a new one.
c. Follow the false trail back to its beginning so that you can rediscover the real trail.
d. Make the signs conspicuous so that you won't be confused when you turn around.
e. Conceal the trail by bending the lighter side of the leaves downward to cover it.

44. Director: Movies require the audience to suspend their disbelief. As such, directors need to create a universe with consistent internal logic. When the subject matter is based on real events and communities, the director must closely mirror reality. For example, characters should talk like people from that specific region and historical period.

Critic: Movies hold immense power in our culture in defining what is and isn't socially acceptable. Consequently, directors have a responsibility not to use language that offends various groups, especially people in vulnerable positions. Censoring hate speech and racial slurs won't break the audience's disbelief.

Which one of the following best describes the main point in dispute between the director and critic?

a. Movie audiences suspend their disbelief.
b. Hate speech and racial slurs offend people.
c. Movies should avoid offending people.
d. Directors enjoy full creative control over their work.
e. Movies have enormous cultural relevancy.

45. Businessman: My cardinal rule is to only invest in privately-held small businesses that exclusively sell tangible goods and have no debt.

Which one of the following is the best investment opportunity according to the businessman's cardinal rule?

a. Jose owns his own grocery store. He's looking for a partner, because he fell behind on his mortgage and owes the bank three months' worth of payments.
b. Elizabeth is seeking a partner with business expertise to help expand her standalone store that sells niche board games. The store isn't currently profitable, but it's never been in debt.
c. A family-owned accounting firm with no outstanding debts is looking for its first outside investor. The firm has turned a profit every year since it opened
d. A multinational corporation is selling high-yield bonds for the first time.
e. A regional chain of liquor stores is selling the licensing rights for a new franchise to help repay its initial small business loan.

46. Ecologist: If we do not act now, more than one hundred animal species will be extinct by the end of the decade. The best way to save them is to sell hunting licenses for endangered species. Hunters can pay for the right to kill old and lame animals. Otherwise, there's no way to fund our conservation efforts.

Which one of the following assumptions does the ecologist's argument rely upon?

a. Hunting licenses for non-endangered species aren't profitable.
b. All one hundred animal species must be saved.
c. The new hunting license revenue will fund conservation efforts.
d. Conservation efforts should've began last decade.
e. It is physically impossible for old and lame animals to reproduce.

47. Politician: Every cigarette smoked cost the city more than $1,000. Smokers are bankrupting our healthcare system. Discarded filters pollute our waterways, and second-hand smoke poisons our airways, threatening all pedestrians. The city must ban tobacco smoking immediately.

Which one of the following, if true, would most strengthen the politician's argument?
a. Placing a high tax on tobacco hasn't reduced smoking at all.
b. Smoking cigarettes is already banned in bars and restaurants.
c. The city's waterways and airways also suffer from heavy industrial pollution.
d. Many tobacco substitutes are readily available.
e. The state government is also considering a ban on tobacco.

Questions 48 – 49 are based off the following passage:

> Rehabilitation, rather than punitive justice, is becoming much more popular in prisons around the world. Prisons in America, especially, where the recidivism rate is 67 percent, would benefit from mimicking prison tactics in Norway, which has a recidivism rate of only 20 percent. In Norway, the idea is that a rehabilitated prisoner is much less likely to offend than one harshly punished. Rehabilitation includes proper treatment for substance abuse, psychotherapy, healthcare and dental care, and education programs.

48. Which of the following best captures the author's purpose?
a. To show the audience one of the effects of criminal rehabilitation by comparison.
b. To persuade the audience to donate to American prisons for education programs.
c. To convince the audience of the harsh conditions of American prisons.
d. To inform the audience of the incredibly lax system of Norway prisons.
e. To entertain the audience with interesting stories and anecdotes.

49. Which of the following describes the word *recidivism* as it is used in the passage?
a. The lack of violence in the prison system.
b. The opportunity of inmates to receive therapy in prison.
c. The event of a prisoner escaping the compound.
d. The likelihood of a convicted criminal to reoffend.
e. The propensity for a person to commit any sort of crime.

50. A reader comes across a word they do not know in the book they are reading, and they need to find out what the word means in order to understand the context of the sentence. Where should the reader look?
a. Table of contents
b. Introduction
c. Index
d. Heading
e. Glossary

Answer Explanations

1. D: Neutrality due to the style of the report. The report is mostly objective; we see very little language that entails any strong emotion whatsoever. The story is told almost as an objective documentation of a sequence of actions—we see the president sitting in his box with his wife, their enjoyment of the show, Booth's walk through the crowd to the box, and Ford's consideration of Booth's movements. There is perhaps a small amount of bias when the author mentions the president's "worthy wife." However, the word choice and style show no signs of excitement, sadness, anger, or apprehension from the author's perspective, so the best answer is Choice *D*.

2. B: Mr. Ford assumed Booth's movement throughout the theater was due to being familiar with the theater. Choice *A* is incorrect; although Booth does eventually make his way to Lincoln's box, Mr. Ford does not make this distinction in this part of the passage. Choice *C* is incorrect; although the passage mentions "companions," it mentions Lincoln's companions rather than Booth's companions. Choice *D* is incorrect; the passage mentions "dress circle," which means the first level of the theater, but this is different from a "dressing room." Finally, Choice *E* is incorrect; the passage mentions a "symptom" but does not signify a symptom from an illness.

3. C: A lead singer leaves their band to begin a solo career, and the band's sales on their next album drop by 50 percent. The original source of the analogy displays someone significant to an event who leaves, and then the event becomes the worst for it. We see Mr. Sothern leaving the theater company, and then the play becoming a "very dull affair." Choice *A* depicts a dancer who backs out of an event before the final performance, so this is incorrect. Choice *B* shows a basketball player leaving an event, and then the team makes it to the championship but then loses. This choice could be a contestant for the right answer; however, we don't know if the team has become worse because of his departure or better. We simply do not have enough information here. Choice *D* is incorrect. The actor departs an event, but there is no assessment of the quality of the movie. It simply states what actors filled in instead. Choice *E* is incorrect because the opposite of the source happens; the professor leaves the entity, and the entity becomes better. Additionally, the betterment of the entity is not due to the individual leaving. Choice *E* is not analogous to the source.

4. A: A chronological account in a fiction novel of a woman and a man meeting for the first time. It's tempting to mark Choice A wrong because the genres are different. Choice *A* is a fiction text, and the original passage is not a fictional account. However, the question stem asks specifically for organizational structure. Choice *A* is a chronological structure just like the passage, so this is the correct answer. The passage does not have a cause and effect, problem/solution, or compare/contrast structure, making Choices *B*, *D*, and *E* incorrect. Choice *C* is tempting because it mentions an autobiography; however, the structure of this text starts at the end and works its way toward the beginning, which is the opposite structure of the original passage.

5. C: The word *adornments* would LEAST change the meaning of the sentence because it's the most closely related word to *festoons*. The other choices don't make sense in the context of the sentence. *Feathers* of flags, *armies* of flags, *buckets* of flags, and *boats* of flags are not as accurate as the word *adornments* of flags. The passage also talks about other décor in the setting, so the word *adornments* fits right in with the context of the paragraph.

6. D: The primary purpose of the passage is to recount in detail the events that led up to Abraham Lincoln's death. Choice *A* is incorrect; the author makes no claims and uses no rhetoric of persuasion towards the audience. Choice *B* is incorrect, though it's a tempting choice; the passage depicts the setting in exorbitant detail, but the setting itself is not the primary purpose of the passage. Choice *C* is incorrect; one could argue this is a narrative, and the passage is about Lincoln's last few hours, but this isn't the *best* choice. The best choice recounts the details that leads up to Lincoln's death. Finally, Choice *E* is incorrect. The author does not try to prove or disprove anything to the audience, and the passage does not even make it to when Lincoln gets shot, so this part of the story is irrelevant.

7. D: The word *deleterious* can be best interpreted as referring to the word *ruinous*. The first paragraph attempts to explain the process of milk souring, so the "acid" would probably prove "ruinous" to the growth of bacteria and cause souring. Choice *A*, *amicable*, means friendly, so this does not make sense in context. Choice *B*, *smoldering*, means to boil or simmer, so this is also incorrect. Choices *C* and *E*, *luminous* and *virtuous*, have positive connotations and don't make sense in the context of the passage. Luminous means shining or brilliant, and virtuous means to be honest or ethical.

8. B: The author begins by explaining a process or phenomenon, then gives the history of the study of this phenomenon, and ends by presenting the effects of this phenomenon. The author explains the process of souring in the first paragraph by informing the reader that "it is due to the action of certain of the milk bacteria upon the milk sugar which converts it into lactic acid, and this acid gives the sour taste and curdles the milk." In the second paragraph, we see how the phenomenon of milk souring was viewed when it was "first studied," and then we proceed to gain insight into "recent investigations" toward the end of the paragraph. Finally, the passage ends by presenting the effects of the phenomenon of milk souring. We see the milk curdling, becoming bitter, tasting soapy, turning blue, or becoming thread-like. All of the other answer choices are incorrect.

9: A: The primary purpose is to inform the reader of the phenomenon, investigation, and consequences of milk souring. Choice *B* is incorrect because the passage states that *Bacillus acidi lactici* is not the only cause of milk souring. Choice *C* is incorrect because, although the author mentions the findings of researchers, the main purpose of the text does not seek to describe their accounts and findings, as we are not even told the names of any of the researchers. Choice *D* is tricky. We do see the author present us with new findings in contrast to the first cases studied by researchers. However, this information is only in the second paragraph, so it is not the primary purpose of the *entire passage*. Finally, Choice *E* is incorrect because the genre of the passage is more informative than narrative, although the author does talk about the phenomenon of milk souring and its subsequent effects.

10. C: Milk souring is caused mostly by a species of bacteria identical to that of *Bacillus acidi lactici* although there are a variety of other bacteria that cause milk souring as well. Choice *A* is incorrect because it contradicts the assertion that the souring is still caused by a variety of bacteria. Choice *B* is incorrect because the ordinary cause of milk souring *is known* to current researchers. Choice *D* is incorrect because this names mostly the effects of milk souring, not the cause. Choice *E* is incorrect because the bacteria itself doesn't have a strange soapy smell or is a different color, but it eventually will cause the milk to produce these effects.

11. C: The study of milk souring has improved throughout the years, as we now understand more of what causes milk souring and what happens afterward. None of the choices here are explicitly stated, so we have to rely on our ability to make inferences. Choice *A* is incorrect because there is no indication from the author that milk researchers in the past have been incompetent—only that recent research has done a better job of studying the phenomenon of milk souring. Choice *B* is incorrect because the author refers to dairymen in relation to the effects of milk souring and their "troubles" surrounding milk souring, and does not compare them to milk researchers. Choice *D* is incorrect because we are told in the second paragraph that only certain types of bacteria are able to sour milk. Choice *E* is incorrect; although we are told that milk souring is a natural occurrence, the author makes no implication that soured milk is safe to consume. Choice *C* is the best answer choice here because although the author does not directly state that the study of milk souring has improved, we can see this might be true due to the comparison of old studies to newer studies, and the fact that the newer studies are being used as a reference in the passage.

12. A: It is most analogous to the chemical change that occurs when a firework explodes. The author tells us that after milk becomes slimy, "it persists in spite of all attempts made to remedy it," which means the milk has gone through a chemical change. It has changed its state from milk to sour milk by changing its odor, color, and material. After a firework explodes, there is nothing one can do to change the substance of a firework back to its original form—the original substance is turned into sound and light. Choice *B* is incorrect because, although the rain overwatered the plant, it's possible that the plant is able to recover from this. Choice *C* is incorrect because although mercury leaking out may be dangerous, the actual substance itself stays the same and does not alter into something else. Choice *D* is incorrect; this situation is not analogous to the alteration of a substance. Choice *E* is also incorrect. Ice melting into a liquid is a physical change, which means it can be undone. Milk turning sour, as the author asserts, cannot be undone.

13. D: It would most likely be a paragraph showing the ways bacteria infiltrate milk and ways to avoid this infiltration. Choices *A, B,* and *C* are incorrect because these are already represented in the third, second, and first paragraphs. Choice *E* is incorrect; this choice isn't impossible. There could be a glossary right after the third paragraph, but this would be an awkward place for a glossary. Choice *D* is the best answer because it follows a sort of problem/solution structure in writing.

14. E: A central question to both passages is: What is the interpretation of the first amendment and its limitations? Choice *A* is incorrect; this is a question for the first passage but it does not apply to the second. Choice *B* is incorrect; a quote mentions this at the end of the first passage, but this question is not found in the second passage. Choice *C* is incorrect, as the passages are not concerned with the definition of freedom of speech, but how to interpret it. Choice *D* is incorrect; this is a question for the second passage, but it is not found in the first passage.

15. C: The authors would most likely disagree over the man thrown in jail for encouraging a riot against the U.S. government for the wartime tactics although no violence ensued. The author of Passage A says that "If a state may properly forbid murder or robbery or treason, it may also punish those who induce or counsel the commission of such crimes." This statement tells us that the author of Passage A would support throwing the man in jail for encouraging a riot, although no violence ensues. The author of Passage B states that "And we can with certitude declare that the First Amendment forbids the punishment of words merely for their injurious tendencies." This is the best answer choice because we are clear on each author's stance in this situation. Choice *A* is tricky; the author of Passage A would definitely agree with this, but it's questionable whether the author of Passage B would also agree. Violence does ensue at the capitol as a result of this man's provocation, and the author of Passage B states "speech should be unrestricted by censorship . . . unless it is clearly liable to cause direct . . . interference with the conduct of war." This answer is close, but it is not the *best* choice. Choice *B* is incorrect because we have no way of knowing what the authors' philosophies are in this situation. Choice *D* is incorrect because, again, we have no way of knowing what the authors would do in this situation, although it's assumed they would probably both agree with this. Choice *E* is something the authors would probably both agree on, because brutal violence ensued, but it has nothing to do with free speech, so we have no way of knowing for sure.

16. E: Choice *E* is the best answer. To figure out the correct answer choice we must find out the relationship between Passage A and Passage B. Between the two passages, we have a general principle (freedom of speech) that is questioned on the basis of interpretation. In Choice *E*, we see that we have a general principle (right to die, or euthanasia) that is questioned on the basis of interpretation as well. Should euthanasia only include passive euthanasia, or euthanasia in any aspect? Choice *A* is a problem/solution relationship; the first option outlines a problem, and the second option delivers a solution, so this choice is incorrect. Choice *B* is incorrect because it does not question the interpretation of a principle, but rather describes the effects of two events that happened in the past involving contamination of radioactive substances. Choice *C* begins with a principle—that of labor laws during wartime—but in the second option, the interpretation isn't questioned. The second option looks at the historical precedent of labor laws in the past during wartime. Choice *D* is incorrect because the two texts disagree over the cause of something rather than the interpretation of it.

17. B: Choice *B* is the best answer choice because the author is trying to demonstrate via the examples that anyone who incites a crime, despite the severity or magnitude of the crime, should be held accountable for that crime in some degree. Choice *A* is incorrect because the crimes mentioned are not being compared to each other, but they are being used to demonstrate a point. Choice *C* is incorrect because the author makes the same point using both of the examples and does not question the definition of freedom of speech but its ability to be limited. Choice *D* is incorrect because this sentiment goes against what the author has been arguing throughout the passage. Choice *E* is incorrect because the author does not suggest that the crimes mentioned be reopened anywhere in the passage.

18. A: The idea that human beings are able and likely to change their mind between the utterance and execution of an event that may harm others most seriously undermines the claim because it brings into question the bad tendency of a crime and points out the difference between utterance and action in moral situations. Choice *B* is incorrect; this idea does not undermine the claim at hand, but introduces an observation irrelevant to the claim. Choices *C, D,* and *E* would most likely strengthen the argument's claim; or, they are at least supported by the author in Passage A.

19. D: The primary purpose is to call upon the interpretation of freedom of speech to be already evident in the First Amendment and to offer a clear perimeter of the principle during war time. Choice *A* is incorrect; the passage calls upon no historical situations as precedent in this passage. Choice *B* is incorrect; we can infer that the author would not agree with this, because the author states that "In war time, therefore, speech should be unrestricted . . . by punishment." Choice *C* is incorrect; this is more consistent with the main idea of the first passage. Choice *E* is incorrect; the passage states a limitation in saying that "speech should be unrestricted . . . unless it is clearly liable to cause direct and dangerous interference with the conduct of war."

20. E: The word that would least change the meaning of the sentence is *grievance. Malcontent* is a complaint or grievance, and in this context would be uttered in advocation of absolute freedom of speech. Choice *A, regimen,* means a pattern of living, and would not make sense in this context. Choice *B, cacophony,* means a harsh noise or mix of discordant noises; someone may express or "urge" a cacophony but it would be an awkward word in this context. Choice *C, anecdote,* is a short account of an amusing story. Since the word is a noun, it fits grammatically inside the sentence, but anecdotes are usually thought out, and this word is considered "unthinking." Choice *D, residua,* means an outcome, and also does not make sense within this context.

21. B: The author says that the classical understanding of poetry dealt with its ability to be used to teach morality. Later, philosophers would define poetry by its ability to imitate life. Finally, during the renaissance, poetry was believed to be an imitative art that instilled morality in its readers. The rest of the answer choices improperly interpret this explanation in the passage. Poetry was never mentioned for use in entertainment, which makes Choices *D* and *E* incorrect. Choices *A* and *C* are incorrect because they mix up the chronological order.

22. C: The author says that although most poetry was written as lyric, epic, or drama, the critics were most focused on the techniques of the epic and drama and their performance of structure and character. This is the best answer choice as portrayed by paragraph three. Choice *A* is incorrect because nowhere in the passage does it say rhetoric was more valued than poetry, although it did seem to have a more definitive purpose than poetry. Choice *B* is incorrect; this almost mirrors Choice *A*, but the critics were *not* focused on the lyric, as the passage indicates. Choice *D* is incorrect because the passage does not mention that the study of poetics was more pleasurable than the study of rhetoric. Choice *E* is incorrect because again, we do not see anywhere in the passage where poetry was reserved for the most elite in society.

23. E: The purpose is to contemplate the differences between classical rhetoric and poetry and to consider their purposes in a particular culture. Choice *A* is incorrect; this thought is discussed in the third paragraph, but it is not the main idea of the passage. Choice *B* is incorrect; although changes in poetics throughout the years is mentioned, this is not the main idea of the passage. Choice *C* is incorrect; although this is partly true—that rhetoric within the education system is mentioned—the subject of poetics is left out of this answer choice. Choice *D* is incorrect; the passage makes no mention of poetics being a subset of rhetoric.

24. B: The correct answer choice is Choice *B*, *instill*. Choice *A*, *imbibe*, means to drink heavily, so this choice is incorrect. Choice *C*, *implode*, means to collapse inward, which does not make sense in this context. Choice *D*, *inquire*, means to investigate. This option is better than the other options, but it is not as accurate as *instill*. Choice *E*, *idolize*, means to admire, which does not make sense in this context.

25. B: The first paragraph presents definitions and examples of a particular subject. The second paragraph presents a second subject in the same way. The third paragraph offers a contrast of the two subjects. In the passage, we see the first paragraph defining rhetoric and offering examples of how the Greeks and Romans taught this subject. In the second paragraph, poetics is defined and examples of its dynamic definition are provided. In the third paragraph, the contrast between rhetoric and poetry is characterized through how each of these were studied in a classical context.

26. D: The best answer is Choice *D:* As a football player, they taught me how to understand the logistics of the game, how my placement on the field affected the rest of the team, and how to run and throw with a mixture of finesse and strength. The content of rhetoric in the passage . . . "taught how to work up a case by drawing valid inferences from sound evidence, how to organize this material in the most persuasive order, and how to compose in clear and harmonious sentences. What we have here is three general principles: 1) it taught me how to understand logic and reason (drawing inferences parallels to understanding the logistics of the game), 2) it taught me how to understand structure and organization (organization of material parallels to organization on the field) and 3) it taught me how to make the end product beautiful (how to compose in harmonious sentences parallels to how to run with finesse and strength). Each part parallels by logic, organization, and style.

27. E: *Treatises* is most closely related to the word *commentary*. Choices *A* and *B* do not make sense because thesauruses and encyclopedias are not written about one single subject. Choice *C* is incorrect; sermons are usually given by religious leaders as advice or teachings. Choice *D* is incorrect; anthems are songs and do not fit within the context of this sentence.

28. D: A city whose population is made up of people who seek quick fortunes rather than building a solid business foundation. Choice *A* is a characteristic of Portland, but not that of a boom city. Choice *B* is close—a boom city is one that becomes quickly populated, but it is not necessarily *always* populated by residents from the east coast. Choice *C* is incorrect because a boom city is not one that catches fire frequently, but one made up of people who are looking to make quick fortunes from the resources provided on the land. Choice *E* is incorrect because although it describes a characteristic of Portland, the passage does not state that in order for a city to be a "boom city," it *must* be located on a river.

29. D: Choice *D* is the best answer because of the surrounding context. We can see that the fact that Portland is a "boom city" means that the "floating class"—a group of people who only have temporary roots put down—go through. This would cause the main focus of the city to be on employment and industry, rather than society and culture; thus, Choice *E* is incorrect. Choice *A* is incorrect, as we are not told about the inhabitants being social or antisocial. Choice *B* is incorrect because the text does not talk about the culture in the East regarding European influence. Finally, Choice *C* is incorrect; this is an assumption that has no evidence in the text to back it up.

30. E: The author would say that it has as much culture as the cities in the East. The author says that Portland has "as fine churches, as complete a system of schools, as fine residences, as great a love of music and art, as can be found at any city of the East of equal size," which proves that the culture is similar in this particular city to the cities in the East.

31. B: Approximately 240,000. We know from the image that San Francisco has around 300,000 inhabitants at this time. From the text (and from the graph) we can see that Portland has 60,000 inhabitants. Subtract these two numbers to come up with 240,000

32. C: This question requires close attention to the passage. Choice *A* can be found where the passage says, "no less than six named and several unnamed varieties of the peach have thus produced several varieties of nectarine, so this choice is incorrect. Choice *B* can be found where the passage says, "it is highly improbable that all these peach-trees . . . are hybrids from the peach and nectarine." Choice *D* is incorrect because we see in the passage that "the production of peaches from nectarines, either by seeds or buds, may perhaps be considered as a case of reversion." Choice *E* can be found in the last paragraph where it says, "descended from an old French variety bearing purple fruit, produced when about ten years old bright yellow plums; these differed in no respect except colour from those on the other trees." Choice *C* is the correct answer because the word "unremarkable" should be changed to "remarkable" in order for it to be consistent with the details of the passage.

33. B: The author's tone in this passage can be considered objective. An objective tone means that the author is open-minded and detached about the subject. Most scientific articles are objective. Choices *A, C, D,* and *E* are incorrect. The author is not very enthusiastic on the paper; the author is not critical, but rather interested in the topic. The author is not desperate in any way here.

34. B: Choice *B* is the correct answer because the meaning holds true even if the words have been switched out or rearranged some. Choice *A* is incorrect because it has trees either bearing peaches or nectarines, and the trees in the original phrase bear both. Choice *C* is incorrect because the statement does not say these trees are "indifferent to bud-variation," but that they have "indifferently [borne] peaches or nectarines." Choices *D* and *E* are incorrect; the statement may use some of the same words, but the meaning is skewed in these sentences.

35. C: Personification. The chapter on Literature and Language Use has a subsection, "Figurative Speech." The sections located under Figurative Speech all have to do with language that uses words or phrases that are different from their literal interpretation. Personification is included in figurative speech, which means giving inanimate objects human characteristics. Nouns, agreement, and syntax all have to do with grammar and usage, and are not considered figurative language. Context has to do with the surrounding words, thoughts, and ideas in which a given word should be interpreted.

36. C: We can infer that the season of this narrative is in the winter time. Some of the evidence here is that "the cold became intense," and people were decorating their shops with "holly sprigs,"—a Christmas tradition. It also mentions that it's Christmastime at the end of the passage. Choice *A* is incorrect. We cannot infer that the passage takes place during the night time. While we do have a statement that says that the darkness thickened, this is the only evidence we have. The darkness could be thickening because it is foggy outside. We don't have enough proof to infer this otherwise. Choice *B* is incorrect; we *can* infer that the narrative is located in a bustling city street by the actions in the story. People are running around trying to sell things, the atmosphere is busy, there is a church tolling the hours, etc. The scene switches to the Mayor's house at the end of the passage, but the answer says "majority," so this is still incorrect. Choice *D* is incorrect; we *can* infer that the Lord Mayor is wealthy—he lives in the "Mansion House" and has fifty cooks. Choice *E* is incorrect because we *can* infer that Scrooge was not kind nor receptive since he scared the caroler away.

37. E: The passage tells us that the poulterers' and grocers' trades were "a glorious pageant, with which it was next to impossible to believe that such dull principles as bargain and sale had anything to do," which means they set up their shops to be entertaining public spectacles in order to increase sales. Choice *A* is incorrect; although the word "joke" is used, it is meant to be used as a source of amusement rather than something made in poor quality. Choice *B* is incorrect; that they put on a "pageant" is figurative for the public spectacle they made with their shops, not a literal play. Choice *C* is incorrect, as this is not mentioned anywhere in the passage. Finally, Choice *D* is incorrect; although it's an appealing option because the poulterers and grocers clearly aimed to spread Christmas cheer, it's not clear that they were working tirelessly to convert non-believers.

38. B: The author, at least in the last few paragraphs, does not attempt to evoke empathy for the character of Scrooge. We see Scrooge lashing out at an innocent, cold boy, with no sign of affection or feeling for his harsh conditions. We see Choice *A* when the author talks about Saint Dunstan. We see Choices *C* and *E*, providing a palpable experience and imaginable setting and character, especially with the "piercing, searching, biting cold," among other statements. Finally, we see Choice *D* when Scrooge chases the young boy away.

39. B: Whatever happened in his life before he had a certain internal change is irrelevant. Choices *A, C, D,* and *E* use some of the same language as the original passage, like "revolution," "speak," and "details," but they do not capture the meaning of the statement. The statement is saying the details of his previous life are not going to be talked about—that he had some kind of epiphany, and moving forward in his life is what the narrator cares about.

40. C: The section that is talked about in the text is blazing the trail, which is Choice *C*. The passage states that one must blaze the trail by "bending down and breaking branches of trees, underbrush, and bushes." The girl in the image is bending a branch in order to break it so that she can use it to "blaze the trail" so she won't get lost.

41. B: Choice *B* is the best answer here; the sentence states "In unknown regions take a responsible guide with you, unless the trail is short, easily followed, and a frequented one." Choice *A* is incorrect; the passage does not state that you should try and explore unknown regions. Choice *C* is incorrect; the passage talks about trails that contain pitfalls, traps, and boggy places, but it does not say that *all* unknown regions contain these things. Choice *D* is incorrect; the passage mentions "rail" and "boat" as means of transport at the beginning, but it does not suggest it is better to travel unknown regions by rail. Choice *E* is incorrect because the passage warns against the challenges and downsides of a potential "false trail;" it does not encourage purposely creating one.

42. D: Choice *D* is correct; it may be real advice an experienced hiker would give to an inexperienced hiker. However, the question asks about details in the passage, and this is not in the passage. Choice *A* is incorrect; we do see the author encouraging the reader to learn about the trail beforehand . . . "wet or dry; where it leads; and its length." Choice *B* is also incorrect, because we do see the author telling us the time will lengthen with boggy or rugged places opposed to smooth places. Choice *C* is incorrect; at the end of the passage, the author tells us "do not go alone through lonely places . . . unless you are quite familiar with the country and the ways of the wild." Choice *E* is incorrect because the detail is found in the passage in the first sentence of the last paragraph.

43. C: The best answer here is Choice *C*: "Follow the false trail back to its beginning so that you can rediscover the real trail." Choices *A* and *D* are represented in the text; but this is advice on how to blaze a trail, not what to do when being led astray by a false trail. Choice *B* is incorrect; this is the opposite of what the text suggests doing. Choice *E* is incorrect because the author suggests bending the branches so that the light side of the leaf points upward to help make the trail clear. This advice is also in reference to blazing the main trail, not what to do should you be led astray on a false trail.

44. C: Choice *C* correctly identifies the main point in dispute. The director and critic are arguing about the director's role. The director argues that directors should be allowed to offend people, if that would accurately reflect reality, so the audience can maintain its suspension of disbelief. The critic would argue that this violates the director's social responsibility to avoid offending people.

Choice *A* is incorrect. Both the director and critic would agree that movie audiences suspend their disbelief. This is the director's main point, and the critic acknowledges its existence by claiming that censoring hate speech and racial slurs won't break the audience's disbelief.

Choice *B* is incorrect. This is the critic's main point, and the director would likely also agree. The director isn't claiming that movies aren't offensive, but that offending people is justified to protect the suspension of disbelief.

Choice *D* is incorrect. This isn't the main point in dispute. In addition, both the director and critic imply that they believe this to be true. For the director, creative control is required to structure a universe where an audience can suspend its disbelief. For the critic, the director would need creative control to censor what the critic deems inappropriate.

Choice *E* is incorrect. The critic would agree that movies have enormous cultural relevancy—that's why the critic is calling for self-censorship—but it's unclear whether the director would agree or disagree.

45. B: Choice *B* correctly identifies the best investment opportunity. The cardinal rule has three requirements—privately held small business, sells tangible goods, and no debt. Elizabeth's store is a privately held small business (standalone and owned by her), it sells tangible goods (board games), and it has no debt. The lack of profitability is irrelevant, acting as a red herring. The cardinal rule doesn't mention it, presumably since the businessman thinks he can increase profitability as long as the business meets those three requirements.

Choice *A* is incorrect. Jose's grocery store owes the bank three months' worth of mortgage payments, so it has debt, violating the cardinal rule.

Choice *C* is incorrect. The accounting firm violates the cardinal rule, because it does not sell a tangible good.

Choice *D* is incorrect. A multinational corporation is not a small business, so it violates the cardinal rule.

Choice *E* is incorrect. The regional chain of liquor stores has debt (small business loan), so it's a worse investment than the board game store according to the businessman's cardinal rule.

46. C: Choice *C* correctly identifies a necessary assumption in the argument. The argument is that hunting licenses for endangered species should be sold to support conservation efforts. If the revenue from those licenses isn't funding conservation efforts, then the ecologist's entire argument falls apart.

Choice *A* is incorrect. Hunting licenses for non-endangered species could be profitable, and the ecologist's argument wouldn't be impacted one way or another. The ecologist could still argue that hunting licenses should be expanded to further increase funding for species that are still endangered.

Choice *B* is incorrect. The ecologist would definitely agree that all one hundred animal species should be saved, but it isn't a necessary assumption. The argument would function the same if the ultimate goal were to save ten endangered animal species.

Choice *D* is incorrect. Like Choice *B*, the ecologist would agree that conservation efforts should've begun earlier, but it isn't a necessary assumption.

Choice *E* is incorrect. The ecologist likely supports hunting licenses for endangered species due to old and lame animals' diminished capacity to reproduce. But reproduction being physically impossible isn't a necessary assumption. The argument would be the same even if those animals were reproducing on a limited basis.

47. A: Choice *A* correctly identifies the statement that most strengthens the argument. The argument is that the city must ban smoking, because every cigarette that's smoked costs the city $1,000. Choice *A* eliminates a possible counterargument for a less extreme measure—taxing tobacco. Since the tax didn't work, the city would be more likely to pursue a total ban.

Choice *B* is incorrect. If smoking cigarettes was already banned in bars and restaurants, it might strengthen the argument by laying the foundation for a total ban. However, a total ban is much more extreme, and Choice *A* is stronger since it eliminates a primary counterargument against changing the law.

Choice *C* is incorrect. Non-smoking related pollution in the waterways and airways might increase the need to avoid additional pollutants, but it's not as strong as Choice *A*.

Choice *D* is incorrect. The existence of tobacco substitutes doesn't justify banning tobacco. It also doesn't necessarily mean that they'll be better for the healthcare system and environment.

Choice *E* is incorrect. The state government's decision to ban tobacco could encourage the city government to do the same, but Choice *A* has a more direct impact on that debate as it pertains to the city.

48. A: To show the audience one of the effects of criminal rehabilitation by comparison. Choice *B* is incorrect because although it is obvious the author favors rehabilitation, the author never asks for donations from the audience. Choice *E* is incorrect because the passage is not intended to be entertaining, but informative in its aim to address serious subject matter. Choices *C* and *D* are also incorrect. We can infer from the passage that American prisons are probably harsher than Norway prisons. However, the best answer that captures the author's purpose is Choice *A*, because we see an effect by the author (recidivism rate of each country) comparing Norwegian and American prisons.

49. D: The likelihood of a convicted criminal to reoffend. The passage explains how a Norwegian prison, due to rehabilitation, has a smaller rate of recidivism. Thus, we can infer that recidivism is probably not a positive attribute. Choices *A* and *B* are both positive attributes, the lack of violence and the opportunity of inmates to receive therapy, so Norway would probably not have a lower rate of these two things. Choice *C* is possible, but it does not make sense in context, because the author does not talk about tactics in which to keep prisoners inside the compound, but ways in which to rehabilitate criminals so that they can live as citizens when they get out of prison. Choice *E* can be ruled out because the passage wouldn't be explaining why the prison system is better in Norway if the likelihood that a citizen would commit a crime was lower. Instead, the passage would explain why the structure or policies in Norway lead to fewer misdemeanors.

50. E: Glossary. A glossary is a section in a book that provides brief definitions/explanations for words that the reader may not know. Choice *A* is incorrect because a table of contents shows where each section of the book is located. Choice *B* is incorrect because the introduction is usually a chapter that introduces the book about to be read. Choice *C* is incorrect because an index is usually a list of alphabetical references at the end of a book that a reader can look up to get more information. Choice *D* is incorrect because a heading would give an idea of the subject matter around which the word appears, which may help, but it would not be as useful as the glossary to find the meaning of the unknown word.

Mathematics

Estimation, Measurement, & Statistical Principles

Estimation and Measurement

Converting Within and Between Standard and Metric Systems

When working with dimensions, sometimes the given units don't match the requirements of formula, and conversions must be made. The metric system has base units of meter for length, kilogram for mass, and liter for liquid volume. This system expands to three places above the base unit and three places below. These places correspond with prefixes with a base of 10.

The following table shows the conversions:

kilo-	**hecto-**	**deka-**	**base**	**deci-**	**centi-**	**milli-**
1,000 times the base	100 times the base	10 times the base		1/10 times the base	1/100 times the base	1/1000 times the base

To convert between units within the metric system, values with a base ten can be multiplied. The decimal can also be moved in the direction of the new unit by the same number of zeros on the number. For example, 3 meters is equivalent to .003 kilometers. The decimal moved three places (the same number of zeros for *kilo-*) to the left (the same direction from base to *kilo-*). Three meters is also equivalent to 3,000 millimeters. The decimal is moved three places to the right because the prefix *milli-* is three places to the right of the base unit.

The English Standard system used in the United States has a base unit of foot for length, pound for weight, and gallon for liquid volume. These conversions aren't as easy as the metric system because they aren't a base ten model. The following table shows the conversions within this system.

Length	**Weight**	**Capacity**
1 foot (ft) = 12 inches (in) 1 yard (yd) = 3 feet 1 mile (mi) = 5280 feet 1 mile = 1760 yards	1 pound (lb) = 16 ounces (oz) 1 ton = 2000 pounds	1 tablespoon (tbsp) = 3 teaspoons (tsp) 1 cup (c) = 16 tablespoons 1 cup = 8 fluid ounces (oz) 1 pint (pt) = 2 cups 1 quart (qt) = 2 pints 1 gallon (gal) = 4 quarts

When converting within the English Standard system, most calculations include a conversion to the base unit and then another to the desired unit. For example, take the following problem: $3\ quarts = \_\_\_\ cups$. There is no straight conversion from quarts to cups, so the first conversion is from quarts to pints. There are 2 pints in 1 quart, so there are 6 pints in 3 quarts. This conversion can be solved as a proportion: $\frac{3\ qt}{x} = \frac{1\ qt}{2\ pints}$. It can also be observed as a ratio 2:1, expanded to 6:3. Then the 6 pints must be converted to cups. The ratio of pints to cups is 1:2, so the expanded ratio is 6:12. For 6 pints, the measurement is 12 cups. This problem can also be set up as one set of fractions to cancel out units. It begins with the given information and cancels out matching units on top and bottom to yield the answer. Consider the following expression:

$$\frac{3\ quarts}{1} \times \frac{2\ pints}{1\ quart} \times \frac{2\ cups}{1\ pint}$$

It's set up so that units on the top and bottom cancel each other out:

$$\frac{3\ \cancel{quarts}}{1} \times \frac{2\ \cancel{pints}}{1\ \cancel{quart}} \times \frac{2\ cups}{1\ \cancel{pint}}$$

The numbers can be calculated as 3 × 3 × 2 on the top and 1 on the bottom. It still yields an answer of 12 cups.

This process of setting up fractions and canceling out matching units can be used to convert between standard and metric systems. A few common equivalent conversions are 2.54 cm = 1 inch, 3.28 feet = 1 meter, and 2.205 pounds = 1 kilogram. Writing these as fractions allows them to be used in conversions. For the fill-in-the-blank problem 5 meters = ___ feet, an expression using conversions starts with the expression $\frac{5\ meters}{1} \times \frac{3.28\ feet}{1\ meter}$, where the units of meters will cancel each other out, and the final unit is feet. Calculating the numbers yields 16.4 feet. This problem only required two fractions. Others may require longer expressions, but the underlying process stays the same. When there's a unit on the top of the fraction that's the same as the unit on the bottom, then they cancel each other out. Using this logic and the conversions given above, many units can be converted between and within the different systems.

The conversion between Fahrenheit and Celsius is found in a formula:

$$°C = (°F - 32) \times \frac{5}{9}$$

For example, to convert 78°F to Celsius, the given temperature would be entered into the formula:

$$°C = (78 - 32) \times \frac{5}{9}$$

Solving the equation, the temperature comes out to be 25.56°C. To convert in the other direction, the formula becomes:

$$°F = °C \times \frac{9}{5} + 32$$

Remember to follow the order of operations when calculating these conversions.

Measuring Length and Perimeter

Measuring and Comparing Lengths of Objects Using Standard Tools

Lengths of objects can be measured using tools such as rulers, yard sticks, meter sticks, and tape measures. Typically, a ruler measures 12 inches, or one foot. For this reason, a ruler is normally used to measure lengths smaller or just slightly more than 12 inches. Rulers may represent centimeters instead of inches. Some rulers have inches on one side and centimeters on the other. Be sure to recognize what units you are measuring in. The standard ruler measurements are divided into units of 1 inch and normally broken down to $\frac{1}{2}$, $\frac{1}{4}$, $\frac{1}{8}$, and even $\frac{1}{16}$ of an inch for more precise measurements. If measuring in centimeters, the centimeter is likely divided into tenths, or millimeters. To measure the size of a picture, for purposes of buying a frame, a ruler is helpful. If the picture is very large, a yardstick, which measures 3 feet, and normally is divided into feet and inches, might be useful. Using metric units, the meter stick measures 1 meter and is divided into 100 centimeters. To measure the size of a window in a home, either a yardstick or meter stick would work. To measure the size of a room, however, a tape measure would be the easiest tool to use. Tape measures can measure up to 10 feet, 25 feet, or more, depending on the particular tape measure.

Perimeter

Perimeter and area are two commonly used geometric quantities that describe objects. **Perimeter** is the distance around an object. The perimeter of an object can be found by adding the lengths of all sides. Perimeter may be used in problems dealing with lengths around objects such as fences or borders. It may also be used in finding missing lengths of shapes, or working backwards. If the perimeter is given, but a length is missing, subtraction can be used to find the missing length. Given a square with side length *s*, the formula for perimeter is $P = 4s$. Given a rectangle with length *l* and width *w*, the formula for perimeter is $P = 2l + 2w$. The perimeter of a triangle is found by adding the three side lengths, and the perimeter of a trapezoid is found by adding the four side lengths. The units for perimeter are always the original units of length, such as meters, inches, miles, etc. When discussing a circle, the distance around the object is referred to as its **circumference,** not perimeter. The formula for circumference of a circle is $C = 2\pi r$, where *r* represents the radius of the circle. This formula can also be written as $C = d\pi$, where *d* represents the diameter of the circle, because the diameter is twice the length of the radius.

Using Estimates of Time to Plan and Achieve Work-Related Objectives

In the real world, projects that can be broken up into individual parts with different timelines and deadlines are assigned to employees. The deadlines are assigned at the beginning of the project and are based on estimates that determine how long each part of the project will take to complete. Sometimes, the amount of time needed complete a project, or any type of work-related objective, is underestimated: not enough time is given to complete the task. Some reasons for underestimations are that the type of work needed to be done is unfamiliar or that other time-consuming aspects of the project are not taken into consideration. In any case, it is important to determine an estimate for completion that is as accurate as possible. The more accurate the estimates are, the more likely the project is to be completed on time and within its budget.

To determine a good estimate, there are a few things that should be considered. Initially, all necessary tasks needed to complete the project should to be listed. The tasks should also be ordered to define which one needs to be completed first, second, etc., and any important deadlines that need to be met should be noted. Anyone who will be working on the project can be included in this ordering process. Finally, each individual task or step needs to be assigned a time estimate. The time allotted for the entire scope of the project is equal to the sum of the individual times of the different tasks or steps.

Once the individual times and deadlines are defined, the people working on the project must adhere to them. Falling behind schedule at the beginning means that time will have to be made up in the end, which might be difficult to do. Working ahead is always better than falling behind, especially because unforeseen circumstances can occur that could possibly delay deadlines from being met.

Estimating the Results of Problems Prior to Computation

Sometimes it is helpful to find an estimated answer to a problem rather than working out an exact answer. An estimation might be much quicker to find, and given the scenario, an estimation might be all that is required. For example, if Aria goes grocery shopping and has only a $100 bill to cover all of her purchases, it might be appropriate for her to estimate the total cost of the items she is purchasing to tell if she has enough money to cover them. Also, an estimation can help determine if an answer makes sense and is reasonable given the problem. For instance, if an answer in the hundreds is expected, but the result is a fraction less than 1, something is probably wrong in the calculation.

The first type of estimation involves rounding. **Rounding** consists of expressing a number in terms of the nearest decimal place like the tenth, hundredth, or thousandth place, or in terms of the nearest whole number unit like tens, hundreds, or thousands place. When rounding to a specific place value, look at the digit to the right of the place. If it is 5 or higher, round the number to its left up to the next value, and if it is 4 or lower, keep that number at the same value. For instance, 1,654.2674 rounded to the nearest thousand is 2,000 because there is a 6 in the hundreds place, and the same number rounded to the nearest thousandth is 1,654.267 because there is a 4 in the ten-thousandths place.

Estimating is also very helpful when working with measurements. Bryan is updating his kitchen and wants to retile the floor. Again, an over-measurement might be useful. Also, rounding to nearest half-unit might be helpful. For instance, one side of the kitchen might have an exact measurement of 14.32 feet, and the most useful measurement needed to buy tile could be estimating this quantity to be 14.5 feet. If the kitchen was rectangular and the other side measured 10.9 feet, Bryan might round the other side to 11 feet. Therefore, Bryan would find the total tile necessary according to the following area calculation: $14.5 \times 11 = 159.5$ square feet. To make sure he purchases enough tile, Bryan would probably want to purchase at least 160 square feet of tile. This is a scenario in which an estimation might be more useful than an exact calculation. Having more tile than necessary is better than having an exact amount, in case any tiles are broken or otherwise unusable.

Finally, estimation is helpful when exact answers are necessary. Consider a situation in which Sabina has many operations to perform on numbers with decimals, and she is allowed to use a calculator to find the result. Even though an exact result can be obtained with a calculator, there is always a possibility that Sabina could make an error while inputting the data. For example, she could miss a decimal place, or misuse a parenthesis, causing a problem with the actual order of operations. In this case, a quick estimation at the beginning would be helpful to make sure the final answer is given with the correct number of units. Sabina has to find the exact total of 10 cars listed for sale at the dealership. Each price has two decimal places included to account for both dollars and cents. If one car is listed at $21,234.43 but Sabina incorrectly inputs into the calculator the price of $2,123.443, this error would throw off the final sum by almost $20,000. A quick estimation at the beginning, by rounding each price to the nearest thousand and finding the sum of the prices would give Sabina a ballpark amount to compare the exact amount to. This comparison would let Sabina see if an error was made in her exact calculation.

Statistical Principles

Performing Arithmetic Operations with Basic Statistical Data Related to Test Scores

A **data set,** such as test scores, can be described by calculating the mean, median, and mode. These values, called **measures of center**, allow the data to be described with a single value that is representative of the data set.

The most common measure of center is the **mean**, also referred to as the **average.**

To calculate the mean,

- Add all data values together
- Divide by the sample size (the number of data points in the set)

The **median** is middle data value, so that half of the data lies below this value and half lies below the data value.

To calculate the median,

- Order the data from least to greatest
- The point in the middle of the set is the median
    - In the event that there is an even number of data points, add the two middle points and divide by 2

The **mode** is the data value that occurs most often.

To calculate the mode,

- Order the data from least to greatest
- Find the value that occurs most often

Example: Amelia is a leading scorer on the school's basketball team. The following data set represents the number of points that Amelia has scored in each game this season. Use the mean, median, and mode to describe the data.

16, 12, 26, 14, 13, 28, 14, 12, 15, 25

Solution:

Mean: $16 + 12 + 26 + 14 + 28 + 14 + 12 + 15 + 25 = 162$

$162 \div 9 = 18$

Amelia averages 18 points per game.

Median: 12, 12, 14, 14, **15**, 16, 25, 26, 28

Amelia's median score is 15.

Mode: 12, 12, 14, 14, 15, 16, 25, 26, 28

12 and 14 each occur twice in the data set, so this set has 2 modes: 12 and 14.

The **range** is the difference between the largest and smallest values in the set. In the example above, the range is 28 – 12 = 16.

In addition to these measures of central tendency and spread, additional values regarding test scores, such as ratios and percentages or questions answered correctly can be calculated. To calculate either, the number of correct responses is set as the first number in the ratio or as the numerator in the fraction. The colon in a ratio, or the fraction bar in a fraction, serves to stand for the words "out of" and then the number that follows the colon or the denominator of the fraction is the total number of questions on the test. For example, imagine a test where a student gets 21 questions correct out of a total of 25. This is written as a ratio of 21:25 or as a fraction of $\frac{21}{25}$. In the latter, dividing the numerator by the denominator and multiplying by 100 yields the percentage of correct answers (84%).

Basic Probability Principles

Probability describes how likely it is that an event will occur. Probabilities are always a number from 0 to 1. If an event has a high likelihood of occurrence, it will have a probability close to 1. If there is only a small chance that an event will occur, the likelihood is close to 0. A fair six-sided die has one of the numbers 1, 2, 3, 4, 5, and 6 on each side. When this die is rolled, there is a one in six chance that it will land on 2. This is because there are six possibilities and only one side has a 2 on it. The probability then is $\frac{1}{6}$ or .167. The probability of rolling an even number from this die is three in six, or ½ or .5. This is because there are three sides on the die with even numbers (2, 4, 6), and there are six possible sides. The probability of rolling a number less than 10 is 1 because every side of the die has a number less than 6, so this is certain to occur. On the other hand, the probability of rolling a number larger than 20 is zero. There are no numbers greater than 20 on the die, so it is certain that this will not occur, thus the probability is zero.

If a teacher says that the probability of anyone passing her final exam is .2, is it highly likely that anyone will pass? No, the probability of anyone passing her exam is low because .2 is closer to 0 than to 1. If another teacher is proud that the probability of students passing his class is .95, how likely is it that a student will pass? It is highly likely that a student will pass because the probability, .95, is very close to 1.

Probability problems require that the total number of events in the sample space must be known. Different methods can be used to count the number of possible outcomes, depending on whether different arrangements of the same items are counted only once or separately. **Permutations** are arrangements in which different sequences are counted separately. Therefore, order matters in permutations. **Combinations** are arrangements in which different sequences are not counted separately. Therefore, order does not matter in combinations. For example, if 123 is considered different from 321, permutations would be discussed. However, if 123 is considered the same as 321, combinations would be considered.

If the sample space contains *n* different permutations of *n* different items and all of them must be selected, there are $n!$ different possibilities. For example, five different books can be rearranged 5! = 120 times. The probability of one person randomly ordering those five books in the same way as another person is $\frac{1}{120}$. A different calculation is necessary if a number less than *n* is to be selected or if order does not matter. In general, the notation $P(n, r)$ represents the number of ways to arrange *r* objects from a set of *n* if order does matter, and:

$$P(n,r) = \frac{n!}{(n-r)!}$$

Therefore, in order to calculate the number of ways five books can be arranged in three slots if order matters, plug *n* = 5 and *r* = 3 in the formula to obtain:

$$P(5,3) = \frac{5!}{(5-3)!} = \frac{5!}{2!} = 60$$

Secondly, $C(n, r)$ represents the total number of *r* combinations selected out of *n* items when order does not matter, and:

$$C(n,r) = \frac{n!}{(n-r)!\ r!}$$

Therefore, the number of ways five books can be arranged in three slots if order does not matter is:

$$C(5,3) = \frac{5!}{(5-3)!\ 3!} = 10$$

The following relationship exists between permutations and combinations:

$$C(n,r) = \frac{P(n,r)}{r!}$$

A **probability experiment** is an action that causes specific results, such as counts or measurements. The result of such an experiment is known as an **outcome**, and the set of all potential outcomes is known as the **sample space.** An **event** consists of one or more of those outcomes. For example, consider the probability experiment of tossing a coin and rolling a six-sided die. The coin has two possible outcomes—a heads or a tails—and the die has six possible outcomes—rolling each number 1–6. Therefore, the sample space has twelve possible outcomes: a heads or a tails paired with each roll of the die.

A **simple event** is an event that consists of a single outcome. For instance, selecting a queen of hearts from a standard fifty-two-card deck is a simple event; however, selecting a queen is not a simple event because there are four possibilities.

Classical, or **theoretical, probability** is when each outcome in a sample space has the same chance to occur. The probability for an event is equal to the number of outcomes in that event divided by the total number of outcomes in the sample space. For example, consider rolling a six-sided die. The probability of rolling a 2 is $\frac{1}{6}$, and the probability of rolling an even number is $\frac{3}{6}$, or $\frac{1}{2}$, because there are three even numbers on the die. This type of probability is based on what should happen in theory but not what actually happens in real life.

Empirical probability is based on actual experiments or observations. For example, if a die is rolled eight times, and a 1 is rolled two times, the empirical probability of rolling a 1 is $\frac{2}{8} = \frac{1}{4}$, which is higher than the theoretical probability. The Law of Large Numbers states that as an experiment is completed repeatedly, the empirical probability of an event should get closer to the theoretical probability of an event.

Again, probabilities range from 0 to 1. The closer something is to 0, the less likely it will occur. The closer it is to 1, the more likely it is to occur.

The **addition rule** is necessary to find the probability of event A or event B occurring or both occurring at the same time. If events A and B are **mutually exclusive** or **disjoint,** which means they cannot occur at the same time, $P(A \text{ or } B) = P(A) + P(B)$. If events A and B are not mutually exclusive, $P(A \text{ or } B) = P(A) + P(B) - P(A \text{ and } B)$ where $P(A \text{ and } B)$ represents the probability of event A and B both occurring at the same time. An example of two events that are mutually exclusive are rolling a 6 on a die and rolling an odd number on a die. The probability of rolling a 6 or rolling an odd number is:

$$\frac{1}{6} + \frac{3}{6} = \frac{4}{6} = \frac{2}{3}$$

Rolling a 6 and rolling an even number are not mutually exclusive because there is some overlap. The probability of rolling a 6 or rolling an even number is:

$$\frac{1}{6}+\frac{3}{6}-\frac{1}{6}=\frac{3}{6}=\frac{1}{2}$$

Conditional Probability

The **multiplication rule** is necessary when finding the probability that an event *A* occurs in a first trial and event *B* occurs in a second trial, which is written as $P(A \text{ and } B)$. This rule differs if the events are independent or dependent. Two events *A* and *B* are **independent** if the occurrence of one event does not affect the probability that the other will occur. If *A* and *B* are not independent, they are **dependent,** and the outcome of the first event somehow affects the outcome of the second. If events *A* and B are independent, $P(A \text{ and } B) = P(A)P(B)$, and if events *A* and *B* are dependent, $P(A \text{ and } B) = P(A)P(B|A)$, where $P(B|A)$ represents the probability event *B* occurs given that event *A* has already occurred.

$P(B|A)$ represents **conditional probability**, or the probability of event *B* occurring given that event *A* has already occurred. $P(B|A)$ can be found by dividing the probability of events *A* and *B* both occurring by the probability of event *A* occurring using the formula $P(B|A) = \frac{P\,(A \text{ and } B)}{P(A)}$ and represents the total number of outcomes remaining for *B* to occur after *A* occurs. This formula is derived from the multiplication rule with dependent events by dividing both sides by $P(A)$. Note that $P(B|A)$ and $P(A|B)$ are not the same. The first quantity shows that event *B* has occurred after event *A,* and the second quantity shows that event *A* has occurred after event *B.* To incorrectly interchange these ideas is known as **confusion of the inverse.**

Consider the case of drawing two cards from a deck of fifty-two cards. The probability of pulling two queens would vary based on whether the initial card was placed back in the deck for the second pull. If the card is placed back in, the probability of pulling two queens is:

$$\frac{4}{52}\times\frac{4}{52}=0.00592$$

If the card is not placed back in, the probability of pulling two queens is:

$$\frac{4}{52}\times\frac{3}{51}=0.00452$$

When the card is not placed back in, both the numerator and denominator of the second probability decrease by 1. This is due to the fact that, theoretically, there is one less queen in the deck, and there is one less card in total in the deck as well.

Conditional probability is used frequently when probabilities are calculated from tables. A **two-way frequency table** displays categorical data with two variables, and it highlights relationships that exist between those two variables. Such tables are used frequently to summarize survey results, and are also known as **contingency tables**. Each cell shows a count pertaining to that individual variable paring, known as a **joint frequency**, and the totals of each row and column also are in the table.

Consider the following two-way frequency table:

Distribution of the Residents of a Particular Village

	70 or older	69 or younger	Totals
Women	20	40	60
Men	5	35	40
Total	25	75	100

The table shows the breakdown of ages and sexes of 100 people in a particular village. The total number of people in the data is shown in the bottom right corner. Each total is shown at the end of each row or column, as well. For instance, there were 25 people aged 70 or older and 60 women in the data. The 20 in the first cell shows that out of 100 total villagers, 20 were women aged 70 or older. The 5 in the cell below shows that out of 100 total villagers, 5 were men aged 70 or older.

A two-way table can also show relative frequencies. If instead of the count, the percentage of people in each category was placed into the cells, the two-way table would show relative frequencies. If each frequency is calculated over the entire total of 100, the first cell would be 20% or 0.2. However, the relative frequencies can also be calculated over row or column totals. If row totals were used, the first cell would be:

$$\frac{20}{60} = 0.333 = 33.3\%.$$

If column totals were used, the first cell would be:

$$\frac{20}{25} = 0.8 = 80\%$$

Such tables can be used to calculate conditional probabilities, which are probabilities that an event occurs, given another event. Consider a randomly-selected villager. The probability of selecting a male 70 years old or older is $\frac{5}{100} = 0.05$ because there are 5 males over the age of 70 and 100 total villagers.

Developing and Using a Probability Model

A **discrete random variable** is a set of values that is either finite or countably infinite. If there are infinitely many values, being **countable** means that each individual value can be paired with a natural number. For example, the number of coin tosses before getting heads could potentially be infinite, but the total number of tosses is countable. Each toss refers to a number, like the first toss, second toss, etc. A **continuous random variable** has infinitely many values that are not countable. The individual items cannot be enumerated; an example of such a set is any type of measurement. There are infinitely many heights of human beings due to decimals that exist within each inch, centimeter, millimeter, etc. Each type of variable has its own **probability distribution**, which calculates the probability for each potential value of the random variable. Probability distributions exist in tables, formulas, or graphs. The expected value of a random variable represents what the mean value should be in either a large sample size or after many trials. According to the Law of Large Numbers, after many trials, the actual mean and that of the probability distribution should be very close to the expected value. The **expected value** is a weighted average that is calculated as $E(X) = \sum x_i p_i$, where x_i represents the value of each outcome, and p_i represents the probability of each outcome.

The expected value if all of the probabilities are equal is:

$$E(X) = \frac{x_1 + x_2 + \cdots + x_n}{n}$$

Expected value is often called the **mean of the random variable** and is known as a **measure of central tendency** like mean and mode.

A **binomial probability distribution** is a probability distribution that adheres to some important criteria. The distribution must consist of a fixed number of trials where all trials are independent, each trial has an outcome classified as either success or failure, and the probability of a success is the same in each trial. Within any binomial experiment, x is the number of resulting successes, n is the number of trials, P is the probability of success within each trial, and $Q = 1 - P$ is the probability of failure within each trial. The probability of obtaining x successes within n trials is:

$$\binom{n}{x} P^x (1 - P)^{n-x}$$

Where:

$$\binom{n}{x} = \frac{n!}{x!\,(n - x)!}$$

is called the **binomial coefficient**. A binomial probability distribution could be used to find the probability of obtaining exactly two heads on five tosses of a coin. In the formula, $x = 2$, $n = 5$, $P = 0.5$, and $Q = 0.5$.

A **uniform probability distribution** exists when there is constant probability. Each random variable has equal probability, and its graph is a rectangle because the height, representing the probability, is constant.

Finally, a **normal probability distribution** has a graph that is symmetric and bell-shaped; an example using body weight is shown here:

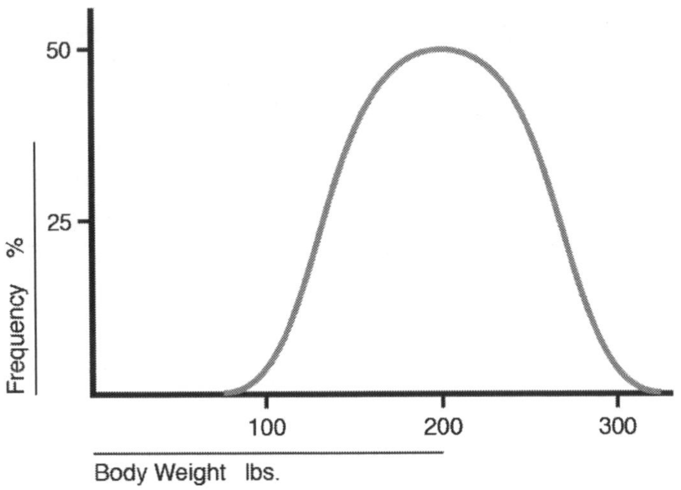

Population percentages can be estimated using normal distributions. For example, the probability that a data point will be less than the mean is 50 percent. The Empirical Rule states that 68 percent of the data falls within 1 standard deviation of the mean, 95 percent falls within 2 standard deviations of the mean, and 99.7 percent falls within 3 standard deviations of the mean. A **standard normal distribution** is a normal distribution with a mean equal to 0 and standard deviation equal to 1. The area under the entire curve of a standard normal distribution is equal to 1.

Interpreting the Meaning of Standardized Test Scores to Determine How Individuals Performed Relative to Other Students

A **standardized test** is one in which test questions are gathered from a common bank of test questions and are scored in the same manner. Because the scoring process is same for each person who takes the test, individual scores allow for easy comparisons of performances from person to person. Some well-known standardized tests include the ACT and SAT tests for admission into colleges.

A common way in which standardized test scores are presented is by using percentiles. A **percentile** is a statistical measure that divides a group into one hundred equal parts. When a percentile is stated, it refers to a percentage that breaks up all values into two parts of the whole group. For example, if a value is in the 65th percentile, sixty-five percent of all other values fall below the value being discussed and thirty-five percent of all other values fall above the value being discussed. When considering standardized test scores, if someone scores in the 80th percentile, eighty percent of people scored lower than that person, and twenty percent of people scored higher.

Standardized tests can also be composed of subsections that have scores presented in the same manner. For instance, the ACT has many parts, including English, Math, Reading, and Science. A student can score in different percentiles in each part. For example, a student can score in the 99th percentile on the Math portion and in the 80th percentile on the English portion. These scores indicate that the student fared better on the Math portion than on the English portion of the test.

Another type of score that is utilized in standardized tests is a **stanine score**. This scoring mechanism uses a nine-point scale to classify scores. A score is a whole number from 0 to 9, and is assigned by using a normal distribution with a mean of five and a standard deviation of two. A bell curve is partitioned into nine equal parts as shown here:

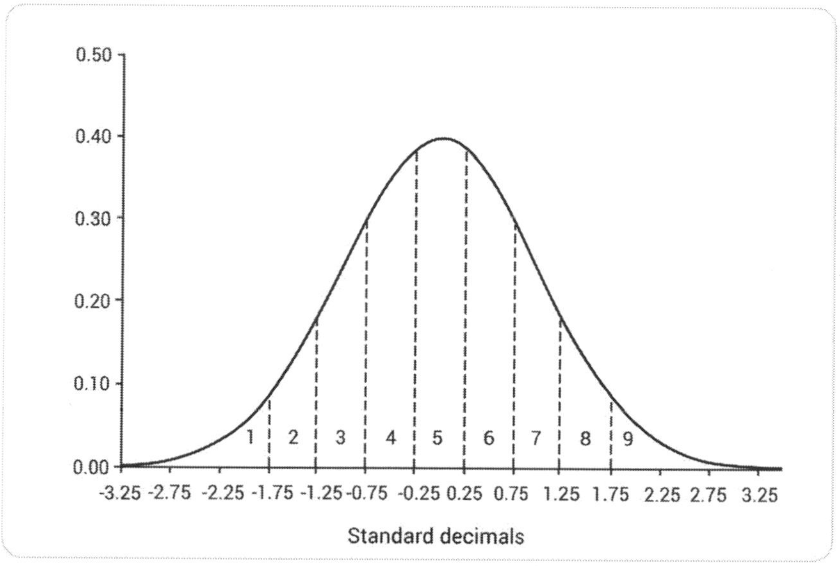

A score of a 9 represents a score in the top four percent of all other scores, and an 8 represents the next seven percent of scores. A 7 represents the next twelve percent of scores, and a 6 represents the next top seventeen percent. A score of a 5 represents the middle twenty percent of all scores. A 4 represents the next seventeen percent that fall below a score of a 5, and a 3 represents the next twelve percent. Finally, a score of a 2 represents the next seven percent, and a 1 represents the bottom four percent.

Computation & Problem Solving

Addition, Subtraction, Multiplication, and Division with Whole Numbers

The four basic operations include addition, subtraction, multiplication, and division. The result of addition is a **sum**, the result of subtraction is a **difference**, the result of multiplication is a **product**, and the result of division is a **quotient**. Each type of operation can be used when working with rational numbers; however, the basic operations need to be understood first while using simpler numbers before working with fractions and decimals.

Performing these operations should first be learned using whole numbers. Addition needs to be done column by column. To add two whole numbers, add the ones column first, then the tens columns, then the hundreds, etc. If the sum of any column is greater than 9, a one must be carried over to the next column. For example, the following is the result of 482 + 924:

$$\begin{array}{r} {\scriptstyle 1} \\ 482 \\ +924 \\ \hline 1406 \end{array}$$

Notice that the sum of the tens column was 10, so a one was carried over to the hundreds column. Subtraction is also performed column by column. Subtraction is performed in the ones column first, then the tens, etc. If the number on top is smaller than the number below, a one must be borrowed from the column to the left. For example, the following is the result of 5,424 – 756:

$$\begin{array}{r} 4\ 13\ 11\ 14 \\ \not{5}\ \not{4}\ \not{2}\ \not{4} \\ -\ 7\ \ 5\ \ 6 \\ \hline 4\ \ 6\ \ 6\ \ 8 \end{array}$$

Notice that a one is borrowed from the tens, hundreds, and thousands place. After subtraction, the answer can be checked through addition. A check of this problem would be to show that 756 + 4,668 = 5,424.

Multiplication of two whole numbers is performed by writing one on top of the other. The number on top is known as the **multiplicand,** and the number below is the **multiplier.** Perform the multiplication by multiplying the multiplicand by each digit of the multiplier. Make sure to place the ones value of each result under the multiplying digit in the multiplier. Each value to the right is then a 0. The product is found by adding each product. For example, the following is the process of multiplying 46 times 37, where 46 is the multiplicand and 37 is the multiplier:

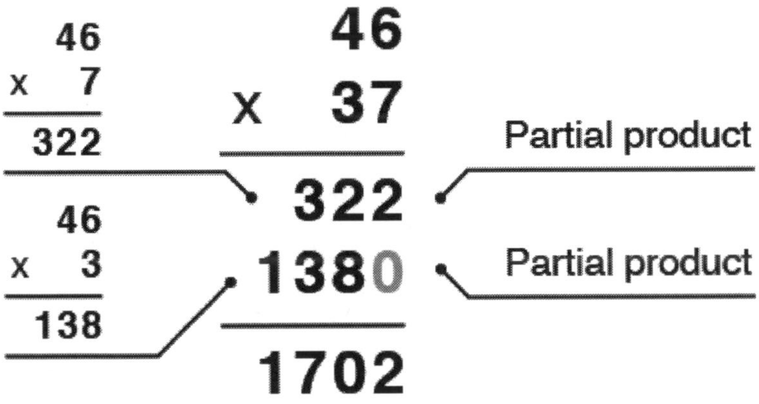

Finally, division can be performed using long division. When dividing a number by another number, the first number is known as the **dividend,** and the second is the **divisor.** For example, with $a \div b = c$, a is the dividend, b is the divisor, and c is the quotient. For long division, place the dividend within the division symbol and the divisor on the outside. For example, with $8{,}764 \div 4$, refer to the first problem in the diagram below. First, there are 2 4's in the first digit, 8. This number 2 gets written above the 8. Then, multiply 4 times 2 to get 8, and that product goes below the 8. Subtract to get 8, and then carry down the 7. Continue the same steps. $7 \div 4 = 1\ \text{R3}$, so 1 is written above the 7. Multiply 4 times 1 to get 4, and write it below the 7. Subtract to get 3, and carry the 6 down next to the 3. Resulting steps give a 9 and a 1. The final subtraction results in a 0, which means that 8,764 is divisible by 4. There are no remaining numbers.

The second example shows that $4{,}536 \div 216 = 21$. The steps are a little different because 216 cannot be contained in 4 or 5, so the first step is placing a 2 above the 3 because there are 2 216's in 453. Finally, the third example shows that $546 \div 31 = 17\text{ R}19$. The 19 is a remainder. Notice that the final subtraction does not result in a 0, which means that 546 is not divisible by 31. The remainder can also be written as a fraction over the divisor to say that $546 \div 31 = 17\frac{19}{31}$.

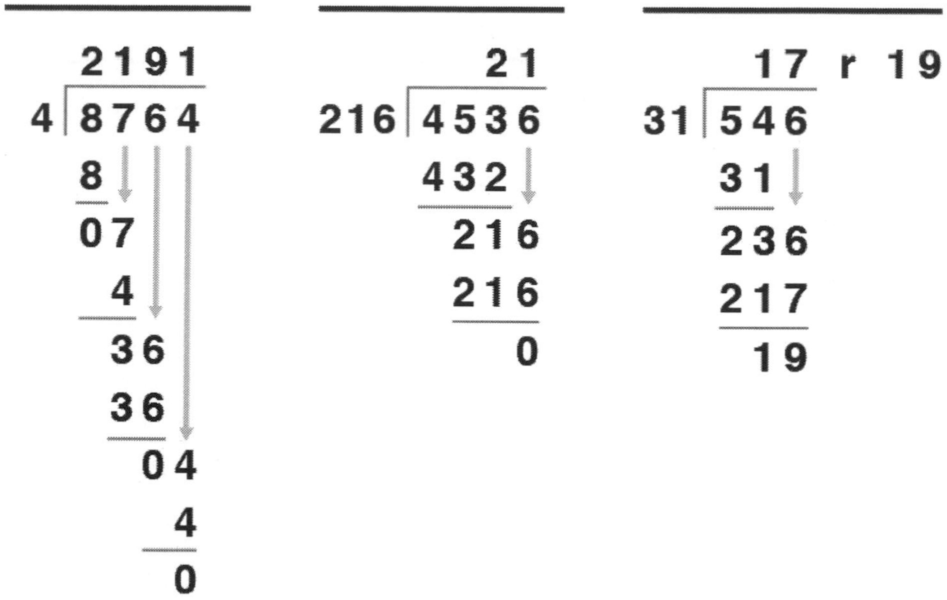

If a division problem relates to a real-world application, and a remainder does exist, it can have meaning. For example, consider the third example, $546 \div 31 = 17R19$. Let's say that we had \$546 to spend on calculators that cost \$31 each, and we wanted to know how many we could buy. The division problem would answer this question. The result states that 17 calculators could be purchased, with \$19 left over. Notice that the remainder will never be greater than or equal to the divisor.

Addition, Subtraction, Multiplication, and Division with Positive and Negative Numbers

Once the operations are understood with whole numbers, they can be used with integers. There are many rules surrounding operations with negative numbers. First, consider addition with integers. The sum of two numbers can first be shown using a number line. For example, to add $-5 + (-6)$, plot the point −5 on the number line. Then, because a negative number is being added, move 6 units to the left. This process results in landing on −11 on the number line, which is the sum of −5 and −6. If adding a positive number, move to the right.

Visualizing this process using a number line is useful for understanding; however, it is not efficient. A quicker process is to learn the rules. When adding two numbers with the same sign, add the absolute values of both numbers, and use the common sign of both numbers as the sign of the sum. For example, to add $-5 + (-6)$, add their absolute values $5 + 6 = 11$. Then, introduce a negative number because both addends are negative. The result is −11. To add two integers with unlike signs, subtract the lesser absolute value from the greater absolute value, and apply the sign of the number with the greater absolute value to the result. For example, the sum $-7 + 4$ can be computed by finding the difference $7 - 4 = 3$ and then applying a negative because the value with the larger absolute value is negative. The result is -3. Similarly, the sum $-4 + 7$ can be found by computing the same difference but leaving it as a positive result because the addend with the larger absolute value is positive. Also, recall that any number plus 0 equals that number. This is known as the **Addition Property of 0.**

Subtracting two integers can be computed by changing to addition to avoid confusion. The rule is to add the first number to the opposite of the second number. The opposite of a number is the number on the other side of 0 on the number line, which is the same number of units away from 0. For example, −2 and 2 are opposites. Consider $4 - 8$. Change this to adding the opposite as follows: $4 + (-8)$. Then, follow the rules of addition of integers to obtain −4. Secondly, consider $-8 - (-2)$. Change this problem to adding the opposite as $-8 + 2$, which equals −6. Notice that subtracting a negative number is really adding a positive number.

Multiplication and division of integers are actually less confusing than addition and subtraction because the rules are simpler to understand. If two factors in a multiplication problem have the same sign, the result is positive. If one factor is positive and one factor is negative, the result, known as the **product,** is negative. For example, $(-9)(-3) = 27$ and $9(-3) = -27$. Also, a number times 0 always results in 0. If a problem consists of more than a single multiplication, the result is negative if it contains an odd number of negative factors, and the result is positive if it contains an even number of negative factors. For example, $(-1)(-1)(-1)(-1) = 1$ and $(-1)(-1)(-1)(-1)(-1) = -1$. These two examples of multiplication also bring up another concept. Both are examples of repeated multiplication, which can be written in a more compact notation using exponents. The first example can be written as $(-1)^4 = 1$, and the second example can be written as $(-1)^5 = -1$. Both are exponential expressions: −1 is the base in both instances, and 4 and 5 are the respective exponents. Note that a negative number raised to an odd power is always negative, and a negative number raised to an even power is always positive. Also, $(-1)^4$ is not the same as -1^4. In the first expression, the negative is included in the parentheses, but it is not in the second expression. The second expression is found by evaluating 1^4 first to get 1 and then applying the negative sign to obtain −1.

A similar theory applies within division. First, consider some vocabulary. When dividing 14 by 2, it can be written in the following ways: $14 \div 2 = 7$ or $\frac{14}{2} = 7$. 14 is the **dividend,** 2 is the **divisor,** and 7 is the **quotient.** If two numbers in a division problem have the same sign, the quotient is positive. If two numbers in a division problem have different signs, the quotient is negative. For example:

$$14 \div (-2) = -7, \text{ and } -14 \div (-2) = 7$$

To check division, multiply the quotient times the divisor to obtain the dividend. Also, remember that 0 divided by any number is equal to 0. However, any number divided by 0 is undefined. It just does not make sense to divide a number by 0 parts.

If more than one operation is to be completed in a problem, follow the **Order of Operations**. The mnemonic device, PEMDAS, for the order of operations states the order in which addition, subtraction, multiplication, and division need to be done. It also includes when to evaluate operations within grouping symbols and when to incorporate exponents. PEMDAS, which some remember by thinking "please excuse my dear Aunt Sally," refers to parentheses, exponents, multiplication, division, addition, and subtraction. First, within an expression, complete any operation that is within parentheses, or any other grouping symbol like brackets, braces, or absolute value symbols. Note that this does not refer to the case when parentheses are used to represent multiplication like $(2)(5)$, wherein an operation is not within parentheses like it is in $(2 \cdot 5)$. Then, any exponents must be computed. Next, multiplication and division are performed from left to right.

Finally, addition and subtraction are performed from left to right. The following is an example in which the operations within the parentheses need to be performed first, so the order of operations must be applied to the exponent, subtraction, addition, and multiplication within the grouping symbol:

$$9-3(3^2-3+4\cdot 3)$$

$$9-3(3^2-3+4\cdot 3)$$ Work within the parentheses first

$$=9-3(9-3+12)$$

$$=9-3(18)$$

$$=9-54$$

$$=-45$$

Addition, Subtraction, Multiplication, and Division with Fractions, Decimals, & Percentages

Operations with Fractions

Once the rules for integers are understood, operations with fractions and decimals can be mastered. Recall that a **rational number** can be written as a fraction and can be converted to a decimal through division. If a rational number is negative, the rules for adding, subtracting, multiplying, and dividing integers must be used. If a rational number is in fraction form, performing addition, subtraction, multiplication, and division is more complicated than when working with integers. First, consider addition. To add two fractions having the same denominator, add the numerators and then reduce the fraction. When an answer is a fraction, it should always be in lowest terms. **Lowest terms** means that every common factor, other than 1, between the numerator and denominator is divided out. For example:

$$\frac{2}{8}+\frac{4}{8}=\frac{6}{8}=\frac{6\div 2}{8\div 2}=\frac{3}{4}$$

Both the numerator and denominator of $\frac{6}{8}$ have a common factor of 2, so 2 is divided out of each number to put the fraction in lowest terms. If denominators are different in an addition problem, the fractions must be converted to have common denominators. The **least common denominator (LCD)** of all the given denominators must be found, and this value is equal to the **least common multiple (LCM)** of the denominators. This non-zero value is the smallest number that is a multiple of both denominators. Then, each original fraction can be written as an equivalent fraction using the new denominator. Once in this form, process of adding with like denominators is completed. For example, consider $\frac{1}{3}+\frac{4}{9}$. The LCD is 9 because 9 is the smallest multiple of both 3 and 9. The fraction $\frac{1}{3}$ must be rewritten with 9 as its denominator. Therefore, multiply both the numerator and denominator by 3. Multiplying by $\frac{3}{3}$ is the same as multiplying times 1, which does not change the value of the fraction. Therefore, an equivalent fraction is $\frac{3}{9}$, and $\frac{1}{3}+\frac{4}{9}=\frac{3}{9}+\frac{4}{9}=\frac{7}{9}$, which is in lowest terms. Subtraction is performed in a similar manner; once the denominators are equal, the numerators are then subtracted. The following is an example of addition of a positive and a negative fraction:

$$-\frac{5}{12}+\frac{5}{9}=-\frac{5\times 3}{12\times 3}+\frac{5\times 4}{9\times 4}=-\frac{15}{36}+\frac{20}{36}=\frac{5}{36}$$

Common denominators are not used in multiplication and division. To multiply two fractions, multiply the numerators together and the denominators together. Then, write the result in lowest terms.

For example:

$$\frac{2}{3}\times\frac{9}{4}=\frac{18}{12}=\frac{3}{2}$$

Alternatively, the fractions could be factored first to cancel out any common factors before performing the multiplication. For example:

$$\frac{2}{3}\times\frac{9}{4}=\frac{2}{3}\times\frac{3\times 3}{2\times 2}=\frac{3}{2}$$

This second approach is helpful when working with larger numbers, as common factors might not be obvious. Multiplication and division of fractions are related because the division of two fractions is changed into a multiplication problem. Division of a fraction is equivalent to multiplication of the **reciprocal** of the second fraction, so that second fraction must be inverted, or "flipped," to be in reciprocal form. For example:

$$\frac{11}{15}\div\frac{3}{5}=\frac{11}{15}\times\frac{5}{3}=\frac{55}{45}=\frac{11}{9}$$

The fraction $\frac{5}{3}$ is the reciprocal of $\frac{3}{5}$. It is possible to multiply and divide numbers containing a mix of integers and fractions. In this case, convert the integer to a fraction by placing it over a denominator of 1. For example, a division problem involving an integer and a fraction is:

$$3\div\frac{1}{2}=\frac{3}{1}\times\frac{2}{1}=\frac{6}{1}=6$$

Finally, when performing operations with rational numbers that are negative, the same rules apply as when performing operations with integers. For example, a negative fraction times a negative fraction results in a positive value, and a negative fraction subtracted from a negative fraction results in a negative value.

Operations with Decimals

Operations can be performed on rational numbers in decimal form. Recall that to write a fraction as an equivalent decimal expression, divide the numerator by the denominator. For example, $\frac{1}{8}=1\div 8=0.125$.

With the case of decimals, it is important to keep track of place value. To add decimals, make sure the decimal places are in alignment so that the numbers are lined up with their decimal points and add vertically. If the numbers do not line up because there are extra or missing place values in one of the numbers, then zeros may be used as placeholders. For example, $0.123+0.23$ becomes:

$$\begin{array}{r} 0.123 \\ \underline{0.230} \\ 0.353 \end{array}$$

Subtraction is done the same way. Multiplication and division are more complicated. To multiply two decimals, place one on top of the other as in a regular multiplication process and do not worry about lining up the decimal points. Then, multiply as with whole numbers, ignoring the decimals. Finally, in the solution, insert the decimal point as many places to the left as there are total decimal values in the original problem. Here is an example of a decimal multiplication:

0.52	*2 decimal places*
x 0.2	*1 decimal place*
0.104	*3 decimal places*

The answer to 52 times 2 is 104, and because there are three decimal values in the problem, the decimal point is positioned three units to the left in the answer.

The decimal point plays an integral role throughout the whole problem when dividing with decimals. First, set up the problem in a long division format. If the divisor is not an integer, the decimal must be moved to the right as many units as needed to make it an integer. The decimal in the dividend must be moved to the right the same number of places to maintain equality. Then, division is completed normally. Here is an example of long division with decimals:

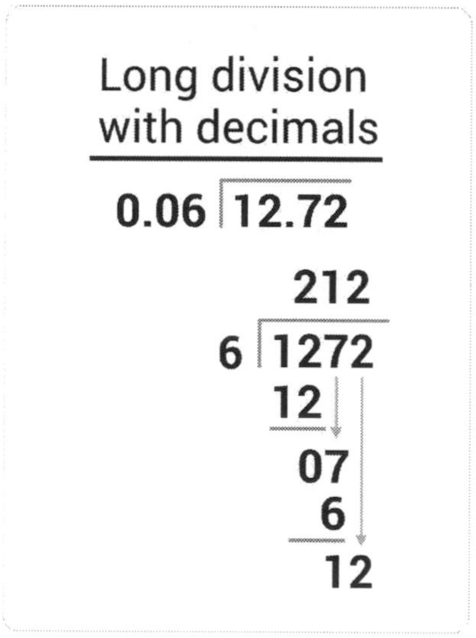

Because the decimal point is moved two units to the right in the divisor of 0.06 to turn it into the integer 6, it is also moved two units to the right in the dividend of 12.72 to make it 1,272. The result is 212, and remember that a division problem can always be checked by multiplying the answer by the divisor to see if the result is equal to the dividend.

Sometimes it is helpful to round answers that are in decimal form. First, find the place to which the rounding needs to be done. Then, look at the digit to the right of it. If that digit is 4 or less, the number in the place value to its left stays the same, and everything to its right becomes a 0. This process is known as **rounding down**. If that digit is 5 or higher, round up by increasing the place value to its left by 1, and every number to its right becomes a 0. If those 0's are in decimals, they can be dropped. For example, 0.145 rounded to the nearest hundredths place would be rounded up to 0.15, and 0.145 rounded to the nearest tenths place would be rounded down to 0.1.

Converting Non-Negative Fractions, Decimals, and Percentages

Within the number system, different forms of numbers can be used. It is important to be able to recognize each type, as well as work with, and convert between, the given forms. The **real number system** comprises natural numbers, whole numbers, integers, rational numbers, and irrational numbers. Natural numbers, whole numbers, integers, and irrational numbers typically are not represented as fractions, decimals, or percentages. Rational numbers, however, can be represented as any of these three forms. A **rational number** is a number that can be written in the form $\frac{a}{b}$, where a and b are integers, and b is not equal to zero. In other words, rational numbers can be written in a fraction form. The value a is the **numerator,** and b is the **denominator.**

If the numerator is equal to zero, the entire fraction is equal to zero. Non-negative fractions can be less than 1, equal to 1, or greater than 1. Fractions are less than 1 if the numerator is smaller (less than) than the denominator. For example, $\frac{3}{4}$ is less than 1. A fraction is equal to 1 if the numerator is equal to the denominator. For instance, $\frac{4}{4}$ is equal to 1. Finally, a fraction is greater than 1 if the numerator is greater than the denominator: the fraction $\frac{11}{4}$ is greater than 1. When the numerator is greater than the denominator, the fraction is called an **improper fraction**. An improper fraction can be converted to a **mixed number**, a combination of both a whole number and a fraction. To convert an improper fraction to a mixed number, divide the numerator by the denominator. Write down the whole number portion, and then write any remainder over the original denominator. For example, $\frac{11}{4}$ is equivalent to $2\frac{3}{4}$. Conversely, a mixed number can be converted to an improper fraction by multiplying the denominator by the whole number and adding that result to the numerator.

Fractions can be converted to decimals. With a calculator, a fraction is converted to a decimal by dividing the numerator by the denominator. For example, $\frac{2}{5} = 2 \div 5 = 0.4$. Sometimes, rounding might be necessary. Consider $\frac{2}{7} = 2 \div 7 = 0.28571429$. This decimal could be rounded for ease of use, and if it needed to be rounded to the nearest thousandth, the result would be 0.286. If a calculator is not available, a fraction can be converted to a decimal manually. First, find a number that, when multiplied by the denominator, has a value equal to 10, 100, 1,000, etc. Then, multiply both the numerator and denominator times that number. The decimal form of the fraction is equal to the new numerator with a decimal point placed as many place values to the left as there are zeros in the denominator. For example, to convert $\frac{3}{5}$ to a decimal, multiply both the numerator and denominator by 2, which results in $\frac{6}{10}$. The decimal is equal to 0.6 because there is one zero in the denominator, and so the decimal place in the numerator is moved one unit to the left.

In the case where rounding would be necessary while working without a calculator, an approximation must be found. A number close to 10, 100, 1,000, etc. can be used. For example, to convert $\frac{1}{3}$ to a decimal, the numerator and denominator can be multiplied by 33 to turn the denominator into approximately 100, which makes for an easier conversion to the equivalent decimal. This process results in $\frac{33}{99}$ and an approximate decimal of 0.33. Once in decimal form, the number can be converted to a percentage. Multiply the decimal by 100 and then place a percent sign after the number. For example, .614 is equal to 61.4%. In other words, move the decimal place two units to the right and add the percentage symbol.

Solving Practical Math Problems

One-step problems take only one mathematical step to solve. For example, solving the equation $5x = 45$ is a one-step problem because the one step of dividing both sides of the equation by 5 is the only step necessary to obtain the solution $x = 9$. The **multiplication principle of equality** is the one step used to isolate the variable. The equation is of the form $ax = b$, where a and b are rational numbers. Similarly, the **addition principle of equality** could be the one step needed to solve a problem. In this case, the equation would be of the form $x + a = b$ or $x - a = b$, for real numbers a and b.

A multi-step problem involves more than one step to find the solution, or it could consist of solving more than one equation. An equation that involves both the addition principle and the multiplication principle is a two-step problem, and an example of such an equation is $2x - 4 = 5$. Solving involves adding 4 to both sides and then dividing both sides by 2. An example of a two-step problem involving two separate equations is $y = 3x, 2x + y = 4$. The two equations form a system of two equations that must be solved together in two variables. The system can be solved by the substitution method. Since y is already solved for in terms of x, plug $3x$ in for y into the equation $2x + y = 4$, resulting in $2x + 3x = 4$. Therefore, $5x = 4$ and $x = \frac{4}{5}$. Because there are two variables, the solution consists of a value for both x and for y. Substitute $x = \frac{4}{5}$ into either original equation to find y. The easiest choice is $y = 3x$. Therefore:

$$y = 3 \times \frac{4}{5} = \frac{12}{5}$$

The solution can be written as the ordered pair $\left(\frac{4}{5}, \frac{12}{5}\right)$.

Real-world problems can be translated into both one-step and multi-step problems. In either case, the word problem must be translated from the verbal form into mathematical expressions and equations that can be solved using algebra. An example of a one-step real-world problem is the following: A cat weighs half as much as a dog living in the same house. If the dog weighs 14.5 pounds, how much does the cat weigh? To solve this problem, an equation can be used. In any word problem, the first step must be defining variables that represent the unknown quantities. For this problem, let x be equal to the unknown weight of the cat. Because two times the weight of the cat equals 14.5 pounds, the equation to be solved is: $2x = 14.5$. Use the multiplication principle to divide both sides by 2. Therefore, $x = 7.25$. The cat weighs 7.25 pounds.

Most of the time, real-world problems are more difficult than this one and are multi-step problems. The following is an example of a multi-step problem: The sum of two consecutive page numbers is equal to 437. What are those page numbers? First, define the unknown quantities. If x is equal to the first page number, then $x + 1$ is equal to the next page number because they are consecutive integers. Their sum is equal to 437, and this statement translates to the equation $x + (x + 1) = 437$. To solve, first collect like terms to obtain $2x + 1 = 437$.

Then, subtract 1 from both sides and then divide by 2. The solution to the equation is $x = 218$. Therefore, the two consecutive page numbers that satisfy the problem are 218 and 219. It is always important to make sure that answers to real-world problems make sense. For instance, if the solution to this same problem resulted in decimals, that should be a red flag indicating the need to check the work. Page numbers are whole numbers; therefore, if decimals are found to be answers, the solution process should be double-checked to see where mistakes were made.

Solving Single- and Multistep Problems Involving Percentages

Percentages are defined to be parts per one hundred. To convert a decimal to a percentage, move the decimal point two units to the left and place the percent sign after the number. Percentages appear in many scenarios in the real world. It is important to make sure the statement containing the percentage is translated to a correct mathematical expression. Be aware that it is extremely common to make a mistake when working with percentages within word problems.

An example of a word problem containing a percentage is the following: 35% of people speed when driving to work. In a group of 5,600 commuters, how many would be expected to speed on the way to their place of employment? The answer to this problem is found by finding 35% of 5,600. First, change the percentage to the decimal 0.35. Then compute the product: $0.35 \times 5{,}600 = 1{,}960$. Therefore, it would be expected that 1,960 of those commuters would speed on their way to work based on the data given. In this situation, the word "of" signals to use multiplication to find the answer. Another way percentage is used is in the following problem: *Teachers work 8 months out of the year. What percent of the year do they work?* To answer this problem, find what percent *of* 12 the number 8 *is*, because there are 12 months in a year. Therefore, divide 8 by 12, and convert that number to a percentage:

$$\frac{8}{12} = \frac{2}{3} = 0.66\bar{6}$$

The percentage rounded to the nearest tenth place tells us that teachers work 66.7% of the year. Percentages also appear in real-world application problems involving finding missing quantities like in the following question: 60% of what number is 75? To find the missing quantity, an equation can be used. Let x be equal to the missing quantity. Therefore, $0.60x = 75$. Divide each side by 0.60 to obtain 125. Therefore, 60% of 125 is equal to 75.

Sales tax is an important application relating to percentages because tax rates are usually given as percentages. For example, a city might have an 8% sales tax rate. Therefore, when an item is purchased with that tax rate, the real cost to the customer is 1.08 times the price in the store. For example, a \$25 pair of jeans costs the customer $\$25 \times 1.08 = \$27$. Sales tax rates can also be determined if they are unknown when an item is purchased. If a customer visits a store and purchases an item for \$21.44, but the price in the store was \$19, they can find the tax rate by first subtracting $\$21.44 - \$19$ to obtain \$2.44, the sales tax amount. The sales tax is a percentage of the in-store price. Therefore, the tax rate is $\frac{2.44}{19} = 0.128$, which has been rounded to the nearest thousandths place. In this scenario, the actual sales tax rate given as a percentage is 12.8%.

Solving Real-World Problems Involving Proportions

Fractions appear in everyday situations, and in many scenarios, they appear in the real-world as ratios and in proportions. A **ratio** is formed when two different quantities are compared. For example, in a group of 50 people, if there are 33 females and 17 males, the ratio of females to males is 33 to 17. This expression can be written in the fraction form, $\frac{33}{17}$, or by using the ratio symbol, 33:17. The order of the number matters when forming ratios. In the same setting, the ratio of males to females is 17 to 33, which is equivalent to $\frac{17}{33}$ or 17:33. A **proportion** is an equation involving two ratios. The equation $\frac{a}{b} = \frac{c}{d}$, or $a{:}b = c{:}d$ is a proportion, for real numbers a, b, c, and d. Usually, in one ratio, one of the quantities is unknown, and cross-multiplication is used to solve for the unknown. Consider $\frac{1}{4} = \frac{x}{5}$. To solve for x, cross-multiply to obtain $5 = 4x$. Divide each side by 4 to obtain the solution $x = \frac{5}{4}$. It is also true that percentages are ratios in which the second term is 100. For example, 65% is 65:100 or $\frac{65}{100}$. Therefore, when working with percentages, one is also working with ratios.

Real-world problems frequently involve proportions. For example, consider the following problem: If 2 out of 50 pizzas are usually delivered late from a local Italian restaurant, how many would be late out of 235 orders? The following proportion would be solved with x as the unknown quantity of late pizzas: $\frac{2}{50} = \frac{x}{235}$. Cross multiplying results in $470 = 50x$. Divide both sides by 50 to obtain $x = \frac{470}{50}$, which in lowest terms is equal to $\frac{47}{5}$. In decimal form, this improper fraction is equal to 9.4. Because it does not make sense to answer this question with decimals (portions of pizzas do not get delivered) the answer must be rounded. Traditional rounding rules would say that 9 pizzas would be expected to be delivered late. However, to be safe, rounding up to 10 pizzas out of 235 would probably make more sense.

Solving Real-World Problems Involving Ratios and Rates of Change

Recall that a **ratio** is the comparison of two different quantities. Comparing 2 apples to 3 oranges results in the ratio 2:3, which can be expressed as the fraction $\frac{2}{3}$. Note that order is important when discussing ratios. The number mentioned first is the numerator, and the number mentioned second is the denominator. The ratio 2:3 does not mean the same quantity as the ratio 3:2. Also, it is important to make sure than when discussing ratios that have units attached to them, the two quantities use the same units. For example, to think of 8 feet to 4 yards, it would make sense to convert 4 yards to feet by multiplying by 3. Therefore, the ratio would be 8 feet to 12 feet, which can be expressed as the fraction $\frac{8}{12}$. Also, note that it is proper to refer to ratios in lowest terms.

Therefore, the ratio of 8 feet to 4 yards is equivalent to the fraction $\frac{2}{3}$. Many real-world problems involve ratios. Often, problems with ratios involve proportions, as when two ratios are set equal to find the missing amount. However, some problems involve deciphering single ratios. For example, consider an amusement park that sold 345 tickets last Saturday. If 145 tickets were sold to adults and the rest of the tickets were sold to children, what would the ratio of the number of adult tickets to children's tickets be? A common mistake would be to say the ratio is 145:345. However, 345 is the total number of tickets sold, not the number of children's tickets. There were 345 – 145 = 200 tickets sold to children. The correct ratio of adult to children's tickets is 145:200. As a fraction, this expression is written as $\frac{145}{200}$, which can be reduced to $\frac{29}{40}$.

While a ratio compares two measurements using the same units, rates compare two measurements with different units. Examples of rates would be \$200 of work for 8 hours, or 500 miles per 20 gallons. Because the units are different, it is important to always include the units when discussing rates. Rates can be easily seen because if they are expressed in words, the two quantities are usually split up using one of the following words: *for, per, on, from, in.* Just as with ratios, it is important to write rates in lowest terms. A common rate that can be found in many real-life situations is cost per unit. This quantity describes how much one item or one unit costs. This rate allows the best buy to be determined, given a couple of different sizes of an item with different costs. For example, if 2 quarts of soup was sold for \$3.50 and 3 quarts was sold for \$4.60, to determine the best buy, the cost per quart should be found. $\frac{\$3.50}{2} = \$1.75$ per quart, and $\frac{\$4.60}{3} = \$1.53$ per quart. Therefore, the better deal would be the 3-quart option.

Rate of change problems involve calculating a quantity per some unit of measurement. Usually the unit of measurement is time. For example, meters per second is a common rate of change. To calculate this measurement, find the amount traveled in meters and divide by total time traveled. The calculation is an average of the speed over the entire time interval. Another common rate of change used in the real world is miles per hour. Consider the following problem that involves calculating an average rate of change in temperature. Last Saturday, the temperature at 1:00 a.m. was 34 degrees Fahrenheit, and at noon, the temperature had increased to 75 degrees Fahrenheit. What was the average rate of change over that time interval? The average rate of change is calculated by finding the change in temperature and dividing by the total hours elapsed. Therefore, the rate of change was equal to $\frac{75-34}{12-1} = \frac{41}{11}$ degrees per hour. This quantity rounded to two decimal places is equal to 3.72 degrees per hour.

A common rate of change that appears in algebra is the slope calculation. Given a linear equation in one variable, $y = mx + b$, the **slope**, *m,* is equal to $\frac{rise}{run}$ or $\frac{change\ in\ y}{change\ in\ x}$. In other words, slope is equivalent to the ratio of the vertical and horizontal changes between any two points on a line. The vertical change is known as the **rise,** and the horizontal change is known as the **run.** Given any two points on a line (x_1, y_1) and (x_2, y_2), slope can be calculated with the formula:

$$m = \frac{y_2 - y_1}{x_2 - x_1} = \frac{\Delta y}{\Delta x}$$

Common real-world applications of slope include determining how steep a staircase should be, calculating how steep a road is, and determining how to build a wheelchair ramp.

Many times, problems involving rates and ratios involve proportions. A proportion states that two ratios (or rates) are equal. The property of cross products can be used to determine if a proportion is true, meaning both ratios are equivalent. If $\frac{a}{b} = \frac{c}{d}$, then to clear the fractions, multiply both sides by the least common denominator, bd. This results in $ac = cd$, which is equal to the result of multiplying along both diagonals. For example, $\frac{4}{40} = \frac{1}{10}$ grants the cross product $4 \cdot 10 = 40 \times 1$. $40 = 40$ shows that this proportion is true. Cross products are used when proportions are involved in real-world problems. Consider the following: If 3 pounds of fertilizer will cover 75 square feet of grass, how many pounds are needed for 375 square feet? To solve this problem, a proportion can be set up using two ratios. Let x equal the unknown quantity, pounds needed for 375 feet. Then, the equation found by setting the two given ratios equal to one another is $\frac{3}{75} = \frac{x}{375}$. Cross-multiplication gives $3 \times 375 = 75x$. Therefore, $1{,}125 = 75x$. Divide both sides by 75 to get $x = 15$. Therefore, 15 gallons of fertilizer are needed to cover 75 square feet of grass.

Another application of proportions involves similar triangles. If two triangles have the same measurement as two triangles in another triangle, the triangles are said to be **similar.** If two are the same, the third pair of angles are equal as well because the sum of all angles in a triangle is equal to 180 degrees. Each pair of equivalent angles are known as **corresponding angles. Corresponding sides** face the corresponding angles, and it is true that corresponding sides are in proportion. For example, consider the following set of similar triangles:

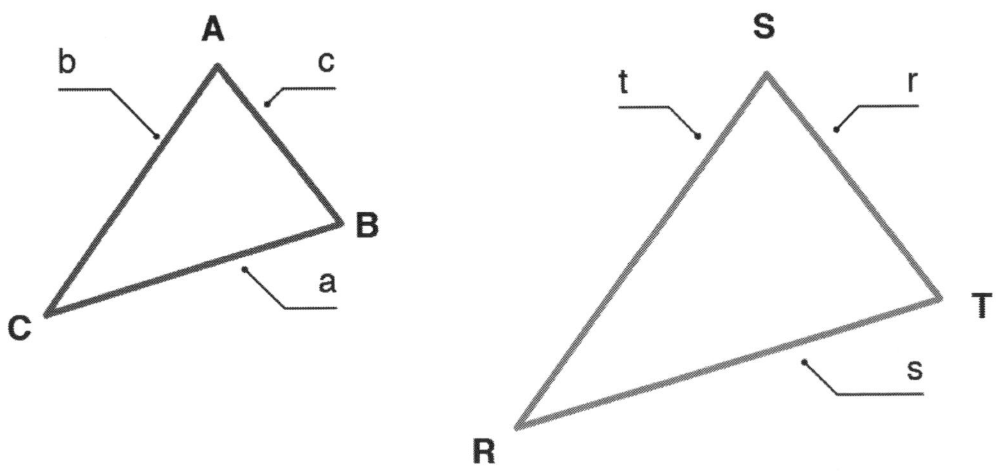

Angles A and R have the same measurement, angles C and T have the same measurement, and angles B and S have the same measurement. Therefore, the following proportion can be set up from the sides:

$$\frac{c}{t} = \frac{a}{r} = \frac{b}{s}$$

This proportion can be helpful in finding missing lengths in pairs of similar triangles. For example, if the following triangles are similar, a proportion can be used to find the missing side lengths, *a* and *b*.

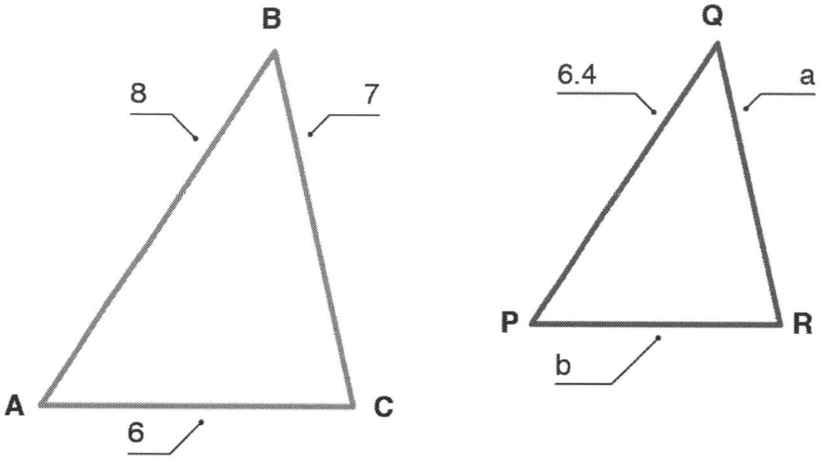

The proportions $\frac{8}{6.4} = \frac{6}{b}$ and $\frac{8}{6.4} = \frac{7}{a}$ can both be cross-multiplied and solved to obtain *a* = 5.6 and *b* = 4.8.

A real-life situation that uses similar triangles involves measuring shadows to find heights of unknown objects. Consider the following problem: A building casts a shadow that is 120 feet long, and at the same time, another building that is 80 feet high casts a shadow that is 60 feet long. How tall is the first building? Each building, together with the sun rays and shadows casted on the ground, forms a triangle. They are similar because each building forms a right angle with the ground, and the sun rays form equivalent angles. Therefore, these two pairs of angles are both equal. Because all angles in a triangle add up to 180 degrees, the third angles are equal as well. Both shadows form corresponding sides of the triangle, the buildings form corresponding sides, and the sun rays form corresponding sides. Therefore, the triangles are similar, and the following proportion can be used to find the missing building length:

$$\frac{120}{x} = \frac{60}{80}$$

Cross-multiply to obtain the cross products, $9600 = 60x$. Then, divide both sides by 60 to obtain $x = 160$. This solution means that the other building is 160 feet high.

Solving Simple Algebraic Problems

Translating Phrases and Sentences into Expressions, Equations, and Inequalities

When presented with a real-world problem that must be solved, the first step is always to determine what the unknown quantity is that must be solved for. Use a variable, such as x or t, to represent that unknown quantity. Sometimes there can be two or more unknown quantities. In these cases, either choose an additional variable, or if a relationship exists between the unknown quantities, express the other quantities in terms of the original variable. After choosing the variables, form algebraic expressions and/or equations that represent the verbal statement in the problem. The following table shows examples of vocabulary used to represent the different operations.

Addition	Sum, plus, total, increase, more than, combined, in all
Subtraction	Difference, less than, subtract, reduce, decrease, fewer, remain
Multiplication	Product, multiply, times, part of, twice, triple
Division	Quotient, divide, split, each, equal parts, per, average, shared

The combination of operations and variables form both mathematical expression and equations. The difference between expressions and equations are that there is no equals sign in an expression, and that expressions are evaluated to find an unknown quantity, while equations are solved to find an unknown quantity. Also, inequalities can exist within verbal mathematical statements. Instead of a statement of equality, expressions state quantities are *less than, less than or equal to, greater than,* or *greater than or equal to.* Another type of inequality is when a quantity is said to be *not equal to* another quantity. The symbol used to represent "not equal to" is $\neq$.

The steps for solving inequalities in one variable are the same steps for solving equations in one variable. The addition and multiplication principles are used. However, to maintain a true statement when using the $<, \leq, >$, and $\geq$ symbols, if a negative number is either multiplied times both sides of an inequality or divided from both sides of an inequality, the sign must be flipped. For instance, consider the following inequality: $3 - 5x \leq 8$. First, 3 is subtracted from each side to obtain $-5x \leq 5$. Then, both sides are divided by -5, while flipping the sign, to obtain $x \geq -1$. Therefore, any real number greater than or equal to -1 satisfies the original inequality.

Solving Problems

To solve problems, follow these steps: Identify the variables that are known, decide which equation should be used, substitute the numbers, and solve. To solve an equation for the amount of time that has elapsed since an event, use the equation $T = L - E$, where T represents the elapsed time, L represents the later time, and E represents the earlier time. For example, the Minnesota Vikings have not appeared in the Super Bowl since 1976. If the year is now 2017, how long has it been since the Vikings were in the Super Bowl? The later time, L, is 2017, $E = 1976$ and the unknown is T. Substituting these numbers, the equation is $T = 2017 - 1976$, and so $T = 41$. It has been 41 years since the Vikings have appeared in the Super Bowl.

Questions involving total cost can be solved using the formula, $C = I + T$, where C represents the total cost, I represents the cost of the item purchased, and T represents the tax amount.

To find the length of a rectangle given the area = 32 square inches and width = 8 inches, the formula $A = L \times W$ can be used. Substitute 32 for A and substitute 8 for W, giving the equation $32 = L \times 8$. This equation is solved by dividing both sides by 8 to find that the length of the rectangle is 4. The formula for volume of a rectangular prism is given by the equation $V = L \times W \times H$. If the length of a rectangular juice box is 4 centimeters, the width is 2 centimeters, and the height is 8 centimeters, what is the volume of this box? Substituting in the formula we find $V = 4 \times 2 \times 8$, so the volume is 64 cubic centimeters. In a similar fashion as those previously shown, the mass of an object can be calculated given the formula, Mass = Density × Volume.

Solving Equations in One Variable

An **equation in one variable** is a mathematical statement where two algebraic expressions in one variable, usually x, are set equal. To solve the equation, the variable must be isolated on one side of the equals sign. The addition and multiplication principles of equality are used to isolate the variable. The **addition principle of equality** states that the same number can be added to or subtracted from both sides of an equation. Because the same value is being used on both sides of the equals sign, equality is maintained. For example, the equation $2x - 3 = 5x$ is equivalent to both $2x - 3 + 2 = 5x + 2$, and $2x - 3 - 5 = 5x - 5$. This principle can be used to solve the following equation: $x + 5 = 4$. The variable x must be isolated, so to move the 5 from the left side, subtract 5 from both sides of the equals sign. Therefore:

$$x + 5 - 5 = 4 - 5$$

So, the solution is $x = -1$. This process illustrates the idea of an **additive inverse** because subtracting 5 is the same as adding -5. Basically, add the opposite of the number that must be removed to both sides of the equals sign.

The **multiplication principle of equality** states that equality is maintained when a number is either multiplied times both expressions on each side of the equals sign, or when both expressions are divided by the same number. For example, $4x = 5$ is equivalent to both $16x = 20$ and $x = \frac{5}{4}$. Multiplying both sides times 4 and dividing both sides by 4 maintains equality. Solving the equation $6x - 18 = 5$ requires the use of both principles. First, apply the addition principle to add 18 to both sides of the equals sign, which results in $6x = 23$. Then use the multiplication principle to divide both sides by 6, giving the solution $x = \frac{23}{6}$. Using the multiplication principle in the solving process is the same as involving a multiplicative inverse. A **multiplicative inverse** is a value that, when multiplied by a given number, results in 1. Dividing by 6 is the same as multiplying by $\frac{1}{6}$, which is both the reciprocal and multiplicative inverse of 6.

When solving a linear equation in one variable, checking the answer shows if the solution process was performed correctly. Plug the solution into the variable in the original equation. If the result is a false statement, something was done incorrectly during the solution procedure. Checking the example above gives the following:

$$6 \times \frac{23}{6} - 18 = 23 - 18 = 5$$

Therefore, the solution is correct.

Some equations in one variable involve fractions or the use of the distributive property. In either case, the goal is to obtain only one variable term and then use the addition and multiplication principles to isolate that variable. Consider the equation $\frac{2}{3}x = 6$. To solve for x, multiply each side of the equation by the reciprocal of $\frac{2}{3}$, which is $\frac{3}{2}$. This step results in:

$$\frac{3}{2} \times \frac{2}{3}x = \frac{3}{2} \times 6$$

This simplifies into the solution $x = 9$. Now consider the equation:

$$3(x + 2) - 5x = 4x + 1$$

Use the distributive property to clear the parentheses. Therefore, multiply each term inside the parentheses by 3. This step results in:

$$3x + 6 - 5x = 4x + 1$$

Next, collect like terms on the left-hand side. **Like terms** are terms with the same variable or variables raised to the same exponent(s). Only like terms can be combined through addition or subtraction. After collecting like terms, the equation is $-2x + 6 = 4x + 1$. Finally, apply the addition and multiplication principles. Add $2x$ to both sides to obtain $6 = 6x + 1$. Then, subtract 1 from both sides to obtain $5 = 6x$. Finally, divide both sides by 6 to obtain the solution $\frac{5}{6} = x$.

Two other types of solutions can be obtained when solving an equation in one variable. The final result could be that there is either no solution or that the solution set contains all real numbers. Consider the equation:

$$4x = 6x + 5 - 2x$$

First, the like terms can be combined on the right to obtain:

$$4x = 4x + 5$$

Next, subtract $4x$ from both sides. This step results in the false statement $0 = 5$. There is no value that can be plugged into x that will ever make this equation true. Therefore, there is no solution. The solution procedure contained correct steps, but the result of a false statement means that no value satisfies the equation. The symbolic way to denote that no solution exists is $\emptyset$.

Next, consider the equation:

$$5x + 4 + 2x = 9 + 7x - 5$$

Combining the like terms on both sides results in:

$$7x + 4 = 7x + 4$$

The left-hand side is exactly the same as the right-hand side. Using the addition principle to move terms, the result is $0 = 0$, which is always true. Therefore, the original equation is true for any number, and the solution set is all real numbers. The symbolic way to denote such a solution set is $\mathbb{R}$, or in interval notation, $(-\infty, \infty)$.

Solving a Linear Inequality in One Variable

A **linear equation in x** can be written in the form $ax + b = 0$. A **linear inequality** is very similar, although the equals sign is replaced by an inequality symbol such as $<, >, \leq,$ or $\geq$. In any case, a can never be 0. Some examples of linear inequalities in one variable are $2x + 3 < 0$ and $4x - 2 \leq 0$. Solving an inequality involves finding the set of numbers that when plugged into the variable, make the inequality a true statement. These numbers are known as the **solution set** of the inequality. To solve an inequality, use the same properties that are necessary in solving equations. First, add or subtract variable terms and/or constants to obtain all variable terms on one side of the equals sign and all constant terms on the other side. Then, either multiply both sides by the same number, or divide both sides by the same number, to obtain an inequality that gives the solution set. When multiplying times, or dividing by, a negative number in an inequality, change the direction of the inequality symbol. The solution set can be graphed on a number line. Consider the linear inequality:

$$-2x - 5 > x + 6$$

First, add 5 to both sides and subtract $-x$ off of both sides to obtain $-3x > 11$. Then, divide both sides by -3, making sure to change the direction of the inequality symbol. These steps result in the solution $x < -\frac{11}{3}$. Therefore, any number less than $-\frac{11}{3}$ satisfies this inequality.

Determining Whether Enough Information is Given to Solve a Problem

In some math problems, initial information is given, and potential conclusions are listed that could possibly stem from the given information. Some conclusions might follow from what is given and some might not. It is your job to determine which of the conclusions are a real consequence from the stated information.

Your first approach in this type of problem could be to pick the conclusion that you think is true and build a proof to show that it is true. One way to do this is to construct a step-by-step reasoning that takes you from the given information to the stated conclusion. In this case, you would have produced a logical argument that shows truth of the conclusion. Through this argument, you have shown that that in any scenario, given the stated information, the conclusion is always true.

A second approach to this type of problem could to show that some of the given conclusions are false. A common way to prove something is false is to provide a counterexample. A **counterexample** is a specific scenario in which the given information is true, but the stated conclusion is false. If this is hard to do, and a counterexample is not found, it does not necessarily mean that the conclusion is true. It might just be the case that another way to disprove the conclusion is needed.

Sometimes conclusions are false if more information is needed in addition to logically produce that conclusion. In this scenario, you might also want to build a step-by-step reasoning to try to prove the conclusion is true. By laying out the information in such a way, you might be able to easily determine the missing information.

Consider the following example: Let's say that Kendra ordered 30 chicken wings, 5 pepperoni pizzas, and 4 salads for her son's fifth birthday party. Wings cost $10 a dozen, small cheese pizzas cost $8, large cheese pizzas cost $10, and salads cost $12. She spent $125 overall. Do we have enough information to determine the following?

- How much Kendra spent on chicken wings
- How much she spent on pizza
- What size pizzas she ordered
- How much she spent on salads

We do have enough information to determine how much Kendra spent on chicken wings. Because she purchased 30 wings, which is equivalent to 2.5 dozen wings, she spent $\$10 \times 2.5 = \$25$ on wings. We also have enough information to determine how much she spent on salads because she ordered 4 at $12 each, which totals $48 dollars. Because we know she spent $125 overall, she spent $125 - $25 - $48 = $52 on pizza. Therefore, we know how much she spent on pizza, but we cannot determine what sizes she ordered. This is because we do not know how much it cost to add pepperoni to a pizza.

Recognizing Alternative Mathematical Methods of Solving a Problem

Depending on the type of math problem, there might be many ways to find the correct answer. Sometimes, there are no definite rules for solving problems, and what makes sense for one person might not make sense for another person. It just takes time to find out what works for you, and that includes practicing on many different types of problems. Here are some typical strategies for solving problems:

- If the problem is a word problem, you might be able to translate the phrase into an algebraic expression to solve for the unknown quantity or into a mathematical expression that needs to be evaluated. Also, some word problems can be translated into a picture, a diagram, or a graph that will help you find the answer.
- If the problem given is in terms of a picture or a graph, you might also be able to translate what is given into an algebraic equation needed to be solved or into a mathematical expression that needs to be evaluated. Also, the graph might need to be slightly altered or adjusted in some manner to solve the given problem.
- Some problems might already be stated in terms of an algebraic equation or a mathematical expression. Simplifying what is given might be all that is necessary to find the answer to the posed question.

Other problem-solving techniques involve identifying a pattern, determining a mathematical relationship, using a trial and error process, estimating a solution, performing a quantitative comparison, and dividing a problem in to different cases and determining a solution to each case.

This is by no means an exhaustive list of problem-solving techniques. However, they are some of the popular approaches to determining a solution to a math problem. You might be able to use more than one of these different approaches on the same problem to determine a correct answer.

Numerical & Graphic Relationships

Relationships in Numerical Data

Sets of numerical patterns can be found by starting with a number and following a given rule. If two sets are generated, the corresponding terms in each set can be found to relate to one another by one or more operations. For example, the following table shows two sets of numbers that each follow their own pattern. The first column shows a pattern of numbers increasing by 1. The second column shows the numbers increasing by 4. Because the numbers are lined up, corresponding numbers are side by side for the two sets. A question to ask is, "How can the number in the first column be turned into the number in the second column?"

1	4
2	8
3	12
4	16
5	20

This answer will lead to the relationship between the two sets. By recognizing the multiples of 4 in the right column and the counting numbers in order in the left column, the relationship of multiplying by four is determined. The first set is multiplied by 4 to get the second set of numbers. To confirm this relationship, each pair of corresponding numbers can be checked. For any two sets of numerical patterns, the corresponding numbers can be lined up to find how each one relates to the other. In some cases, the relationship is simply addition or subtraction, multiplication or division. In other relationships, these operations are used in conjunction with each together. As seen in the following table, the relationship uses multiplication and addition. The following expression shows this relationship: $3x + 2$. The x represents the numbers in the first column.

1	5
2	8
3	11
4	14

The following table presents another linear relationship. The first thing to observe from the table is that the y-values increase by the same amount of 3 each time. As the x-values increase by 1, the y-values increase by 3. This pattern shows that the relationship is linear. If this table shows the money earned, y-value, for the hours worked, x-value, then it can be used to predict how much money will be earned for future hours. If 6 hours are worked, then the pay would be $19. For further hours and money to be determined, it would be helpful to have an equation that models this table of values. The equation will show the relationship between x and y. The y-value can each time be determined by multiplying the x-value by 3, then adding 1. The following equation models this relationship: $y = 3x + 1$. Now that there is an equation, any number of hours, x can be substituted into the equation to find the amount of money earned, y.

y = 3x + 1	
x	y
0	1
1	4
2	7
4	13
5	16

Not all data can be accurately described by a linear relationship. When given data in ordered pairs, choosing an appropriate function or equation to model the data is important. Besides linear relationships, other common relationships that exist are quadratic and exponential. A helpful way to determine what type of function to use is to find the difference between consecutive dependent variables. Basically, find pairs of ordered pairs where the x-values increase by 1, and take the difference of the y-values. If the differences between subsequent y-values are always the same value, then the function is **linear.** If the differences between subsequent y-values are not the same, the function could be quadratic or exponential. In **quadratic** functions, when the differences between the x-values are the same (for example, increasing by 1), the differences between subsequent y-values will not be the same. Instead, the difference of the differences between subsequent y-values will be the same. For example, in the simplest quadratic function, $y = x^2$, as the x-values increase by 1, the y-values increase by different amounts, but the difference between the difference is constant (2).

x	y=x^2
0	0
1	1
2	4
3	9
4	16
5	25
6	36

difference of y-values

- 1-0 =1
- 4-1 =3
- 9-4 =5
- 16-9 =7
- 25-16 =9
- 36-25 =11

difference of differences

- 3-1 =2
- 5-3 =2
- 7-5 =2
- 9-7 =2
- 11-9 =2

If consecutive differences between the differences are not the same, try taking ratios of consecutive y-values. If the ratios are the same, the data have an **exponential** relationship and an exponential function should be used.

For example, the ordered pairs (1, 4), (2, 6), (3 ,8), and (4,10) have a linear relationship because the difference in y-values is 2. The ordered pairs (1, 0), (2, 3), (3, 10), and (4, 21) have a nonlinear relationship. The first differences in y-values are 3, 7, and 11, however, consecutive second differences are both 4, so the function is quadratic. Third, the ordered pairs (1, 10), (2, 30), (3, 90), and (4, 270) have an exponential relationship. Taking ratios of consecutive y-values leads to a common ratio of 4.

The general form of a **quadratic equation** is $y = ax^2 + bx + c$, and its **vertex form** is $y = a(x - h)^2 + k$, with vertex (h, k). If the vertex and one other point are known, the vertex form should be used to solve for a. If three points, not the vertex, are known, the general form should be used. The three points create a system of three equations in three unknowns that can be solved for.

The general form of an **exponential function** is $y = b \times a^x$, where a is the **base** and b is the y**-intercept**.

The Position of Numbers in Relation to Each Other

Whole numbers are the numbers 0, 1, 2, 3, ... Examples of other whole numbers would be 413 and 8,431. Notice that numbers such as 4.13 and $\frac{1}{4}$ are not included in whole numbers. **Counting numbers**, also known as **natural numbers**, consist of all whole numbers except for the zero. In set notation, the natural numbers are the set $\{1, 2, 3, \ldots\}$. The entire set of whole numbers and negative versions of those same numbers comprise the set of numbers known as **integers.** Therefore, in set notation, the integers are $\{\ldots, -3, -2, -1, 0, 1, 2, 3, \ldots\}$. Examples of other integers are −4,981 and 90,131. A number line is a great way to visualize the integers. Integers are labeled on the following number line:

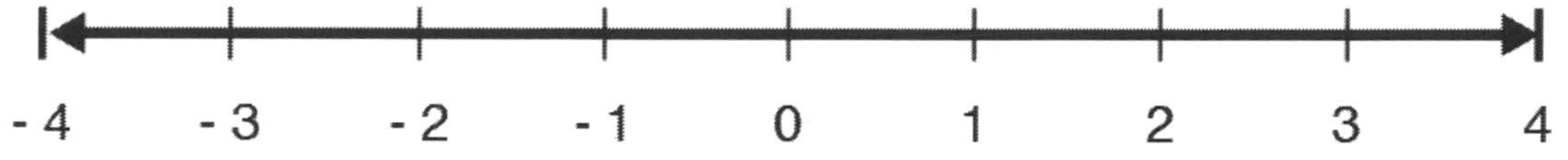

The arrows on the right- and left-hand sides of the number line show that the line continues indefinitely in both directions.

Fractions also exist on the number line as parts of a whole. For example, if an entire pie is cut into two pieces, each piece is half of the pie, or $\frac{1}{2}$. The top number in any fraction, known as the **numerator,** defines how many parts there are. The bottom number, known as the **denominator,** states how many pieces the whole is divided into. Fractions can also be negative or written in their corresponding decimal form.

A **decimal** is a number that uses a decimal point and numbers to the right of the decimal point representing the part of the number that is less than 1. For example, 3.5 is a decimal and is equivalent to the fraction $\frac{7}{2}$ or mixed number $3\frac{1}{2}$. The decimal is found by dividing 2 into 7. Other examples of fractions are $\frac{2}{7}, \frac{-3}{14}$, and $\frac{14}{27}$.

Any number that can be expressed as a fraction is known as a **rational number.** Basically, if a and b are any integers and $b \neq 0$, then $\frac{a}{b}$ is a rational number. Any integer can be written as a fraction where the denominator is 1, so therefore the rational numbers consist of all fractions and all integers.

Any number that is not rational is known as an **irrational number.** Consider the number $\pi = 3.141592654 \ldots$. The decimal portion of that number extends indefinitely. In that situation, a number can never be written as a fraction. Another example of an irrational number is $\sqrt{2} = 1.414213662 \ldots$. Again, this number cannot be written as a ratio of two integers.

Together, the set of all rational and irrational numbers makes up the **real numbers.** The number line contains all real numbers. To graph a number other than an integer on a number line, it needs to be plotted between two integers. For example, 3.5 would be plotted halfway between 3 and 4.

Comparing integers is a straightforward process, especially when using the number line, but the comparison of decimals and fractions is not as obvious. When comparing two non-negative decimals, compare digit by digit, starting from the left. The larger value contains the first larger digit. For example, 0.1456 is larger than 0.1234 because the value 4 in the hundredths place in the first decimal is larger than the value 2 in the hundredths place in the second decimal. When comparing a fraction with a decimal, convert the fraction to a decimal and then compare in the same manner. Finally, there are a few options when comparing multiple fractions. If two non-negative fractions have the same denominator, the fraction with the larger numerator is the larger value. If they have the same numerator but different denominators (such as $\frac{3}{5}$ and $\frac{3}{10}$), the fraction whose denominator is a smaller number (in this case, the $\frac{3}{5}$ because 5 is less than 10) is larger.

If the two fractions have different numerators and denominators, they can be converted to equivalent fractions with a common denominator to be compared, or they can be converted to decimals to be compared. When comparing two negative decimals or fractions, a different approach must be used. It is important to remember that the smaller number exists to the left on the number line. Therefore, when comparing two negative decimals by place value, the number with the larger first place value is smaller due to the negative sign. Whichever value is closer to 0 is larger. For instance, -0.456 is larger than -0.498 because of the values in the hundredth places. If two negative fractions have the same denominator, the fraction with the larger numerator is smaller because of the negative sign.

Using the Relations Less Than, Greater Than, or Equal To, and Their Associated Symbols to Express a Numerical Relationship

Ordering rational numbers is a way to compare two or more different numerical values. Determining whether two amounts are equal, or if one is less than or greater than the other is the basis for comparing both positive and negative numbers. Also, a group of numbers can be compared by ordering them from the smallest value to the largest value. A few symbols are necessary to use when ordering rational numbers. The equals sign, =, shows that the two quantities on either side of the symbol have the same value. For example, $\frac{12}{3} = 4$ because both values are equivalent.

Another symbol that is used to compare numbers is <, which represents "less than." With this symbol, the smaller number is placed on the left and the larger number is placed on the right. Always remember that the symbol's "mouth" opens up to the larger number. When comparing negative and positive numbers, it is important to remember that the number occurring to the left on the number line is always smaller and is placed to the left of the symbol. This idea might seem confusing because some values could appear at first glance to be larger, even though they are not. For example, $-5 < 4$ is read "negative 5 is less than 4." Here is an image of a number line to help visualize relationships:

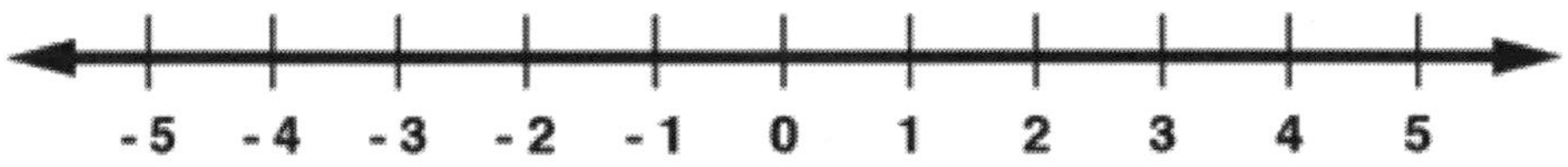

The symbol $\leq$ represents "less than or equal to," and it joins < with equality. Therefore, both $-5 \leq 4$ and $-5 \leq -5$ are true statements and "-5 is less than or equal to both 4 and -5." Other symbols are $>$ and $\geq$, which represent "greater than" and "greater than or equal to." Both $4 \geq -1$ and $-1 \geq -1$ are correct ways to use these symbols.

Here is a chart of these four inequality symbols:

Symbol	Definition
$<$	less than
$\leq$	less than or equal to
$>$	greater than
$\geq$	greater than or equal to

Identifying Numbers, Formulas, and Mathematical Expressions that are Mathematically Equivalent

As mentioned, fractions can be converted to decimals and vice versa, and in either form, these numbers would be mathematically equivalent. For example, $\frac{3}{5} = 3 \div 5 = 0.6$. Similarly, improper fractions and their equivalent mixed number version are equivalent. Remember that to convert an improper fraction to a mixed number, divide the numerator by the denominator. Write down the whole number portion, and then write any remainder over the original denominator. For example, $\frac{10}{3}$ is equivalent to $3\frac{1}{3}$. Conversely, a mixed number can be converted to an improper fraction by multiplying the denominator times the whole number and adding that result to the numerator.

Two algebraic expressions are equivalent if, even though they look different, they represent the same expression. Therefore, plugging in the same values into the variables in each expression will result in the same result in both expressions. To obtain an equivalent form of an algebraic expression, laws of algebra must be followed. For instance, addition and multiplication are both commutative and associative. Therefore, terms in an algebraic expression can be added in any order and multiplied in any order. For instance, $4x + 2y$ is equivalent to $2y + 4x$ and $y \times 2 + x \times 4$. Also, the distributive law allows a number to be distributed throughout parentheses, as in the following: $a(b + c) = ab + ac$. The two expressions on both sides of the equals sign are equivalent. Also, collecting like terms is important when working with equivalent forms. The simplest version of an expression is always the one easiest to work with, so all like terms (those with the same variables raised to the same powers) must be combined.

Note that an expression is not an equation; therefore, expressions cannot be multiplied by numbers, divided by numbers, or have numbers added to them or subtracted from them and still have equivalent expressions. These processes can only happen in equations when the same step is performed on both sides of the equals sign.

As just mentioned, the **distributive property** is a way of taking a factor and multiplying it through a given expression in parentheses. Each term inside the parentheses is multiplied by the outside factor, eliminating the parentheses. This property, written as $a(b + c) = ab + ac$, allows one to generate equivalent algebraic expressions. The following example shows how to distribute the number 3 to all the terms inside the parentheses.

Example: Use the distributive property to write an equivalent algebraic expression:

$3(2x + 7y + 6)$	
$3(2x) + 3(7y) + 3(6)$	Distributive property
$6x + 21y + 18$	Simplify

Because $a - b$ can be written $a + (-b)$, the distributive property can be applied in the example below:

Example: Use the distributive property to write an equivalent algebraic expression.

$7(5m - 8)$	
$7[5m + (-8)]$	Rewrite subtraction as addition of -8
$7(5m) + 7(-8)$	Distributive property
$35m - 56$	Simplify

In the following example, note that the factor of 2 is written to the right of the parentheses but is still distributed as before.

Example: Use the distributive property to write an equivalent algebraic expression:

$(3m + 4x - 10)2$	
$(3m)2 + (4x)2 + (-10)2$	Distributive property
$6m + 8x - 20$	Simplify

Example: $-(-2m + 6x)$

In this example, the negative sign in front of the parentheses can be interpreted as $-1(-2m + 6x)$

$-1(-2m + 6x)$	
$-1(-2m) + (-1)(6x)$	Distributive property
$2m - 6x$	Simplify

Using Rounding Rules when Solving Problems

As mentioned, **rounding** consists of expressing a number in terms of the nearest decimal place like the tenth, hundredth, or thousandth place, or in terms of the nearest whole number unit like tens, hundreds, or thousands place. When rounding to a specific place value, look at the digit to the right of the place. If it is 5 or higher, round the number to its left up to the next value, and if it is 4 or lower, keep that number at the same value. For instance, 2,783.764 rounded to the nearest hundred is 2,800, and the same number rounded to the nearest hundredth is 2,783.76. Rounding can be used in the scenario when grocery totals need to be estimated. Items can be rounded to the nearest dollar. For example, a can of corn that costs $0.79 can be rounded to $1.00, and then all other items can be rounded in a similar manner and added together. When working with larger numbers, it might make more sense to round to higher place values. For example, when estimating the total value of a dealership's car inventory, it would make sense to round the car values to the nearest thousands place. The price of a car that is on sale for $15,654 can be estimated at $16,000. All other cars on the lot could be rounded in the same manner, and then their sum can be found. Depending on the situation, it might make sense to calculate an overestimate. For example, to make sure Aria has enough money at the grocery store, rounding up every time for each item would ensure that she will have enough money when it comes time to pay. A $.40 item rounded up to $1.00 would ensure that there is a dollar to cover that item. Traditional rounding rules would round $0.40 to $0, which does not make sense in this particular real-world setting. Aria might not have a dollar available at checkout to pay for that item if she uses traditional rounding. It is up to the customer to decide the best approach when estimating.

Applying the Meaning of Logical Connectives and Quantifiers

To be successful in performing mathematical operations, you should be able to talk and write about mathematics as well. When communication mathematics verbally, the basic building block is a statement. A **statement** is a sentence that declares something to be true or false. For instance, "the students went to the gymnasium" is a statement. Questions, directions, mathematical expressions (not equations), and equations involving variables are not statements.

Statements, can be joined together using logical connectives such as "and," "or," and "if-then." For example, you could say, "the area of the garden has to be greater than 60 square feet *and* the perimeter of the garden has to be less than 100 feet." Also, you could say, "the area of the garden has to be greater than 60 square feet *or* the perimeter of the garden has to be less than 100 feet." Finally, you could also say "*if* the area of the garden has to be greater than 60 square feet, *then* the perimeter of the garden has to be less than 100 feet." All three of these logical connectives connect two distinct statements. The meanings change based on the connecting word or words used.

The **truth value** of the entire sentence depends on the truth of each individual statement. If the logical connective "and" is used, the entire sentence is true if both of the statements are true. If the logical connective "or" is used, the entire sentence is true if at least one of the statements is true. If the logical connective "if-then" is used, the entire sentence is false if both statements are false. Otherwise, all other scenarios are true.

Statements can also include quantifiers such as "all," "some," and "none." **Quantifiers** are words that are used when we want to give someone information concerning the amount of something. When using "all," the entire amount is being discussed. "Some" means an unknown quantity, and "none" means not even one.

Identifying a Missing Entry From a Table of Data

Tables summarize data. They can organize large amounts of data, and they can allow viewers to make conclusions that might not be seen if the data were not organized in such a manner. Quantities and measures such as totals, means, medians, and modes can be included in tables. A user can manipulate the data and organize the table in such a way that makes sense for the setting at hand. Here is an example of a table that is built in MS Excel:

Region	**Sport**	**Tickets Sold**
East	Basketball	5,004
East	Basketball	4,226
	Basketball Total	**9,230**
East	Football	4,752
East	Football	2,543
	Football Total	**7,295**
East Total		**16,525**
West	Basketball	4,288
West	Basketball	6,012
	Basketball Total	**10,300**
West	Football	3,876
West	Football	3,019
	Football Total	**6,895**
West Total		**17,195**

Notice that different totals exist throughout the table. There are two regions: East and West, and each region shows a total number of tickets sold for both for basketball and football. The total number of basketball tickets sold in the East region was 9,230, and the total number of football tickets sold in the East region was 7,295. Each of these amounts is known as a subtotal. Any total that is found before the entire sum of all the data listed in a table is referred to as a **subtotal**. The entire **total** is the sum of all the data listed. We could add the total number of tickets sold in both the East region and the West region to obtain the total number of tickets sold: 16,525 + 17,195 = 33,720. The person who built this table is not only interested in the total number of tickets sold in each region but also the total number of tickets sold in each sport.

Sometimes, a table might have a missing entry. If the table includes totals and subtotals, the missing amounts can be found through addition and subtraction. If the East Total was missing in the table shown above, we would just need to find the sum of the tickets sold for both football and basketball in that region. If the football subtotal in the East region was missing, we would just need to subtract the basketball subtotal from the East total to obtain the missing amount.

Using Information in Tables and Graphs to Solve Problems

Tables, charts, and graphs can be used to convey information about different variables. They are all used to organize, categorize, and compare data, and they all come in different shapes and sizes. Each type has its own way of showing information, whether it is in a column, shape, or picture. To answer a question relating to a table, chart, or graph, some steps should be followed. First, the problem should be read thoroughly to determine what is being asked to determine what quantity is unknown. Then, the title of the table, chart, or graph should be read. The title should clarify what actual data is being summarized in the table. Next, look at the key and both the horizontal and vertical axis labels, if they are given. These items will provide information about how the data is organized. Finally, look to see if there is any more labeling inside the table. Taking the time to get a good idea of what the table is summarizing will be helpful as it is used to interpret information.

Tables are a good way of showing a lot of information in a small space. The information in a table is organized in columns and rows. For example, a table may be used to show the number of votes each candidate received in an election. By interpreting the table, one may observe which candidate won the election and which candidates came in second and third. In using a bar chart to display monthly rainfall amounts in different countries, rainfall can be compared between countries at different times of the year. Graphs are also a useful way to show change in variables over time, as in a line graph, or percentages of a whole, as in a pie graph.

The table below relates the number of items to the total cost. The table shows that 1 item costs $5. By looking at the table further, 5 items cost $25, 10 items cost $50, and 50 items cost $250. This cost can be extended for any number of items. Since 1 item costs $5, then 2 items would cost $10. Though this information isn't in the table, the given prices can be used to calculate unknown information.

Number of Items	1	5	10	50
Cost ($)	5	25	50	250

A **bar graph** is a graph that summarizes data using bars of different heights. It is useful when comparing two or more items or when seeing how a quantity changes over time. It has both a horizontal and vertical axis. Interpreting bar graphs includes recognizing what each bar represents and connecting that to the two variables. The bar graph below shows the scores for six people on three different games. The color of the bar shows which game each person played, and the height of the bar indicates their score for that game. William scored 25 on game 3, and Abigail scored 38 on game 3. By comparing the bars, it's obvious that Williams scored lower than Abigail.

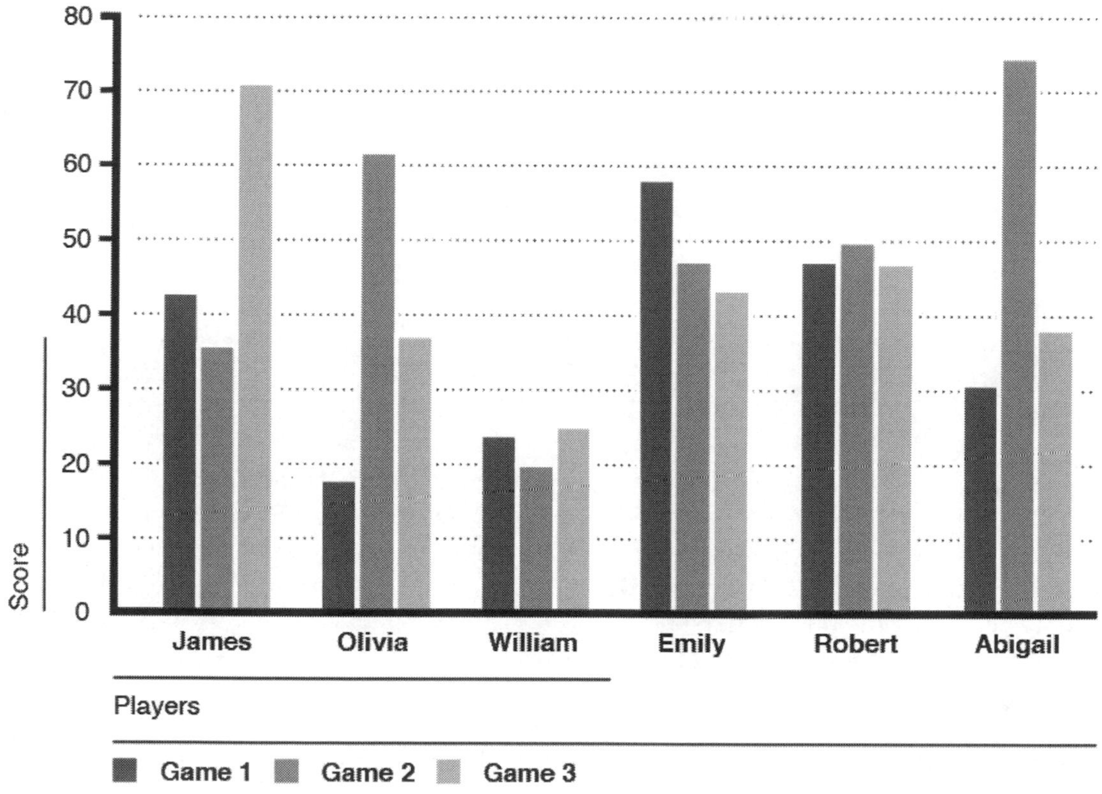

A **line graph** is a way to compare two variables. Each variable is plotted along an axis, and the graph contains both a horizontal and a vertical axis. On a line graph, the line indicates a continuous change. The change can be seen in how the line rises or falls, known as its slope, or rate of change. Often, in line graphs, the horizontal axis represents a variable of time. Readers can quickly see if an amount has grown or decreased over time. The bottom of the graph, or the x-axis, shows the units for time, such as days, hours, months, etc.

If there are multiple lines, a comparison can be made between what the two lines represent. For example, the following line graph, shown previously, displays the change in temperature over five days. The top line represents the high, and the bottom line represents the low for each day. Looking at the top line alone, the high decreases for a day, then increases on Wednesday. Then it decreased on Thursday and increases again on Friday. The low temperatures have a similar trend, shown in bottom line. The range in temperatures each day can also be calculated by finding the difference between the top line and bottom line on a particular day. On Wednesday, the range was 14 degrees, from 62 to 76° F.

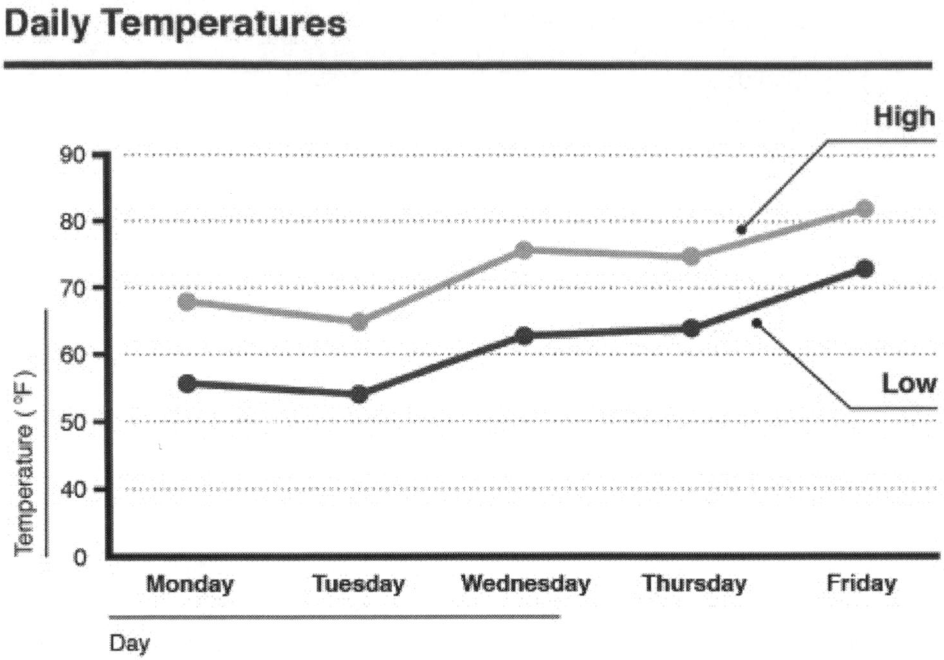

Pie charts are used to show percentages of a whole, as each category is given a piece of the pie, and together all the pieces make up a whole. They are a circular representation of data that are used to highlight numerical proportions. The arc length of each pie slice is proportional to the amount it individually represents. When a pie chart is shown, a reader can quickly make comparisons by comparing the sizes of the pieces of the pie. They can be useful for comparison between different categories. The following pie chart is a simple example of three different categories shown in comparison to each other.

Light gray represents cats, dark gray represents dogs, and the gray shade between those two represents other pets. As the pie is cut into three equal pieces, each value represents just more than 33 percent, or $\frac{1}{3}$ of the whole. Values 1 and 2 may be combined to represent $\frac{2}{3}$ of the whole. In an example where the total pie represents 75,000 animals, then cats would be equal to $\frac{1}{3}$ of the total, or 25,000. Dogs would equal 25,000, and other pets would hold equal 25,000.

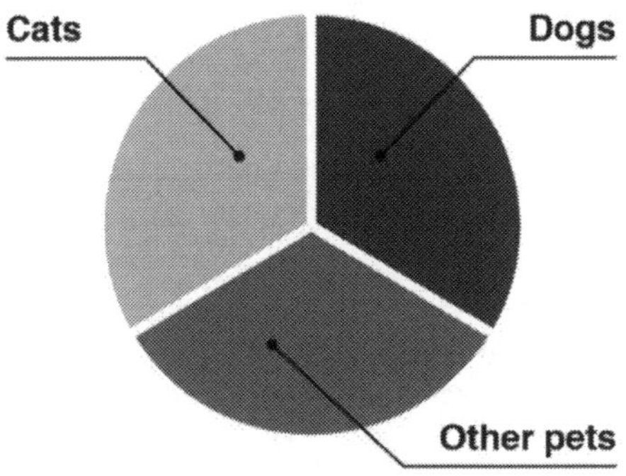

The fact that a circle is 360 degrees is used to create a pie chart. Because each piece of the pie is a percentage of a whole, that percentage is multiplied times 360 to get the number of degrees each piece represents. In the example above, each piece is 1/3 of the whole, so each piece is equivalent to 120 degrees. Together, all three pieces add up to 360 degrees.

Stacked bar graphs are also used fairly frequently when comparing multiple variables at one time. They combine some elements of both pie charts and bar graphs, using the organization of bar graphs and the proportionality aspect of pie charts. The following is an example of a stacked bar graph that represents the number of students in a band playing drums, flute, trombone, and clarinet. Each bar graph is broken up further into girls and boys.

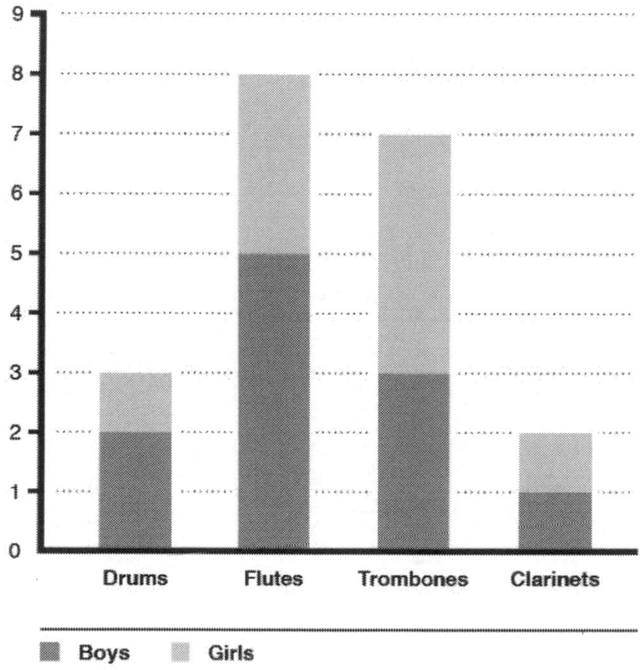

To determine how many boys play trombone, refer to the darker portion of the trombone bar, which indicates 3 boys.

As mentioned, a **scatterplot** is another way to represent paired data. It uses Cartesian coordinates, like a line graph, meaning it has both a horizontal and vertical axis. Each data point is represented as a dot on the graph. The dots are never connected with a line. For example, the following is a scatterplot showing people's age versus height.

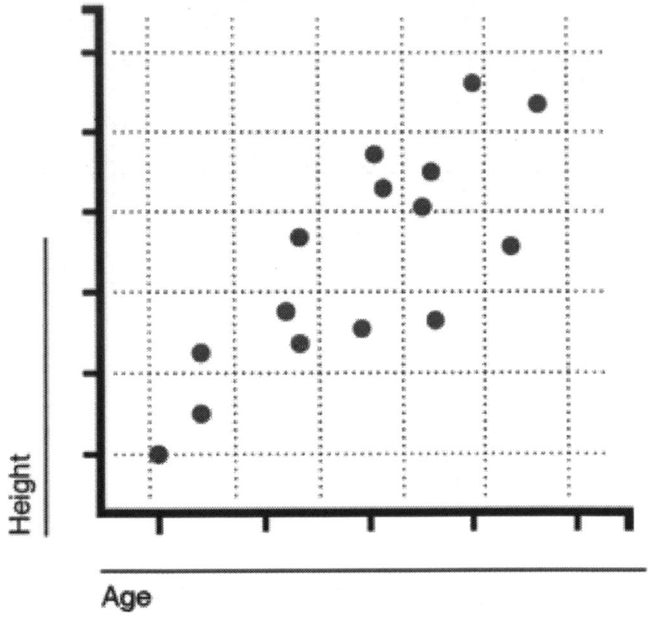

A scatterplot, also known as a **scattergram,** can be used to predict another value and to see if a correlation exists between a set of data. If the data resembles a straight line, the data is **associated** or correlated. The following is an example of a scatterplot in which the data does not seem to have an association:

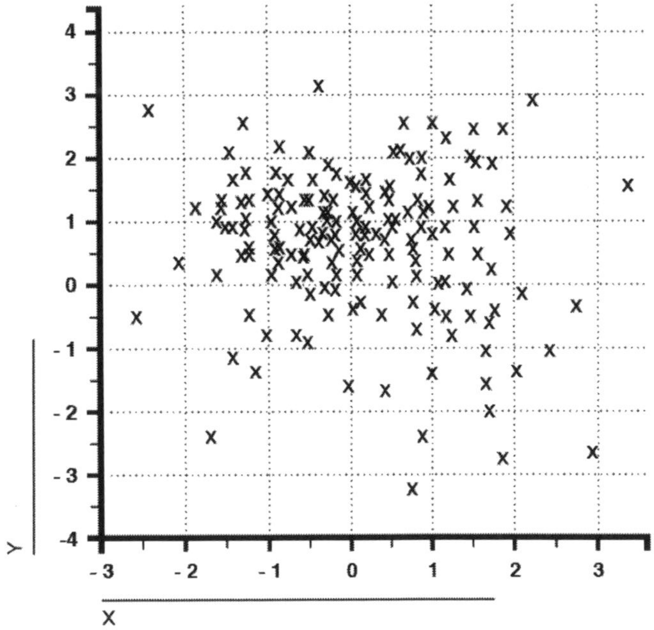

Sets of numbers and other similarly organized data can also be represented graphically. Venn diagrams are a common way to do so. A **Venn diagram** represents each set of data as a circle. The circles overlap, showing that each set of data is overlapping. A Venn diagram is also known as a **logic diagram** because it visualizes all possible logical combinations between two sets. Common elements of two sets are represented by the area of overlap. The following is an example of a Venn diagram of two sets A and B:

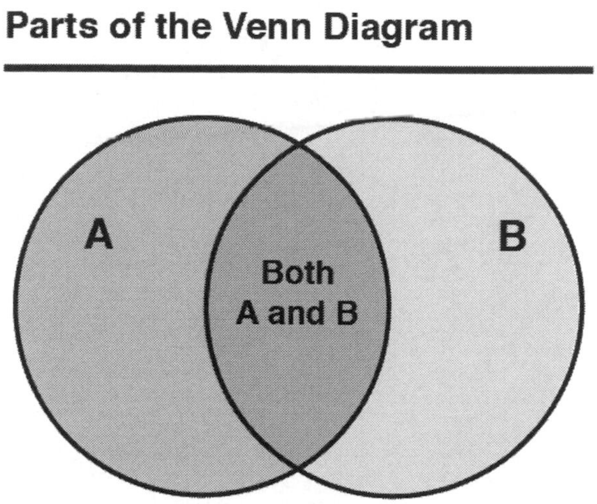

Another name for the area of overlap is the **intersection.** The intersection of A and B, written $A \cap B$, contains all elements that are in both sets A and B. The **union** of A and B, $A \cup B$, contains all elements that are in either set A or set B. Finally, the **complement** of $A \cup B$ is equal to all elements that are not in either set A or set B. These elements are placed outside of the circles.

The following is an example of a Venn diagram in which 22 students were surveyed asking about their siblings. Ten students only had a brother, 7 students only had a sister, and 5 had both a brother and a sister. This number 5 is the intersection and is placed where the circles overlap. Two students did not have a brother or a sister. Therefore, two is the complement and is placed outside of the circles.

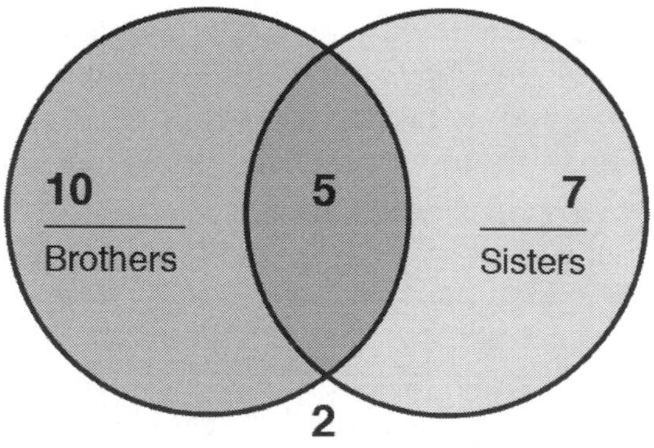

Venn diagrams can have more than two sets of data. The more circles, the more logical combinations are represented by the overlapping. The following is a Venn diagram that represents sock colors worn by a class of students. There were 30 students surveyed. The innermost region represents those students that had green, pink, and blue on their socks (perhaps in a striped pattern). Therefore, 2 students had all three colors. In this example, all students had at least one color on their socks, so no one exists in the complement.

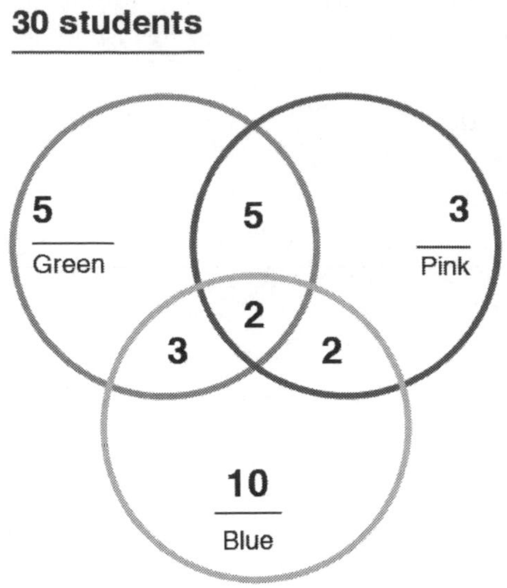

Venn diagrams are typically not drawn to scale, but if they are and their area is proportional to the amount of data it represents, it is known as an **area-proportional Venn diagram**.

Evaluating the Information in Tables, Charts, and Graphs Using Statistics

One way information can be interpreted from tables, charts, and graphs is through statistics. The three most common calculations for a set of data are the mean, median, and mode. These three are called **measures of central tendency**. Measures of central tendency are helpful in comparing two or more different sets of data. The **mean** refers to the average and is found by adding up all values and dividing the total by the number of values. In other words, the mean is equal to the sum of all values divided by the number of data entries. For example, if you bowled a total of 532 points in 4 bowling games, your mean score was $\frac{532}{4} = 133$ points per game. A common application of mean useful to students is calculating what he or she needs to receive on a final exam to receive a desired grade in a class.

The **median** is found by lining up values from least to greatest and choosing the middle value. If there's an even number of values, then the mean of the two middle amounts must be calculated to find the median. For example, the median of the set of dollar amounts \$5, \$6, \$9, \$12, and \$13 is \$9. The **median** of the set of dollar amounts \$1, \$5, \$6, \$8, \$9, \$10 is \$7, which is the mean of \$6 and \$8. The **mode** is the value that occurs the most. The mode of the data set {1, 3, 1, 5, 5, 8, 10} actually refers to two numbers: 1 and 5. In this case, the data set is bimodal because it has two modes. A data set can have no mode if no amount is repeated. Another useful statistic is range. The **range** for a set of data refers to the difference between the highest and lowest value.

In some cases, some numbers in a list of data might have weights attached to them. In that case, a weighted mean can be calculated. A common application of a weighted mean is GPA. In a semester, each class is assigned a number of credit hours, its weight, and at the end of the semester each student receives a grade. To compute GPA, an A is a 4, a B is a 3, a C is a 2, a D is a 1, and an F is a 0. Consider a student that takes a 4-hour English class, a 3-hour math class, and a 4-hour history class and receives all

B's. The weighted mean, GPA, is found by multiplying each grade times its weight, number of credit hours, and dividing by the total number of credit hours. Therefore, the student's GPA is:

$$\frac{3 \times 4 + 3 \times 3 + 3 \times 4}{11} = \frac{33}{1} = 3.0.$$

The following bar chart shows how many students attend a cycle on each day of the week. To find the mean attendance for the week, each day's attendance can be added together, $10 + 7 + 6 + 9 + 8 + 14 + 4 = 58$, and the total divided by the number of days, $58 \div 7 = 8.3$. The mean attendance for the week was 8.3 people. The median attendance can be found by putting the attendance numbers in order from least to greatest: 4, 6, 7, 8, 9, 10, 14, and choosing the middle number: 8 people. The mode for attendance is none for this set of data because no numbers repeat. The range is 10, which is found by finding the difference between the lowest number, 4, and the highest number, 14.

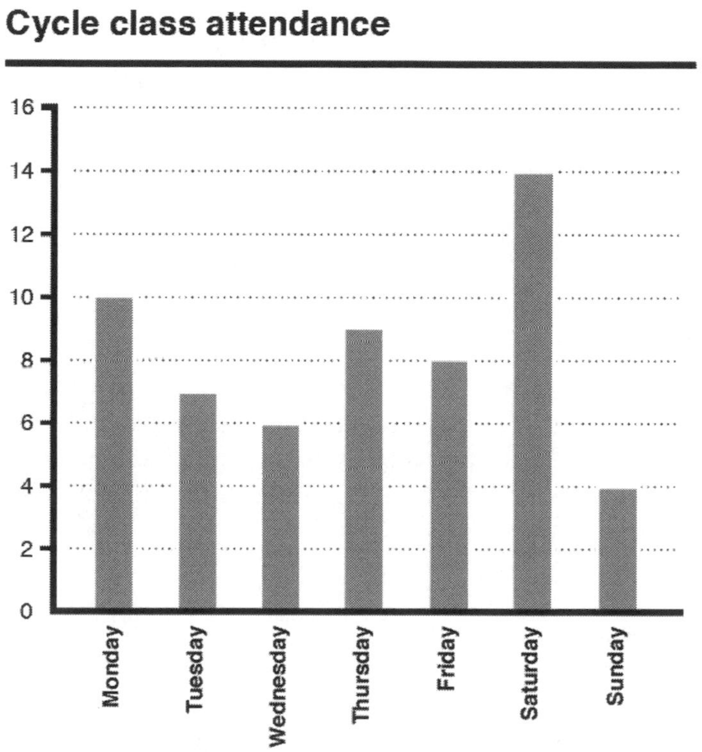

A **histogram** is a bar graph used to group data into "bins" that cover a range on the horizontal, or x-axis. Histograms consist of rectangles whose height is equal to the frequency of a specific category. The horizontal axis represents the specific categories. Because they cover a range of data, these bins have no gaps between bars, unlike the bar graph above. In a histogram showing the heights of adult golden retrievers, the bottom axis would be groups of heights, and the y-axis would be the number of dogs in each range. Evaluating this histogram would show the height of most golden retrievers as falling within a certain range. It also provides information to find the average height and range for how tall golden retrievers may grow.

The following is a histogram that represents exam grades in a given class. The horizontal axis represents ranges of the number of points scored, and the vertical axis represents the number of students. For example, approximately 33 students scored in the 60 to 70 range.

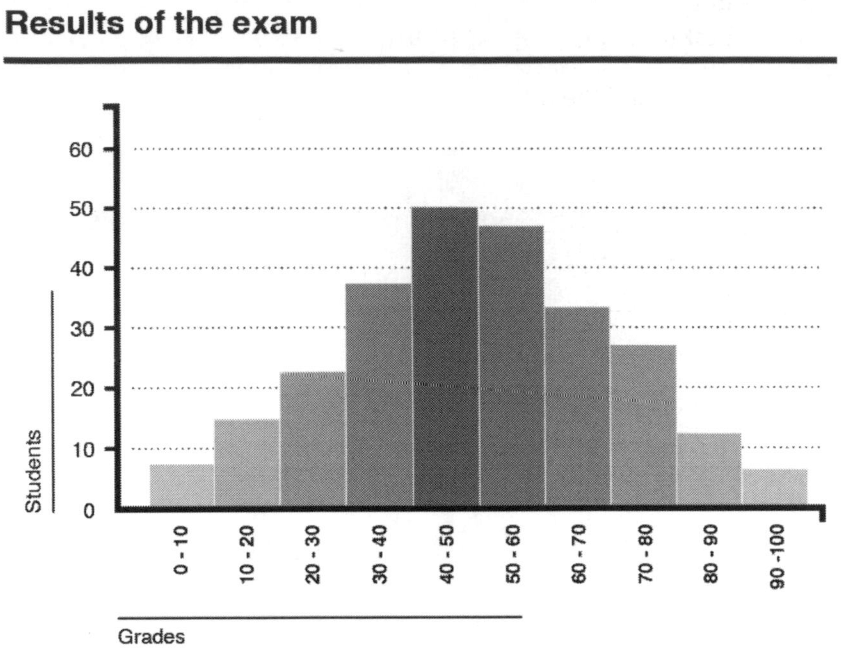

Measures of central tendency can be discussed using a histogram. If the points scored were shown with individual rectangles, the tallest rectangle would represent the mode. A bimodal set of data would have two peaks of equal height. Histograms can be classified as having data **skewed to the left, skewed to the right,** or **normally distributed**, which is also known as **bell-shaped**. These three classifications can be seen in the following chart:

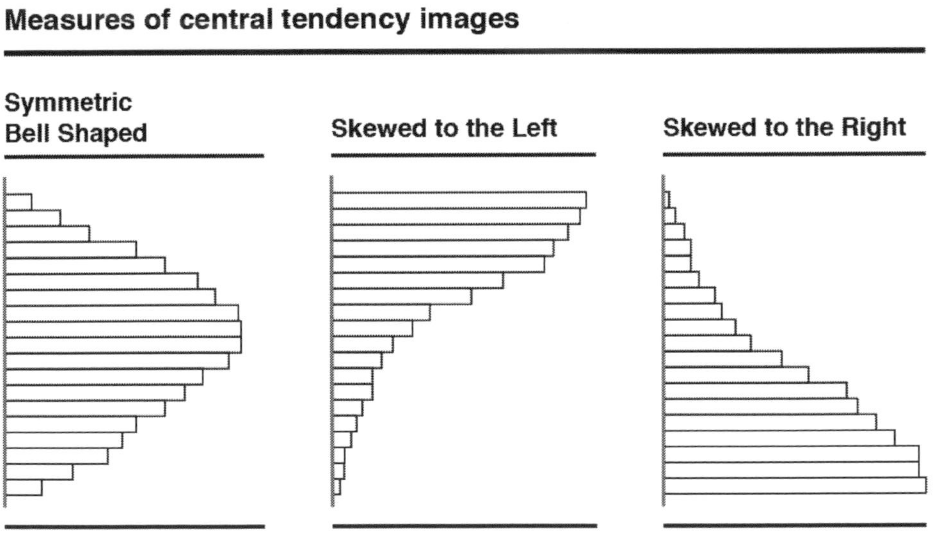

When the data is normal, the mean, median, and mode are all very close. They all represent the most typical value in the data set. The mean is typically used as the best measure of central tendency in this case because it does include all data points. However, if the data is skewed, the mean becomes less meaningful. The median is the best measure of central tendency because it is not affected by any outliers, unlike the mean. When the data is skewed, the mean is dragged in the direction of the skew. Therefore, if the data is not normal, it is best to use the median as the measure of central tendency.

The measures of central tendency and the range may also be found by evaluating information on a line graph.

In the line graph from a previous example that showed the daily high and low temperatures, the average high temperature can be found by gathering data from each day on the triangle line. The days' highs are 82, 78, 75, 65, and 70. The average is found by adding them together to get 370, then dividing by 5 (because there are 5 temperature values). The average high for the five days is 74. If 74 degrees is found on the graph, then it falls in the middle of the values on the triangle line. The mean low temperature can be found in the same way.

Given a set of data, the **correlation coefficient**, *r*, measures the association between all the data points. If two values are correlated, there is an association between them. However, correlation does not necessarily mean causation, or that that one value causes the other. There is a common mistake made that assumes correlation implies causation. Average daily temperature and number of sunbathers are both correlated and have causation. If the temperature increases, that change in weather causes more people to want to catch some rays. However, wearing plus-size clothing and having heart disease are two variables that are correlated but do not have causation. The larger someone is, the more likely he or she is to have heart disease. However, being overweight does not cause someone to have the disease.

Practice Questions

1. What is $\frac{12}{60}$ converted to a percentage?
   a. 0.20
   b. 20%
   c. 25%
   d. 12%
   e. 1.2%

2. Which of the following is the correct decimal form of the fraction $\frac{14}{33}$ rounded to the nearest hundredths place?
   a. 0.420
   b. 0.14
   c. 0.424
   d. 0.140
   e. 0.42

3. Which of the following represents the correct sum of $\frac{14}{15}$ and $\frac{2}{5}$?
   a. $\frac{20}{15}$
   b. $\frac{4}{3}$
   c. $\frac{16}{20}$
   d. $\frac{4}{5}$
   e. $\frac{16}{15}$

4. What is the product of $\frac{5}{14}$ and $\frac{7}{20}$?
   a. $\frac{1}{8}$
   b. $\frac{35}{280}$
   c. $\frac{12}{34}$
   d. $\frac{1}{2}$
   e. $\frac{7}{140}$

5. What is the result of dividing 24 by $\frac{8}{5}$?

a. $\frac{5}{3}$

b. $\frac{3}{5}$

c. $\frac{120}{8}$

d. 15

e. $\frac{24}{5}$

6. Subtract $\frac{5}{14}$ from $\frac{5}{24}$. Which of the following is the correct result?

a. $\frac{25}{168}$

b. 0

c. $-\frac{25}{168}$

d. $\frac{1}{10}$

e. $-\frac{1}{10}$

7. Which of the following is a correct mathematical statement?

a. $\frac{1}{3} < -\frac{4}{3}$

b. $-\frac{1}{3} > \frac{4}{3}$

c. $\frac{1}{3} > \frac{4}{3}$

d. $-\frac{1}{3} \geq \frac{4}{3}$

e. $\frac{1}{3} > -\frac{4}{3}$

8. Which of the following is INCORRECT?

a. $-\frac{1}{5} < \frac{4}{5}$

b. $\frac{4}{5} > -\frac{1}{5}$

c. $-\frac{1}{5} > \frac{4}{5}$

d. $\frac{1}{5} > -\frac{4}{5}$

e. $\frac{4}{5} > \frac{1}{5}$

9. What is the solution to the equation $3(x+2)=14x-5$?

a. $x=1$
b. $x=-1$
c. $x=0$
d. All real numbers
e. No solution

10. What is the solution to the equation $10-5x+2=7x+12-12x$?

a. $x=12$
b. $x=1$
c. $x=0$
d. All real numbers
e. No solution

11. Which of the following is the result when solving the equation $4(x+5)+6=2(2x+3)$?

a. $x=6$
b. $x=1$
c. $x=26$
d. All real numbers
e. No solution

12. How many cases of cola can Lexi purchase if each case is $3.50 and she has $40?

a. 10
b. 12
c. 11.4
d. 11
e. 12.5

13. Two consecutive integers exist such that the sum of three times the first and two less than the second is equal to 411. What are those integers?

a. 103 and 104
b. 104 and 105
c. 102 and 103
d. 100 and 101
e. 101 and 102

14. In a neighborhood, 15 out of 80 of the households have children under the age of 18. What percentage of the households have children?

a. 0.1875%
b. 18.75%
c. 1.875%
d. 15%
e. 1.50%

15. Gina took an algebra test last Friday. There were 35 questions, and she answered 60% of them correctly. How many correct answers did she have?

a. 35
b. 20
c. 21
d. 25
e. 18

16. Paul took a written driving test, and he got 12 of the questions correct. If he answered 75% of the total questions correctly, how many problems were on the test?

a. 25
b. 15
c. 20
d. 18
e. 16

17. If a car is purchased for $15,395 with a 7.25% sales tax, how much is the total price?

a. $15,395.07
b. $16,511.14
c. $16,411.13
d. $15,402
e. $16,113.10

18. A car manufacturer usually makes 15,412 SUVs, 25,815 station wagons, 50,412 sedans, 8,123 trucks, and 18,312 hybrids a month. About how many cars are manufactured each month?

a. 120,000
b. 200,000
c. 300,000
d. 12,000
e. 20,000

19. Each year, a family goes to the grocery store every week and spends $105. About how much does the family spend annually on groceries?

a. $10,000
b. $50,000
c. $500
d. $5,000
e. $1,200

20. Bindee is having a barbeque on Sunday and needs 12 packets of ketchup for every 5 guests. If 60 guests are coming, how many packets of ketchup should she buy?

a. 100
b. 12
c. 144
d. 60
e. 300

21. A grocery store sold 48 bags of apples in one day, and 9 of the bags contained Granny Smith apples. The rest contained Red Delicious apples. What is the ratio of bags of Granny Smith to bags of Red Delicious that were sold?

a. 48:9
b. 39:9
c. 9:48
d. 9:39
e. 39:48

22. If Oscar's bank account totaled $4,000 in March and $4,900 in June, what was the rate of change in his bank account total over those three months?

a. $900 a month
b. $300 a month
c. $4,900 a month
d. $100 a month
e. $4,000 a month

23. Erin and Katie work at the same ice cream shop. Together, they always work less than 21 hours a week. In a week, if Katie worked two times as many hours as Erin, how many hours could Erin work?

a. Less than 7 hours
b. Less than or equal to 7 hours
c. More than 7 hours
d. Less than 8 hours
e. More than 8 hours

24. From the chart below, which two are preferred by more men than women?

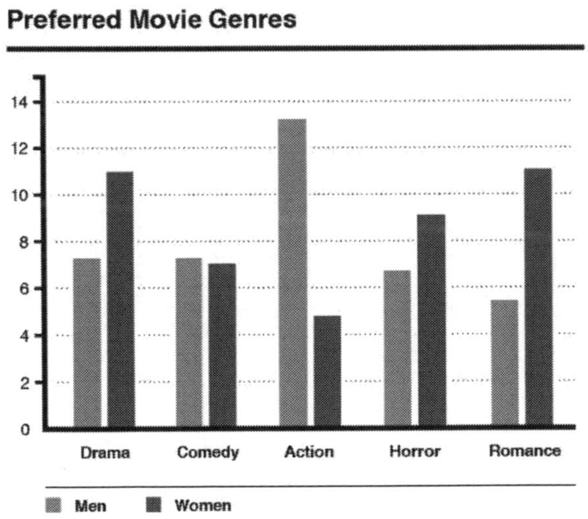

a. Comedy and Action
b. Drama and Comedy
c. Action and Horror
d. Action and Romance
e. Romance and Comedy

25. Which type of graph best represents a continuous change over a period of time?
    a. Stacked bar graph
    b. Bar graph
    c. Pie graph
    d. Histogram
    e. Line graph

26. Using the graph below, what is the mean number of visitors for the first 4 hours?

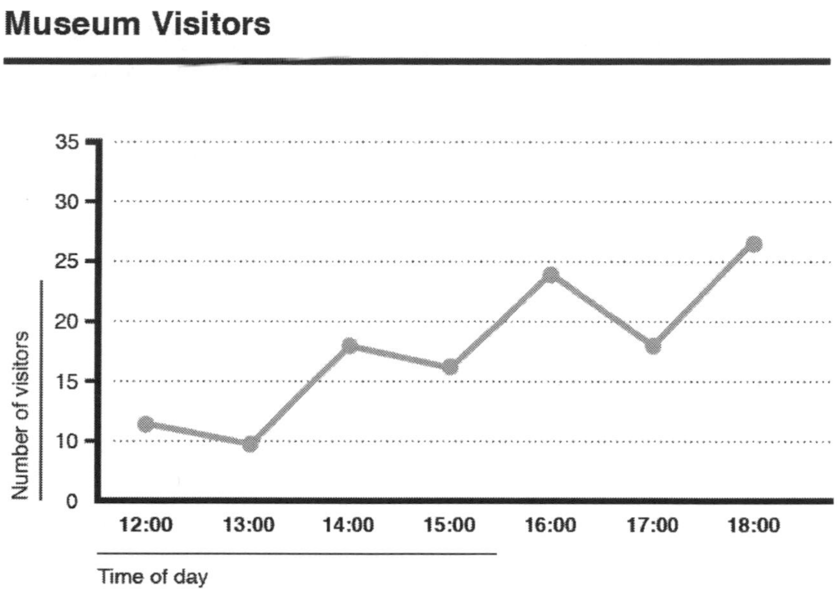

a. 12
b. 13
c. 14
d. 15
e. 16

27. What is the mode for the grades shown in the chart below?

Science Grades	
Jerry	65
Bill	95
Anna	80
Beth	95
Sara	85
Ben	72
Jordan	98

a. 65
b. 33
c. 95
d. 90
e. 84.3

28. The following set represents the test scores from a university class: {35, 79, 80, 87, 87, 90, 92, 95, 95, 98, 99}. If the outlier is removed from this set, which of the following is TRUE?

a. The mean and the median will decrease.
b. The mean and the median will increase.
c. The mean and the mode will increase.
d. The mean and the mode will decrease.
e. The mean, median, and mode will increase.

29. The percentage of smokers above the age of 18 in 2000 was 23.2 percent. The percentage of smokers above the age of 18 in 2015 was 15.1 percent. Find the average rate of change in the percent of smokers above the age of 18 from 2000 to 2015.

a. -.54 percent
b. -8.1 percent
c. -5.4 percent
d. -15 percent
e. -1.5 percent

30. A study of adult drivers finds that it is likely that an adult driver wears his seatbelt. Which of the following could be the probability that an adult driver wears his seat belt?

a. 0.90
b. 0.05
c. 0.25
d. 0
e. 1.5

31. In order to estimate deer population in a forest, biologists obtained a sample of deer in that forest and tagged each one of them. The sample had 300 deer in total. They returned a week later and harmlessly captured 400 deer, and 5 were tagged. Use this information to estimate how many total deer were in the forest.

a. 24,000 deer
b. 30,000 deer
c. 40,000 deer
d. 100,000 deer
e. 120,000 deer

32. Use the graph below entitled "Projected Temperatures for Tomorrow's Winter Storm" to answer the question.

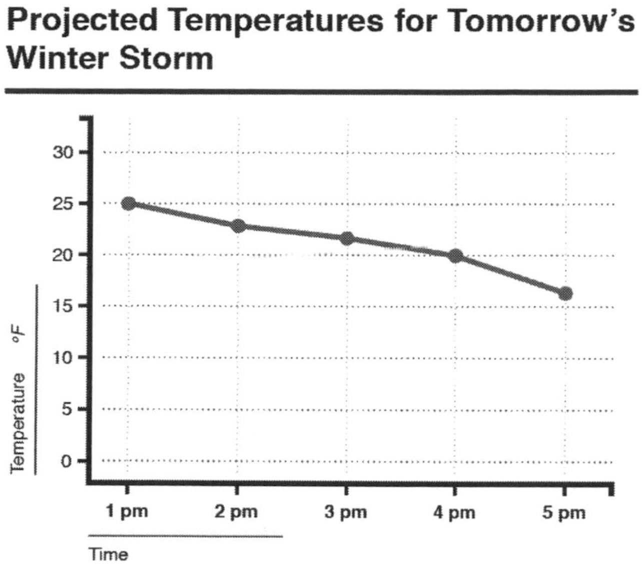

What is the expected temperature at 3:00 p.m.?

a. 25 degrees
b. 22 degrees
c. 20 degrees
d. 16 degrees
e. 18 degrees

33. The number of members of the House of Representatives varies directly with the total population in a state. If the state of New York has 19,600,000 residents and has 27 total representatives, how many should Ohio have with a population of 11,700,000?

a. 10
b. 9
c. 11
d. 5
e. 7

34. Which of the statements below is a statistical question?

a. What was your grade on the last test?
b. What were the grades of the students in your class on the last test?
c. What kind of car do you drive?
d. What was Sam's time in the marathon?
e. What textbooks does Marty use this semester?

35. Eva Jane is practicing for an upcoming 5K run. She has recorded the following times (in minutes):
25, 18, 23, 28, 30, 22.5, 23, 33, 20

Use the above information to answer the next three questions to the closest minute. What is Eva Jane's mean time?

a. 26 minutes
b. 19 minutes
c. 24 minutes
d. 23 minutes
e. 25 minutes

36. What is the mode of Eva Jane's time?

a. 16 minutes
b. 20 minutes
c. 23 minutes
d. 33 minutes
e. 25 minutes

37. What is Eva Jane's median time?

a. 23 minutes
b. 17 minutes
c. 28 minutes
d. 19 minutes
e. 25 minutes

38. What is the perimeter of the following figure?

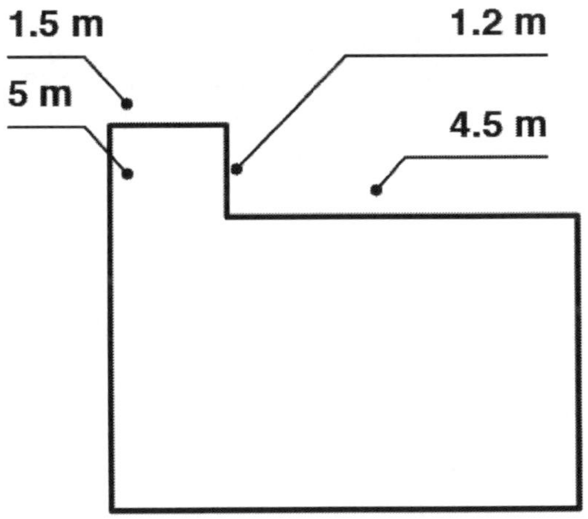

a. 13.4 m
b. 22 m
c. 12.2 m
d. 22.5 m
e. 24.4 m

39. Which of the following measures always corresponds to the 50th percentile on a standardized test?
  a. The mean
  b. The median
  c. The mode
  d. The minimum
  e. The maximum

40. Joe washed his car yesterday. Joe did not go to the grocery store yesterday. Determine which of the following is FALSE:
  a. Joe washed his car yesterday or Joe went to the grocery store yesterday.
  b. If Joe went to the grocery store yesterday, then Joe washed his car yesterday.
  c. Joe washed his car yesterday and Joe did not go to the grocery store yesterday.
  d. If Joe went to the grocery store yesterday, then Joe did not wash his car yesterday.
  e. Joe washed his car yesterday or Joe did not go to the grocery store yesterday.

41. Determine the missing subtotal in gray:

Location	**Type of Clothing**	**Sales**
High St.	Men's	$591
High St.	Men's	$879
	Men's Total	**$1,470**
High St.	Women's	$522
High St.	Women's	$788
	Women's	
High St. Total		$2,780
Main St.	Men's	$607
Main St.	Men's	$981
	Men's Total	**$1,588**
Main St.	Women's	$342
Main St.	Women's	$287
	Women's	$629
Main St. Total		**$2,217**

  a. $1,310
  b. $2,780
  c. $1,470
  d. $788
  e. $266

42. Which of these percentiles falls within a standardized test score range that would have a stanine score of 5?

a. 75th percentile
b. 35th percentile
c. 10th percentile
d. 55th percentile
e. 85th percentile

43. Consider the following problem:

A garden is built in such a way that its width is twice as long as its length and the total perimeter is 50 feet. How long is the width of the garden?

Which of the following two techniques could be used to solve this problem?

a. Evaluating a mathematical expression and drawing a picture
b. Solving an equation and trial and error
c. Identifying a pattern and estimating
d. Evaluating a mathematical expression and estimating
e. Trial and error and estimating

44. A taxi costs a flat rate of $4.00 plus $2.25 per mile in New York City. If Tal has $21, what is the maximum number of miles he can ride in this taxi?

a. 5
b. 6
c. 7
d. 8
e. 9

45. According to your everyday life, which one of the following statements is always FALSE?

a. Some cats have four legs.
b. All flowers are not trees.
c. Some books have pictures
d. No cats are insects.
e. All insects are ants.

46. Ms. Katy is wrapping end-of-the-year gifts for her class. There are 27 students in the class and each gift needs 2 feet, 4 inches of ribbon to tie around the package. What is the total length of ribbon that she needs to wrap all the gifts?

a. 63 inches
b. 63 feet
c. 54 inches
d. 65 feet
e. 54 feet

47. Use the information in the box to determine which of the following conclusions can be made.

- The second-grade classroom has four more boys than girls.
- The second-grade classroom has an even number of boys.

a. The second-grade classroom has an odd number of girls.
b. The second-grade classroom has an even number of girls.
c. The second-grade classroom has 16 boys and 12 girls.
d. The second-grade classroom has no more than 20 boys and 16 girls.
e. The second-grade classroom has a total number of students that is odd.

48. Determine the missing subtotal:

Trees	**Plants Sold**
Maple	12
Oak	45
Pine	33
Subtotal	**90**
Flowers	
Magnolia	45
Marigold	75
Daffodils	22
Subtotal	
Total	**232**

a. 90
b. 322
c. 142
d. 92
e. 374

49. Using the information in the box, which of the following can be determined?

Annie is training for a marathon. She ran 60 miles in one week. She ran 5 miles on Monday, 12 miles on Tuesday, 8 miles on Wednesday, and 14 miles on Thursday.

a. The number of miles she ran on Friday.
b. The number of miles she ran from Friday to Sunday.
c. The number of miles she ran on Saturday and Sunday.
d. The number of miles she runs every Monday.
e. The total number of miles in her training plan.

50. Use the ruler shown below to answer the question regarding the piano:

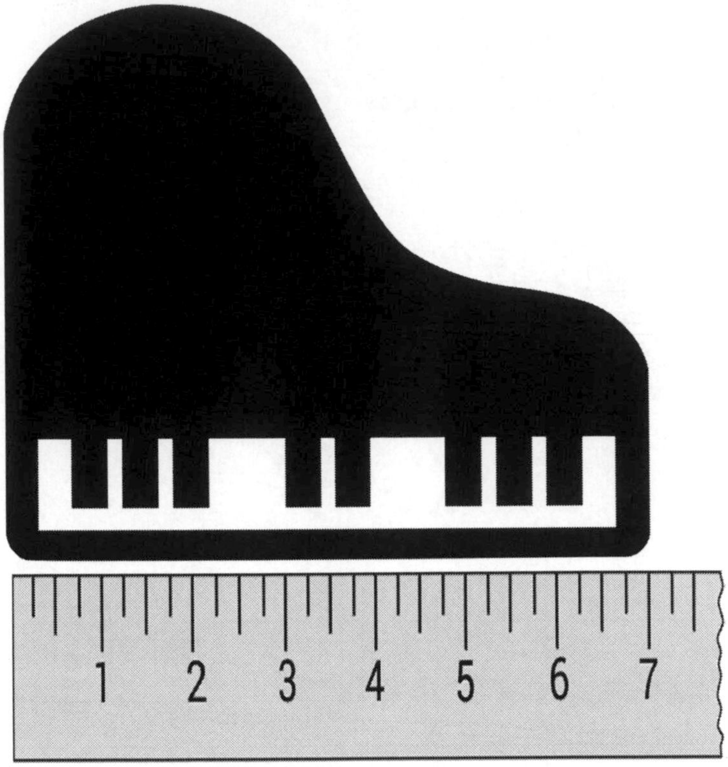

If the actual piano is 3.5 meters long, what is the scale of the picture of the piano?

a. 1 unit = 1 meter
b. 1 unit = 0.5 meter
c. 1 unit = 2 meters
d. 1 unit = 20 centimeters
e. 1 unit = 10 centimeters

Answer Explanations

1. B: The fraction $\frac{12}{60}$ can be reduced to $\frac{1}{5}$, in lowest terms. First, it must be converted to a decimal. Dividing 1 by 5 results in 0.2. Then, to convert to a percentage, move the decimal point two units to the right and add the percentage symbol. The result is 20%.

2. E: If a calculator is used, divide 33 into 14 and keep two decimal places. If a calculator is not used, multiply both the numerator and denominator by 3. This results in the fraction $\frac{42}{99}$, and hence a decimal of 0.42.

3. B: A common denominator must be used to add fractions. The LCD is 15, and $\frac{2}{5} = \frac{6}{15}$.

Therefore, $\frac{14}{15} + \frac{6}{15} = \frac{20}{15}$, and in lowest terms the answer is $\frac{4}{3}$. A common factor of 5 was divided out of both the numerator and denominator.

4. A: A product is found by multiplication. Multiplying two fractions together is easier when common factors are cancelled first to avoid working with larger numbers.

$$\frac{5}{14} \times \frac{7}{20}$$

$$\frac{\cancel{5}}{2 \times \cancel{7}} \times \frac{\cancel{7}}{\cancel{5} \times 4} = \frac{1}{2} \times \frac{1}{4} = \frac{1}{8}$$

5. D: Division is completed by multiplying times the reciprocal. Therefore:

$$24 \div \frac{8}{5}$$

$$\frac{24}{1} \times \frac{5}{8}$$

$$\frac{3 \times \cancel{8}}{1} \times \frac{5}{\cancel{8}} = \frac{15}{1} = 15$$

6. C: A common denominator must be used to subtract fractions. The LCD is 168, so each fraction must be converted to have 168 as the denominator.

$$\frac{5}{24} - \frac{5}{14}$$

$$\frac{5}{24} \times \frac{7}{7} - \frac{5}{14} \times \frac{12}{12}$$

$$\frac{35}{168} - \frac{60}{168} = -\frac{25}{168}$$

7. E: The correct mathematical statement is the one in which the number to the left on the number line is less than the number to the right on the number line. It is written in answer *E* that $\frac{1}{3} > -\frac{4}{3}$, which is the same as $-\frac{4}{3} < \frac{1}{3}$, a correct statement.

8. C: $-\frac{1}{5} > \frac{4}{5}$ is incorrect. The expression on the left is negative, which means that it is smaller than the expression on the right. As it is written, the inequality states that the expression on the left is greater than the expression on the right, which is not true.

9. A: First, the distributive property must be used on the left side. This results in $3x + 6 = 14x - 5$. The addition property is then used to add 5 to both sides, and then to subtract $3x$ from both sides, resulting in $11 = 11x$. Finally, the multiplication property is used to divide each side by 11. Therefore, $x = 1$ is the solution.

10. D: First, like terms are collected to obtain $12 - 5x = -5x + 12$. Then, if the addition principle is used to move the terms with the variable, $5x$ is added to both sides and the mathematical statement $12 = 12$ is obtained. This is always true; therefore, all real numbers satisfy the original equation.

11. E: The distributive property is used on both sides to obtain $4x + 20 + 6 = 4x + 6$. Then, like terms are collected on the left, resulting in $4x + 26 = 4x + 6$. Next, the addition principle is used to subtract $4x$ from both sides, and this results in the false statement $26 = 6$. Therefore, there is no solution.

12. D: This is a one-step real-world application problem. The unknown quantity is the number of cases of cola to be purchased. Let x be equal to this amount. Because each case costs $3.50, the total number of cases times $3.50 must equal $40. This translates to the mathematical equation $3.5x = 40$. Divide both sides by 3.5 to obtain $x = 11.4286$, which has been rounded to four decimal places. Because cases are sold whole (the store does not sell portions of cases), and there is not enough money to purchase 12 cases, there is only enough money to purchase 11.

13. A: First, the variables have to be defined. Let x be the first integer and therefore $x + 1$ is the second integer. This is a two-step problem. The sum of three times the first and two less than the second is translated into the following expression:

$$3x + (x + 1 - 2)$$

This expression is set equal to 411 to obtain:

$$3x + (x + 1 - 2) = 411$$

The left-hand side is simplified to obtain $4x - 1 = 411$. The addition and multiplication properties are used to solve for x. First, add 1 to both sides and then divide both sides by 4 to obtain $x = 103$. The next consecutive integer is 104.

14. B: First, the information is translated into the ratio $\frac{15}{80}$. To find the percentage, translate this fraction into a decimal by dividing 15 by 80. The corresponding decimal is 0.1875. Move the decimal point two units to the right to obtain the percentage 18.75%.

15. C: Gina answered 60% of 35 questions correctly; 60% can be expressed as the decimal 0.60. Therefore, she answered $0.60 \times 35 = 21$ questions correctly.

16. E: The unknown quantity is the number of total questions on the test. Let x be equal to this unknown quantity. Therefore, $0.75x = 12$. Divide both sides by 0.75 to obtain $x = 16$.

17. B: If sales tax is 7.25%, the price of the car must be multiplied by 1.0725 to account for the additional sales tax. This is the same as multiplying the initial price by 0.0725 (the tax) and adding that to the initial cost. Therefore:

$$15{,}395 \times 1.0725 = 16{,}511.1375$$

This amount is rounded to the nearest cent, which is $16,511.14.

18. A: Rounding can be used to find the best approximation. All of the values can be rounded to the nearest thousand. 15,412 SUVs can be rounded to 15,000. 25,815 station wagons can be rounded to 26,000. 50,412 sedans can be rounded to 50,000. 8,123 trucks can be rounded to 8,000. Finally, 18,312 hybrids can be rounded to 18,000. The sum of the rounded values is 117,000, which is closest to 120,000.

19. D: There are 52 weeks in a year, and if the family spends $105 each week, that amount is close to $100. A good approximation is $100 a week for 50 weeks, which is found through the product $50 \times 100 =$ $5,000.

20. C: This problem involves ratios and percentages. If 12 packets are needed for every 5 people, this statement is equivalent to the ratio $\frac{12}{5}$. The unknown amount x is the number of ketchup packets needed for 60 people. The proportion $\frac{12}{5} = \frac{x}{60}$ must be solved. Cross-multiply to obtain $12 \times 60 = 5x$. Therefore, $720 = 5x$. Divide each side by 5 to obtain $x = 144$ packets.

21. D: There were 48 total bags of apples sold. If 9 bags were Granny Smith and the rest were Red Delicious, then 48 – 9 = 39 bags were Red Delicious. Therefore, the ratio of Granny Smith to Red Delicious is 9:39.

22. B: The average rate of change is found by calculating the difference in dollars over the elapsed time. Therefore, the rate of change is equal to $4,900 – $4,000 ÷ 3 months, which is equal to $900 ÷ 3 or $300 a month.

23. A: Let x be the unknown, the number of hours Erin can work. We know Katie works $2x$, and the sum of all hours is less than 21. Therefore, $x + 2x < 21$, which simplifies into $3x < 21$. Solving this results in the inequality $x < 7$ after dividing both sides by 3. Therefore, Erin can work less than 7 hours.

24. A: The chart is a bar graph showing how many men and women prefer each genre of movies. The dark gray bars represent the number of women, while the light gray bars represent the number of men. The light gray bars are higher and represent more men than women for the genres of comedy and action.

25. E: A line graph represents continuous change over time. The line on the graph is continuous and not broken, as on a scatter plot. Stacked bar graphs are used when comparing multiple variables at one time. They combine some elements of both pie charts and bar graphs, using the organization of bar graphs and the proportionality aspect of pie charts. A bar graph may show change but isn't necessarily continuous over time. A pie graph is better for representing percentages of a whole. Histograms are best used in grouping sets of data into bins to show the frequency of a certain variable.

26. C: The mean for the number of visitors during the first 4 hours is 14. The mean is found by calculating the average for the four hours. Adding up the total number of visitors during those hours gives:

$$12 + 10 + 18 + 16 = 56$$

Then $56 \div 4 = 14$.

27. C: The mode for a set of data is the value that occurs the most frequently. The grade that appears the most is 95. It's the only value that repeats in the set. The mean is around 84.3.

28. B: The outlier is 35. When a small outlier is removed from a data set, the mean and the median increase. The first step in this process is to identify the outlier, which is the number that lies away from the given set. Once the outlier is identified, the mean and median can be recalculated. The mean will be affected because it is the average of all of the numbers. The median will be affected because it finds the middle number, which is subject to change because a number is lost. The mode will most likely not change because it is the number that occurs the most, which will not be the outlier if there is only one outlier.

29. A: The formula for the rate of change is the same as slope: change in *y* over change in *x*. The *y*-value in this case is percentage of smokers and the *x*-value is years. The change in percentage of smokers from 2000 to 2015 was -8.1 percent (15.1% – 23.2%). The change in *x* was 2015 – 2000 = 15. Therefore:

$$-8.1\% / 15 = -0.54\%$$

The percentage of smokers decreased 0.54 percent each year.

30. A: The probability of .9 is closer to 1 than any of the other answers. The closer a probability is to 1, the greater the likelihood that the event will occur. The probability of 0.05 shows that it is very unlikely that an adult driver will wear their seatbelt because it is close to zero. A zero probability means that it will not occur. The probability of 0.25 is closer to zero than to one, so it shows that it is unlikely an adult will wear their seatbelt. Choice *E* is wrong because probability must fall between 0 and 1.

31. A: A proportion should be used to solve this problem. The ratio of tagged to total deer in each instance is set equal, and the unknown quantity is a variable x. The proportion is $\frac{300}{x} = \frac{5}{400}$. Cross-multiplying gives $120{,}000 = 5x$, and dividing through by 5 results in 24,000.

32. B: Look on the horizontal axis to find 3:00 p.m. Move up from 3:00 p.m. to reach the dot on the graph. Move horizontally to the left to the horizontal axis to between 20 and 25; the best answer choice is 22. The answer of 25 is too high above the projected time on the graph, and the answers of 20 and 16 degrees are too low.

33. B: The number of representatives varies directly with the population, so the equation necessary is $N = k \times P$, where *N* is number of representatives, *k* is the variation constant, and *P* is total population in millions. Plugging in the information for New York allows *k* to be solved for. This process gives $19.6 = k \times 27$, so $k = 0.73$. Therefore, the formula for number of representatives given total population in billions is:

$$N = .73 \times P$$

Plugging in $P = 11.7$ for Ohio results in $N = 8.5$, which rounds up to 9 total Representatives.

34. B: "What were the grades of the students in your class on the last test?" is a statistical question because to determine this answer one would need to collect data from each person in the class and it is expected the answers would vary. The other answers do not require data to be collected from multiple sources; therefore, the answers will not vary.

35. E: The mean is found by adding all the times together and dividing by the number of times recorded. 25 + 18 + 23 + 28 + 30 + 22.5 + 23 + 33 + 20 = 222.5, divided by 9 = 24.7. Rounding to the nearest minute, the mean is 25 minutes.

36. C: The mode is the time from the data set that occurs most often. The number 23 occurs twice in the data set, while all others occur only once, so the mode is 23 minutes.

37. A: To find the median of a data set, you must first list the numbers from smallest to largest, and then find the number in the middle. If there are two numbers in the middle, as in this data set, add the two numbers in the middle together and divide by 2. Putting this list in order from smallest to greatest yields 18, 20, 22.5, 23, 23, 25, 28, 30, and 33, where 23 is the middle number.

38. B: The perimeter is found by adding the length of all the exterior sides. When the given dimensions are added, the perimeter is 22 meters. Start off by adding the listed lengths: 5 + 1.5 + 1.2 + 4.5

The right side can be calculated by subtracting 1.2 from 5 to get 3.8.

The bottom can be calculated by adding 1.5 to 4.5 to get 6.

That gives us:

$$P = 5 + 1.5 + 1.2 + 4.5 + 3.8 + 6 = 22$$

39. B: The median is the value that is located halfway between the minimum and the maximum value of the scores. Therefore, fifty percent of the scores lie below it and fifty percent of the scores lie above it. It corresponds to the 50th percentile.

40. D: When using an *if-then* connective, the only time it is false is when both statements are false. Joe did not go to the grocery store yesterday and he did wash his car yesterday. Therefore, both statements in Choice *D* are false. Therefore, Choice *D* is false. All other choices are true.

41. A: The missing entry is a subtotal for the sales in women's clothing at the High St. location.

$522 + $788 = $1,310

42. D: A stanine score of 5 has a value that falls in the middle twenty percent of the scores, which means between the 40th percentile and the 60th percentile. The 55th percentile is located within this region.

43. B: Choice *B* is the only option with two different techniques that will both work. Estimation does not work because the problem is looking for an exact answer. However, trial and error will work on this problem. There is no pattern to identify, and there is no expression to evaluate because we do not know the dimensions of the garden. We can, however, can set up an algebraic equation that needs to be solved to find the missing dimensions. A picture could be helpful in solving the problem, but it does not give us an answer.

44. C: There are a few ways in which this problem can be answered. A trial and error method can be used. Second, a direct mathematical expression could be used. Subtract the flat rate $4 from $21 and divide by $2.25 to obtain 7.56 miles. Finally, the algebraic equation $2.25m + 4 = 21$ can be solved to obtain $m = 7.56$ miles. Since the question asks for whole miles, this answer rounds down to 7 miles, because 8 miles would be too expensive.

45. E: All insects are ants is false. A counterexample is a ladybug. A ladybug is an insect that is not an ant. The rest of the options are always true.

46. B: Each package needs 2 feet, 4 inches, which is equal to $2\frac{1}{3} = \frac{7}{3}$ feet of ribbon. Because there are 27 students in the class, Ms. Kay needs $27 \times \frac{7}{3} = 63$ feet of ribbon to wrap all of the gifts.

47. B: The total number of girls must be even. This is true because the number of boys is even and adding 4 to an even number results in another even number. Choices *A* and *E* are false. Choices *C* and *D* cannot be concluded because there is not enough information given.

48. C: To determine the missing subtotal, which is the total number of flowers sold, either add up the three types of flowers or subtract the tree subtotal from the overall total. Either way results in 142.

49. B: We know how far Annie ran from Monday to Thursday, which was 5 + 12 + 8 + 14 = 39 miles. We also know that she ran 60 miles over the entire week. Therefore, she ran 60 – 39 = 21 miles from Friday through Sunday. We do not have enough information to determine the other conclusions.

50. B: The picture of the piano is 7 units long. The actual piano is 3.5 meters long. That means that one unit is equal to $\frac{3.5}{7} = \frac{1}{2}$ of a meter.

Writing

Composing and/or Analyzing Writing in Different Genres

Argumentative Writing: The purpose of an **argumentative writing** is to prove or disprove a particular thesis or hypothesis, using various claims and inferences that challenge one or many previous claims or inferences. Most argumentative pieces are more formal and academic than persuasive pieces. They are not trying to persuade an audience through subjective tropes, but rather are trying to argue a particular point using objective evidence.

Opinion Writing: The purpose of **opinion writing** is to carry out the single-minded goal of voicing one's thoughts and letting one's opinion be heard. Opinion pieces differ from persuasive pieces because they are not trying to sway the readers' opinions; rather, they are simply trying to communicate the writer's own opinion.

Persuasive Writing: The purpose of **persuasive writing** is to blend personal opinions with facts in order to sway or convince readers to take a particular side or stance (usually in some sort of larger societal, political, or ethical debate). Political speeches can sometimes be persuasive in nature for this reason.

Informative/Explanatory Writing: The purpose of **informative** or **explanatory writing** is to communicate concrete intelligence to the reader. Accordingly, the tone is typically formal and the language should be objective. Informative writing does not usually appeal to pathos, logos, or ethos. Instead, it simply aims to provide facts, evidence, observations, and objective descriptions of the subject matter in an organized, understandable fashion.

Summaries, letters, and research reports are examples of subgenres that fall within these larger genres. **Summaries** are traditionally informational/explanatory types of writing that simply remove extraneous details in order to create a shorter, less wordy version of a particular topic, text, or other form of communication. **Letters** are interpersonal or intrapersonal forms of writing that can potentially be argumentative, opinionated, persuasive, or informative. This category is all-encompassing because, at its core, it is a very intimate form of writing that takes on the personal goals or objectives of the author, which can range from venting to informing. **Research reports** are generally argumentative forms of writing that feature thesis statements or testing hypotheses. An entirely opinionated report would likely not maintain the academic standards necessary to pass a course in college, for instance.

Writing Arguments to Support Claims Using Valid Reasoning and Relevant and Sufficient Evidence

Selecting the most relevant material to support a written text is a necessity in producing quality writing and for the credibility of an author. Arguments lacking in reasons or examples won't work in persuading the audience later on, because their brains have not been convinced and their hearts have not been pulled. Using examples to support ideas also gives the writing rhetorical effects such as **pathos** (emotion), **logos** (logic), or **ethos** (credibility), all three of which are necessary for a successful persuasive essay.

Arguments need supporting reasons and examples to support the points the author is trying to make. Unsubstantiated claims can weaken an argument because they give reason to question the credibility and accuracy of the writer's ideas and points. Tangible details and relatable examples also help readers connect with the ideas and "buy in" to the author's ideas. They help bring the ideas to life and provide evidence of their validity. It's particularly important to provide details that facilitate the ability of readers follow the logic of an argument and connect the points made and their implications. Writers should use a variety of credible primary and secondary sources to substantiate their points. It is important to credit the source and cite it appropriately to give the original author due credit, and so that readers can locate the source of their own, should they be interested in further information.

There are a few steps in determining how to support an idea:

Types of Examples
Think about the audience. Are they indifferent? Use a personal story or anecdote in order stir empathy. Are they resistant? Use logical reasoning based in factual evidence so they will be convinced. Personal stories or testimonials, statistics, or documentary evidence are various types of examples that one can use for their writing.

Source and Validity
For libraries or online sources, make sure the research you find is within a credible, scholarly journal and is peer-reviewed. **Peer-reviewed sources** are sources that have been reviewed by other experts in the field. If scholarly journals do not have the information you are looking for, be sure to research the author, date, and website of the source you find, identifying any credibility issues in the process. Sources must also be relevant by being up-to-date, especially those within the science or technology fields.

For example, let's say we want to talk about pesticides and the collapse of bees. An argument without relevant examples would look like this:

> With the use of the world's most popular pesticides, bees are becoming extinct. This is also causing ecological devastation. We must do something soon about the bee population, or else we will chase bees to extinction and lose valuable resources as a result.

Here is the same argument with factual examples. The added examples are in italics:

> With the use of the world's most popular pesticides, bees are becoming extinct. *Beekeepers have reported losing 55 to 95 percent of their colony in just two short years due to toxic poisoning.* This is also causing ecological devastation. *Bees are known for pollinating more than two-thirds of the world's most essential crops.* We must do something soon about the bee population, or else we will chase bees to extinction and lose valuable resources as a result.

Adding examples to the above argument brings life to the bees—they are living, dying, pollinating—and readers feel more compelled to act as a result of adding relevant examples to the argument.

Formal and Informal Language

Formal language is less personal than informal language. It is more "buttoned-up" and business-like, adhering to proper grammatical rules. It is used in professional or academic contexts, to convey respect or authority. For example, one would use formal language to write an informative or argumentative essay for school or to address a superior. Formal language avoids contractions, slang, colloquialisms, and first-person pronouns. Formal language uses sentences that are usually more complex and often in passive voice. Punctuation can differ as well. For example, **exclamation points** *(!)* are used to show strong emotion or can be used as an interjection, but should be used sparingly in formal writing situations.

Informal language is often used when communicating with family members, friends, peers, and those known more personally. It is more casual, spontaneous, and forgiving in its conformity to grammatical rules and conventions. Informal language is used for personal emails and correspondence between coworkers or other familial relationships. The tone is more relaxed. In informal writing, slang, contractions, clichés, and the first- and second-person are often used.

Elements of the Writing Process

Skilled writers undergo a series of steps that comprise the writing process. The purpose of adhering to a structured approach to writing is to develop clear, meaningful, coherent work.

The stages are pre-writing or planning, organizing, drafting/writing, revising, and editing. Not every writer will necessarily follow all five stages for every project but will judiciously employ the crucial components of the stages for most formal or important work. For example, a brief informal response to a short reading passage may not necessitate the need for significant organization after idea generation, but larger assignments and essays will likely mandate the use of the full process.

Pre-Writing/Planning

Brainstorming

One of the most important steps in writing is pre-writing. Before drafting an essay or other assignment, it's helpful to think about the topic for a moment or two, in order to gain a more solid understanding of what the task is. Then, spend about five minutes jotting down the immediate ideas that could work for the essay. Brainstorming is a way to get some words on the page and offer a reference for ideas when drafting. Scratch paper is provided for writers to use any pre-writing techniques such as webbing, freewriting, or listing. Some writers prefer using graphic organizers during this phase. The goal is to get ideas out of the mind and onto the page.

Freewriting

Like brainstorming, freewriting is another prewriting activity to help the writer generate ideas. This method involves setting a timer for two or three minutes and writing down all ideas that come to mind about the topic using complete sentences. Once time is up, writers should review the sentences to see what observations have been made and how these ideas might translate into a more unified direction for the topic. Even if sentences lack sense as a whole, freewriting is an excellent way to get ideas onto the page in the very beginning stages of writing. Using complete sentences can make this a bit more challenging than brainstorming, but overall it is a worthwhile exercise, as it may force the writer to come up with more complete thoughts about the topic.

Once the ideas are on the page, it's time for the writer to turn them into a solid plan for the essay. The best ideas from the brainstorming results can then be developed into a more formal outline.

Organizing

Although sometimes it is difficult to get going on the brainstorming or prewriting phase, once ideas start flowing, writers often find that they have amassed too many thoughts that will not make for a cohesive and unified essay. During the organization stage, writers should examine the generated ideas, hone in on the important ones central to their main idea, and arrange the points in a logical and effective manner. Writers may also determine that some of the ideas generated in the planning process need further elaboration, potentially necessitating the need for research to gather information to fill the gaps.

Once a writer has chosen his or her thesis and main argument, selected the most applicable details and evidence, and eliminated the "clutter," it is time to strategically organize the ideas. This is often accomplished with an outline.

Outlining

An **outline** is a system used to organize writing. When composing essays, outlining is important because it helps writers organize important information in a logical, deliberate pattern and order. Usually, outlines start out with the main ideas and then branch out into subgroups or subsidiary thoughts or subjects. Not only do outlines provide a visual tool for writers to reflect on how events, ideas, evidence, or other key parts of the argument relate to one another, but they can also lead writers to a stronger conclusion.

The sample below demonstrates what a general outline looks like:

- I. Introduction
  - 1. Background
  - 2. Thesis statement
- II. Body
  - 1. Point A
    - a. Supporting evidence
    - b. Supporting evidence
  - 2. Point B
    - a. Supporting evidence
    - b. Supporting evidence
  - 3. Point C
    - a. Supporting evidence
    - b. Supporting evidence
- III. Conclusion
  - 1. Restate main points of the paper.
  - 2. End with something memorable.

Drafting/Writing

Now it comes time to actually write the essay. In this stage, writers should follow the outline they developed in the brainstorming process and try to incorporate the useful sentences penned in the freewriting exercise. The main goal of this phase is to put all the thoughts together in cohesive sentences and paragraphs.

It is helpful for writers to remember that their work here does not have to be perfect. This process is often referred to as *drafting* because writers are just creating a rough draft of their work. Because of this, writers should avoid getting bogged down on the small details.

Referencing Sources

Anytime writers quote or paraphrase another text, they need to include a citation. A **citation** is a short description of the work that a quote or information came from. The style manual your teacher wants you to follow will dictate exactly how to format that citation. For example, this is how one would cite a book according to the APA manual of style:

- *Format*: Last name, First initial, Middle initial. (Year Published) *Book Title*. City, State: Publisher.
- *Example*: Sampson, M. R. (1989). *Diaries from an Alien Invasion. Springfield, IL*: Campbell Press.

Revising

Revising offers an opportunity for writers to polish things up. Putting one's self in the reader's shoes and focusing on what the essay actually says helps writers identify problems—it's a movement from the mindset of writer to the mindset of editor. The goal is to have a clean, clear copy of the essay.

The main goal of the revision phase is to improve the essay's flow, cohesiveness, readability, and focus. For example, an essay will make a less persuasive argument if the various pieces of evidence are scattered and presented illogically or clouded with unnecessary thought. Therefore, writers should consider their essay's structure and organization, ensuring that there are smooth transitions between sentences and paragraphs. There should be a discernable introduction and conclusion as well, as these crucial components of an essay provide readers with a blueprint to follow.

Additionally, if the writer includes copious details that do little to enhance the argument, they may actually distract readers from focusing on the main ideas and detract from the strength of their work. The ultimate goal is to retain the purpose or focus of the essay and provide a reader-friendly experience. Because of this, writers often need to delete parts of their essay to improve its flow and focus. Removing sentences, entire paragraphs, or large chunks of writing can be one of the toughest parts of the writing process because it is difficult to part with work one has done. However, ultimately, these types of cuts can significantly improve one's essay.

Lastly, writers should consider their voice and word choice. The voice should be consistent throughout and maintain a balance between an authoritative and warm style, to both inform and engage readers. One way to alter voice is through word choice. Writers should consider changing weak verbs to stronger ones and selecting more precise language in areas where wording is vague. In some cases, it is useful to modify sentence beginnings or to combine or split up sentences to provide a more varied sentence structure.

Editing

Rather than focusing on content (as is the aim in the revising stage), the editing phase is all about the mechanics of the essay: the syntax, word choice, and grammar. This can be considered the proofreading stage. Successful editing is what sets apart a messy essay from a polished document.

The following areas should be considered when proofreading:

- Sentence fragments
- Awkward sentence structure
- Run-on sentences
- Incorrect word choice
- Grammatical agreement errors
- Spelling errors
- Punctuation errors
- Capitalization errors

One of the most effective ways of identifying grammatical errors, awkward phrases, or unclear sentences is to read the essay out loud. Listening to one's own work can help move the writer from simply the author to the reader.

During the editing phase, it's also important to ensure the essay follows the correct formatting and citation rules as dictated by the assignment.

Recursive Writing Process

While the writing process may have specific steps, the good news is that the process is recursive, meaning the steps need not be completed in a particular order. Many writers find that they complete steps at the same time such as drafting and revising, where the writing and rearranging of ideas occur simultaneously or in very close order. Similarly, a writer may find that a particular section of a draft needs more development and will go back to the prewriting stage to generate new ideas. The steps can be repeated at any time, and the more these steps of the recursive writing process are employed, the better the final product will be.

Practice Makes Prepared Writers

Like any other useful skill, writing only improves with practice. While writing may come more easily to some than others, it is still a skill to be honed and improved. Regardless of a person's natural abilities, there is always room for growth in writing. Practicing the basic skills of writing can aid in preparations for the exam.

One way to build vocabulary and enhance exposure to the written word is through reading. This can be through reading books, but reading of any materials such as newspapers, magazines, and even social media count towards practice with the written word. This also helps to enhance critical reading and thinking skills, through analysis of the ideas and concepts read. Think of each new reading experience as a chance to sharpen these skills.

Developing a Well-Organized Paragraph

A **paragraph** is a series of connected and related sentences addressing one topic. Writing good paragraphs benefits writers by helping them to stay on target while drafting and revising their work. It benefits readers by helping them to follow the writing more easily. Regardless of how brilliant their ideas may be, writers who do not present them in organized ways will fail to engage readers—and fail to accomplish their writing goals. A fundamental rule for paragraphing is to confine each paragraph to a single idea. When writers find themselves transitioning to a new idea, they should start a new paragraph. However, a paragraph can include several pieces of evidence supporting its single idea; and it can include several points if they are all related to the overall paragraph topic. When writers find each point becoming lengthy, they may choose instead to devote a separate paragraph to every point and elaborate upon each more fully.

An effective paragraph should have these elements:

- Unity: One major discussion point or focus should occupy the whole paragraph from beginning to end.
- Coherence: For readers to understand a paragraph, it must be coherent. Two components of coherence are logical and verbal bridges. In logical bridges, the writer may write consecutive sentences with parallel structure or carry an idea over across sentences. In verbal bridges, writers may repeat key words across sentences.
- A topic sentence: The paragraph should have a sentence that generally identifies the paragraph's thesis or main idea.
- Sufficient development: To develop a paragraph, writers can use the following techniques after stating their topic sentence:
    - Define terms
    - Cite data
    - Use illustrations, anecdotes, and examples
    - Evaluate causes and effects
    - Analyze the topic
    - Explain the topic using chronological order

A **topic sentence** identifies the main idea of the paragraph. Some are explicit, some implicit. The topic sentence can appear anywhere in the paragraph. However, many experts advise beginning writers to place each paragraph topic sentence at or near the beginning of its paragraph to ensure that their readers understand what the topic of each paragraph is. Even without having written an explicit topic sentence, the writer should still be able to summarize readily what subject matter each paragraph addresses. The writer must then fully develop the topic that is introduced or identified in the topic sentence. Depending on what the writer's purpose is, they may use different methods for developing each paragraph.

Two main steps in the process of organizing paragraphs and essays should both be completed after determining the writing's main point, while the writer is planning or outlining the work. The initial step is to give an order to the topics addressed in each paragraph. Writers must have logical reasons for putting one paragraph first, another second, etc. The second step is to sequence the sentences in each paragraph. As with the first step, writers must have logical reasons for the order of sentences. Sometimes the work's main point obviously indicates a specific order.

Topic Sentences

To be effective, a topic sentence should be concise so that readers get its point without losing the meaning among too many words. As an example, in *Only Yesterday: An Informal History of the 1920s* (1931), author Frederick Lewis Allen's topic sentence introduces his paragraph describing the 1929 stock market crash: "The Bull Market was dead." This example illustrates the criteria of conciseness and brevity. It is also a strong sentence, expressed clearly and unambiguously. The topic sentence also introduces the paragraph, alerting the reader's attention to the main idea of the paragraph and the subject matter that follows the topic sentence.

Experts often recommend opening a paragraph with the topic sentences to enable the reader to realize the main point of the paragraph immediately. Application letters for jobs and university admissions also benefit from opening with topic sentences. However, positioning the topic sentence at the end of a paragraph is more logical when the paragraph identifies a number of specific details that accumulate evidence and then culminates with a generalization. While paragraphs with extremely obvious main ideas need no topic sentences, more often—and particularly for students learning to write—the topic sentence is the most important sentence in the paragraph. It not only communicates the main idea quickly to readers; it also helps writers produce and control information.

Conventions of Standard English Spelling

Homophones

Homophones are words that have different meanings and spellings, but sound the same. These can be confusing for English Language Learners (ELLs) and beginning students, but even native English-speaking adults can find them problematic unless informed by context. Whereas listeners must rely entirely on context to *differentiate* spoken homophone meanings, readers with good spelling knowledge have a distinct advantage since homophones are spelled differently. For instance, *their* means belonging to them; *there* indicates location; and *they're* is a contraction of *they are*; despite different meanings, they all sound the same. *Lacks* can be a plural noun or a present-tense, third-person singular verb; either way it refers to absence—*deficiencies* as a plural noun, and *is deficient in* as a verb. But *lax* is an adjective that means loose, slack, relaxed, uncontrolled, or negligent. These two spellings, derivations, and meanings are completely different. With speech, listeners cannot know spelling and must use context; but with print, readers with spelling knowledge can differentiate them with or without context.

Homonyms and Homographs

Homophones are words that sound the same in speech but have different spellings and meanings. For example, *to, too,* and *two* all sound alike, but have three different spellings and meanings. Homophones with different spellings are also called **heterographs. Homographs** are words that are spelled identically but have different meanings. If they also have different pronunciations, they are **heteronyms.** For instance, *tear* pronounced one way means a drop of liquid formed by the eye; pronounced another way, it means to rip. Homophones that are also homographs are **homonyms**. For example, *bark* can mean the outside of a tree or a dog's vocalization; both meanings have the same spelling. *Stalk* can mean a plant stem or to pursue and/or harass somebody; these are spelled and pronounced the same. *Rose* can mean a flower or the past tense of *rise.* Many non-linguists confuse things by using "homonym" to mean sets of words that are homophones but not homographs, and also those that are homographs but not homophones.

The word *row* can mean to use oars to propel a boat; a linear arrangement of objects or print; or an argument. It is pronounced the same with the first two meanings, but differently with the third. Because it is spelled identically regardless, all three meanings are homographs. However, the two meanings pronounced the same are homophones, whereas the one with the different pronunciation is a heteronym. By contrast, the word *read* means to peruse language, whereas the word *reed* refers to a marsh plant. Because these are pronounced the same way, they are homophones; because they are spelled differently, they are **heterographs**. Homonyms are both homophones and homographs—pronounced and spelled identically, but with different meanings. One distinction between homonyms is of those with separate, unrelated etymologies, called "true" homonyms, e.g. *skate* meaning a fish or *skate* meaning to glide over ice/water. Those with common origins are called polysemes or polysemous homonyms, e.g. the *mouth* of an animal/human or of a river.

Irregular Plurals

One type of irregular English plural involves words that are spelled the same whether they are singular or plural. These include *deer, fish, salmon, trout, sheep, moose, offspring, species, aircraft,* etc. The spelling rule for making these words plural is simple: they do not change. Another type of irregular English plurals does change from singular to plural form, but it does not take regular English *–s* or *–es* endings. Their irregular plural endings are largely derived from grammatical and spelling conventions in the other languages of their origins, like Latin, German, and vowel shifts and other linguistic mutations. Some examples of these words and their irregular plurals include *child* and *children; die* and *dice; foot* and *feet; goose* and *geese; louse* and *lice; man* and *men; mouse* and *mice; ox* and *oxen; person* and *people; tooth* and *teeth;* and *woman* and *women.*

Contractions

Contractions are formed by joining two words together, omitting one or more letters from one of the component words, and replacing the omitted words with an apostrophe. An obvious yet often forgotten rule for spelling contractions is to place the apostrophe where the letters were omitted; for example, spelling errors like *did'nt* for *didn't. Didn't* is a contraction of *did not.* Therefore, the apostrophe replaces the "o" that is omitted from the "not" component. Another common error is confusing contractions with **possessives** because both include apostrophes, e.g. spelling the possessive *its* as "it's," which is a contraction of "it is"; spelling the possessive *their* as "they're," a contraction of "they are"; spelling the possessive *whose* as "who's," a contraction of "who is"; or spelling the possessive *your* as "you're," a contraction of "you are."

Frequently Misspelled Words

One source of spelling errors is not knowing whether to drop the final letter *e* from a word when its form is changed by adding an ending to indicate the past tense or progressive participle of a verb, converting an adjective to an adverb, a noun to an adjective, etc. Some words retain the final *e* when another syllable is added; others lose it. For example, *true* becomes *truly, argue* becomes *arguing, come* becomes *coming, write* becomes *writing,* and *judge* becomes *judging.* In these examples, the final *e* is dropped before adding the ending. But *severe* becomes *severely, complete* becomes *completely, sincere* becomes *sincerely, argue* becomes *argued,* and *care* becomes *careful.* In these instances, the final *e* is retained before adding the ending. Note that some words, like *argue* in these examples, drops the final *e* when the *–ing* ending is added to indicate the participial form; but the regular past tense ending of *–ed* makes it *argued,* in effect, replacing the final *e* so that *arguing* is spelled without an *e* but *argued* is spelled with one.

Some English words contain the vowel combination of *ei,* while some contain the reverse combination of *ie.* Many people confuse these. Some examples include these:

> *ceiling, conceive, leisure, receive, weird, their, either, foreign, sovereign, neither, neighbors, seize, forfeit, counterfeit, height, weight, protein,* and *freight*

Words with *ie* include *piece, believe, chief, field, friend, grief, relief, mischief, siege, niece, priest, fierce, pierce, achieve, retrieve, hygiene, science,* and *diesel.* A rule that also functions as a mnemonic device is "I before E except after C, or when sounded like A as in 'neighbor' or 'weigh'." However, it is obvious from the list above that many exceptions exist.

Many people often misspell certain words by confusing whether they have the vowel *a, e,* or *i,* frequently in the middle syllable of three-syllable words or beginning the last syllables that sound the same in different words. For example, in the following correctly-spelled words, the vowel in boldface is the one people typically get wrong by substituting one or either of the others for it:

> _cem**e**tery, quant**i**ties, ben**e**fit, priv**i**lege, unpleas**a**nt, sep**a**rate, independ**e**nt, excell**e**nt, cat**e**gories, indispens**a**ble,_ and _irrelev**a**nt_

The words with final syllables that sound the same when spoken but are spelled differently include *unpleasant, independent, excellent,* and *irrelevant.* Another source of misspelling is whether or not to double consonants when adding suffixes. For example, we double the last consonant before *–ed* and *–ing* endings in *controlled, beginning, forgetting, admitted, occurred, referred,* and *hopping;* but we do not double the last consonant before the suffix in *shining, poured, sweating, loving, hating, smiling,* and *hoping.*

One way in which people misspell certain words frequently is by failing to include letters that are silent. Some letters are articulated when pronounced correctly but elided in some people's speech, which then transfers to their writing. Another source of misspelling is the converse: people add extraneous letters. For example, some people omit the silent *u* in _g**u**arantee,_ overlook the first *r* in _su**r**prise,_ leave out the *z* in _reali**z**e,_ fail to double the *m* in _recom**m**end,_ leave out the middle *i* from _asp**i**rin,_ and exclude the *p* from _tem**p**erature._ The converse error, adding extra letters, is common in words like *until* by adding a second *l* at the end; or by inserting a superfluous syllabic *a* or *e* in the middle of *athletic,* reproducing a common mispronunciation.

Use Grammar to Enhance Clarity in Writing

Using Correct Capitalization

The first word of any document, and of each new sentence, is capitalized. Proper nouns, like names and adjectives derived from proper nouns, should also be capitalized. Here are some examples:

- Grand Canyon
- Pacific Palisades
- Golden Gate Bridge
- Freudian slip
- Shakespearian, Spenserian, or Petrarchan sonnet
- Irish song

Some exceptions are adjectives, originally derived from proper nouns, which through time and usage are no longer capitalized, like *quixotic, herculean*, or *draconian*. Capitals draw attention to specific instances of people, places, and things. Some categories that should be capitalized include the following:

- Brand names
- Companies
- Weekdays
- Months
- Governmental divisions or agencies
- Historical eras
- Major historical events
- Holidays
- Institutions
- Famous buildings
- Ships and other manmade constructions
- Natural and manmade landmarks
- Territories
- Nicknames
- Epithets
- Organizations
- Planets
- Nationalities
- Tribes
- Religions
- Names of religious deities
- Roads
- Special occasions, like the Cannes Film Festival or the Olympic Games

Exceptions

Related to American government, capitalize the noun Congress but not the related adjective congressional. Capitalize the noun U.S. Constitution, but not the related adjective constitutional. Many experts advise leaving the adjectives federal and state in lowercase, as in federal regulations or state water board, and only capitalizing these when they are parts of official titles or names, like Federal Communications Commission or State Water Resources Control Board. While the names of the other planets in the solar system are capitalized as names, Earth is more often capitalized only when being described specifically as a planet, like Earth's orbit, but lowercase otherwise since it is used not only as a proper noun but also to mean *land, ground, soil*, etc. While the name of the Bible should be capitalized, the adjective biblical should not. Regarding biblical subjects, the words heaven, hell, devil, and satanic should not be capitalized. Although race names like Caucasian, African-American, Navajo, Eskimo, East Indian, etc. are capitalized, white and black as races are not.

Names of animal species or breeds are not capitalized unless they include a proper noun. Then, only the proper noun is capitalized. Antelope, black bear, and yellow-bellied sapsucker are not capitalized. However, Bengal tiger, German shepherd, Australian shepherd, French poodle, and Russian blue cat are capitalized.

Other than planets, celestial bodies like the sun, moon, and stars are not capitalized. Medical conditions like tuberculosis or diabetes are lowercase; again, exceptions are proper nouns, like Epstein-Barr syndrome, Alzheimer's disease, and Down syndrome. Seasons and related terms like winter solstice or autumnal equinox are lowercase. Plants, including fruits and vegetables, like poinsettia, celery, or avocados, are not capitalized unless they include proper names, like Douglas fir, Jerusalem artichoke, Damson plums, or Golden Delicious apples.

Titles and Names
When official titles precede names, they should be capitalized, except when there is a comma between the title and name. But if a title follows or replaces a name, it should not be capitalized. For example, "the president" without a name is not capitalized, as in "The president addressed Congress." But with a name it is capitalized, like "President Obama addressed Congress." Or, "Chair of the Board Janet Yellen was appointed by President Obama." One exception is that some publishers and writers nevertheless capitalize President, Queen, Pope, etc., when these are not accompanied by names to show respect for these high offices. However, many writers in America object to this practice for violating democratic principles of equality. Occupations before full names are not capitalized, like owner Mark Cuban, director Martin Scorsese, or coach Roger McDowell.

Some universal rules for capitalization in composition titles include capitalizing the following:

- The first and last words of the title
- Forms of the verb *to be* and all other verbs
- Pronouns
- The word *not*

Universal rules for NOT capitalizing in titles include the articles *the, a,* or *an;* the conjunctions *and, or,* or *nor,* and the preposition *to,* or *to* as part of the infinitive form of a verb. The exception to all of these is UNLESS any of them is the first or last word in the title, in which case they are capitalized. Other words are subject to differences of opinion and differences among various stylebooks or methods. These include *as, but, if,* and *or,* which some capitalize and others do not. Some authorities say no preposition should ever be capitalized; some say prepositions five or more letters long should be capitalized. The *Associated Press Stylebook* advises capitalizing prepositions longer than three letters (like *about, across,* or *with*).

Using Apostrophes with Possessive Nouns Correctly
Possessive forms indicate possession, i.e. that something belongs to or is owned by someone or something. As such, the most common parts of speech to be used in possessive form are adjectives, nouns, and pronouns. The rule for correctly spelling/punctuating possessive nouns and proper nouns is with *-'s,* like "the woman's briefcase" or "Frank's hat." With possessive adjectives, however, apostrophes are not used: these include *my, your, his, her, its, our,* and *their,* like "my book," "your friend," "his car," "her house," "its contents," "our family," or "their property." Possessive pronouns include *mine, yours, his,*

hers, its, ours, and *theirs.* These also have no apostrophes. The difference is that possessive adjectives take direct objects, whereas possessive pronouns replace them. For example, instead of using two possessive adjectives in a row, as in "I forgot my book, so Blanca let me use her book," which reads monotonously, replacing the second one with a possessive pronoun reads better: "I forgot my book, so Blanca let me use hers."

Pronouns

There are three pronoun cases: subjective case, objective case, and possessive case. Pronouns as subjects are pronouns that replace the subject of the sentence, such as *I, you, he, she, it, we, they* and *who.* Pronouns as objects replace the object of the sentence, such as *me, you, him, her, it, us, them,* and *whom.* Pronouns that show possession are *mine, yours, hers, its, ours, theirs,* and *whose.* The following are examples of different pronoun cases:

- **Subject pronoun:** She ate the cake for her birthday. I saw the movie.
- **Object pronoun:** You gave me the card last weekend. She gave the picture to him.
- **Possessive pronoun:** That bracelet you found yesterday is mine. His name was Casey.

Adjectives

Adjectives are descriptive words that modify nouns or pronouns. They may occur before or after the nouns or pronouns they modify in sentences. For example, in "This is a big house," *big* is an adjective modifying or describing the noun *house.* In "This house is big," the adjective is at the end of the sentence rather than preceding the noun it modifies.

A rule of punctuation that applies to adjectives is to separate a series of adjectives with commas. For example, "Their home was a large, rambling, old, white, two-story house." A comma should never separate the last adjective from the noun, though.

Adverbs

Whereas adjectives modify and describe nouns or pronouns, **adverbs** modify and describe adjectives, verbs, or other adverbs. Adverbs can be thought of as answers to questions in that they describe when, where, how, how often, how much, or to what extent.

Many (but not all) adjectives can be converted to adverbs by adding *–ly.* For example, in "She is a quick learner," *quick* is an adjective modifying *learner.* In "She learns quickly," *quickly* is an adverb modifying *learns.* One exception is *fast. Fast* is an adjective in "She is a fast learner." However, *–ly* is never added to the word *fast*; it retains the same form as an adverb in "She learns fast."

Verbs

A **verb** is a word or phrase that expresses action, feeling, or state of being. Verbs explain what their subject is *doing.* Three different types of verbs used in a sentence are action verbs, linking verbs, and helping verbs.

Action verbs show a physical or mental action. Some examples of action verbs are *play, type, jump, write, examine, study, invent, develop,* and *taste.* The following example uses an action verb:

> Kat *imagines* that she is a mermaid in the ocean.

The verb *imagines* explains what Kat is doing: she is imagining being a mermaid.

Linking verbs connect the subject to the predicate without expressing an action. The following sentence shows an example of a linking verb:

> The mango *tastes* sweet.

The verb *tastes* is a linking verb. The mango doesn't *do* the tasting, but the word *taste* links the mango to its predicate, sweet. Most linking verbs can also be used as action verbs, such as *smell, taste, look, seem, grow,* and *sound.* Saying something *is* something else is also an example of a linking verb. For example, if we were to say, "Peaches is a dog," the verb *is* would be a linking verb in this sentence, since it links the subject to its predicate.

Helping verbs are verbs that help the main verb in a sentence. Examples of helping verbs are *be, am, is, was, have, has, do, did, can, could, may, might, should,* and *must,* among others. The following are examples of helping verbs:

> Jessica *is* planning a trip to Hawaii.
>
> Brenda *does* not like camping.
>
> Xavier *should* go to the dance tonight.

Notice that after each of these helping verbs is the main verb of the sentence: *planning, like,* and *go.* Helping verbs usually show an aspect of time.

Subject-Verb Agreement

Lack of subject-verb agreement is a very common grammatical error. One of the most common instances is when people use a series of nouns as a compound subject with a singular instead of a plural verb. Here is an example:

> Identifying the best books, locating the sellers with the lowest prices, and paying for them *is* difficult

instead of saying "*are* difficult." Additionally, when a sentence subject is compound, the verb is plural:

> He and his cousins *were* at the reunion.

However, if the conjunction connecting two or more singular nouns or pronouns is "or" or "nor," the verb must be singular to agree:

> That pen or another one like it is in the desk drawer.

If a compound subject includes both a singular noun and a plural one, and they are connected by "or" or "nor," the verb must agree with the subject closest to the verb: "Sally or her sisters go jogging daily"; but "Her sisters or Sally goes jogging daily."

Simply put, singular subjects require singular verbs and plural subjects require plural verbs. A common source of agreement errors is not identifying the sentence subject correctly. For example, people often write sentences incorrectly like, "The group of students *were* complaining about the test." The subject is not the plural "students" but the singular "group." Therefore, the correct sentence should read, "The group of students *was* complaining about the test." The converse also applies, for example, in this incorrect sentence: "The facts in that complicated court case *is* open to question." The subject of the sentence is not the singular "case" but the plural "facts." Hence the sentence would correctly be written:

"The facts in that complicated court case *are* open to question." New writers should not be misled by the distance between the subject and verb, especially when another noun with a different number intervenes as in these examples. The verb must agree with the subject, not the noun closest to it.

Pronoun-Antecedent Agreement

Pronouns within a sentence must refer specifically to one noun, known as the **antecedent.** Sometimes, if there are multiple nouns within a sentence, it may be difficult to ascertain which noun belongs to the pronoun. It's important that the pronouns always clearly reference the nouns in the sentence so as not to confuse the reader. Here's an example of an unclear pronoun reference:

> After Catherine cut Libby's hair, David bought her some lunch.

The pronoun in the examples above is *her*. The pronoun could either be referring to *Catherine* or *Libby*. Here are some ways to write the above sentence with a clear pronoun reference:

> After Catherine cut Libby's hair, David bought Libby some lunch.

> David bought Libby some lunch after Catherine cut Libby's hair.

But many times the pronoun will clearly refer to its antecedent, like the following:

> After David cut Catherine's hair, he bought her some lunch.

Conventions of Standard English Punctuation

Ellipses

Ellipses (. . .) signal omitted text when quoting. Some writers also use them to show a thought trailing off, but this should not be overused outside of dialogue. An example of an ellipses would be if someone is quoting a phrase out of a professional source but wants to omit part of the phrase that isn't needed: "Dr. Skim's analysis of pollen inside the body is clearly a myth . . . that speaks to the environmental guilt of our society."

Commas

Commas separate words or phrases in a series of three or more. The Oxford comma is the last comma in a series. Many people omit this last comma, but many times it causes confusion. Here is an example:

> I love my sisters, the Queen of England and Madonna.

This example without the comma implies that the "Queen of England and Madonna" are the speaker's sisters. However, if the speaker was trying to say that they love their sisters, the Queen of England, as well as Madonna, there should be a comma after "Queen of England" to signify this.

Commas also separate two coordinate adjectives ("big, heavy dog") but not cumulative ones, which should be arranged in a particular order for them to make sense ("beautiful ancient ruins").

A comma ends the first of two independent clauses connected by conjunctions. Here is an example:

> I ate a bowl of tomato soup, and I was hungry very shortly after.

Here are some brief rules for commas:

- Commas follow introductory words like however, furthermore, well, why, and actually, among others.
- Commas go between city and state: Houston, Texas.
- If using a comma between a surname and Jr. or Sr. or a degree like M.D., also follow the whole name with a comma: "Martin Luther King, Jr., wrote that."
- A comma follows a dependent clause beginning a sentence: "Although she was very small, . . ."
- Nonessential modifying words/phrases/clauses are enclosed by commas: "Wendy, who is Peter's sister, closed the window."
- Commas introduce or interrupt direct quotations: "She said, 'I hate him.' 'Why,' I asked, 'do you hate him?'"

Semicolons

Semicolons are used to connect two independent clauses, but should never be used in the place of a comma. They can replace periods between two closely connected sentences: "Call back tomorrow; it can wait until then." When writing items in a series and one or more of them contains internal commas, separate them with semicolons, like the following:

> People came from Springfield, Illinois; Alamo, Tennessee; Moscow, Idaho; and other locations.

Hyphens

Here are some rules concerning **hyphens**:

- Compound adjectives like state-of-the-art or off-campus are hyphenated.
- Original compound verbs and nouns are often hyphenated, like "throne-sat," "video-gamed," "no-meater."
- Adjectives ending in *–ly* are often hyphenated, like "family-owned" or "friendly-looking."
- "Five years old" is not hyphenated, but singular ages like "five-year-old" are.
- Hyphens can clarify. For example, in "stolen vehicle report," "stolen-vehicle report" clarifies that "stolen" modifies "vehicle," not "report."
- Compound numbers twenty-one through ninety-nine are spelled with hyphens.
- Prefixes before proper nouns/adjectives are hyphenated, like "mid-September" and "trans-Pacific."

Parentheses

Parentheses enclose information such as an aside or more clarifying information: "She ultimately replied (after deliberating for an hour) that she was undecided." They are also used to insert short, in-text definitions or acronyms: "His FBS (fasting blood sugar) was higher than normal." When parenthetical information ends the sentence, the period follows the parentheses: "We received new funds ($25,000)." Only put periods within parentheses if the whole sentence is inside them: "Look at this. (You'll be astonished.)" However, this can also be acceptable as a clause: "Look at this (you'll be astonished)." Although parentheses appear to be part of the sentence subject, they are not, and do not change subject-verb agreement: "Will (and his dog) was there."

Quotation Marks
Quotation marks are typically used when someone is quoting a direct word or phrase someone else writes or says. Additionally, quotation marks should be used for the titles of poems, short stories, songs, articles, chapters, and other shorter works. When quotations include punctuation, periods and commas should *always* be placed inside of the quotation marks.

When a quotation contains another quotation inside of it, the outer quotation should be enclosed in double quotation marks and the inner quotation should be enclosed in single quotation marks. For example: "Timmy was begging, 'Don't go! Don't leave!'" When using both double and single quotation marks, writers will find that many word-processing programs may automatically insert enough space between the single and double quotation marks to be visible for clearer reading. But if this is not the case, the writer should write/type them with enough space between to keep them from looking like three single quotation marks. Additionally, non-standard usages, terms used in an unusual fashion, and technical terms are often clarified by quotation marks. Here are some examples:

> My "friend," Dr. Sims, has been micromanaging me again.
>
> This way of extracting oil has been dubbed "fracking."

Apostrophes
One use of the **apostrophe** is followed by an *s* to indicate possession, like *Mrs. White's home* or *our neighbor's dog*. When using the *'s* after names or nouns that also end in the letter *s*, no single rule applies: some experts advise adding both the apostrophe and the *s*, like "the Jones's house," while others prefer using only the apostrophe and omitting the additional *s*, like "the Jones' house." The wisest expert advice is to pick one formula or the other and then apply it consistently. Newspapers and magazines often use *'s* after common nouns ending with *s*, but add only the apostrophe after proper nouns or names ending with *s*. One common error is to place the apostrophe before a name's final *s* instead of after it: "Ms. Hasting's book" is incorrect if the name is Ms. Hastings.

Plural nouns should not include apostrophes (e.g. "apostrophe's"). Exceptions are to clarify atypical plurals, like verbs used as nouns: "These are the do's and don'ts." Irregular plurals that do not end in *s* always take apostrophe-*s*, not *s*-apostrophe—a common error, as in "childrens' toys," which should be "children's toys." Compound nouns like mother-in-law, when they are singular and possessive, are followed by apostrophe-*s*, like "your mother-in-law's coat." When a compound noun is plural and possessive, the plural is formed before the apostrophe-*s*, like "your sisters-in-laws' coats." When two people named possess the same thing, use apostrophe-*s* after the second name only, like "Dennis and Pam's house."

Sentence Structures

<u>Incomplete Sentences</u>
Four types of incomplete sentences are sentence fragments, run-on sentences, subject-verb and/or pronoun-antecedent disagreement, and non-parallel structure.

Sentence fragments are caused by absent subjects, absent verbs, or dangling/uncompleted dependent clauses. Every sentence must have a subject and a verb to be complete. An example of a fragment is "Raining all night long," because there is no subject present. "It was raining all night long" is one correction. Another example of a sentence fragment is the second part in "Many scientists think in unusual ways. Einstein, for instance." The second phrase is a fragment because it has no verb. One correction is "Many scientists, like Einstein, think in unusual ways." Finally, look for "cliffhanger" words like *if, when, because,* or *although* that introduce dependent clauses, which cannot stand alone without an independent clause. For example, to correct the sentence fragment "If you get home early," add an independent clause: "If you get home early, we can go dancing."

Run-On Sentences

A **run-on sentence** combines two or more complete sentences without punctuating them correctly or separating them. For example, a run-on sentence caused by a lack of punctuation is the following:

> There is a malfunction in the computer system however there is nobody available right now who knows how to troubleshoot it.

One correction is, "There is a malfunction in the computer system; however, there is nobody available right now who knows how to troubleshoot it." Another is, "There is a malfunction in the computer system. However, there is nobody available right now who knows how to troubleshoot it."

An example of a comma splice of two sentences is the following:

> Jim decided not to take the bus, he walked home.

Replacing the comma with a period or a semicolon corrects this. Commas that try and separate two independent clauses without a contraction are considered **comma splices**.

Parallel Sentence Structures

Parallel structure in a sentence matches the forms of sentence components. Any sentence containing more than one description or phrase should keep them consistent in wording and form. Readers can easily follow writers' ideas when they are written in parallel structure, making it an important element of correct sentence construction. For example, this sentence lacks parallelism: "Our coach is a skilled manager, a clever strategist, and works hard." The first two phrases are parallel, but the third is not. Correction: "Our coach is a skilled manager, a clever strategist, and a hard worker." Now all three phrases match in form. Here is another example:

> Fred intercepted the ball, escaped tacklers, and a touchdown was scored.

This is also non-parallel. Here is the sentence corrected:

> Fred intercepted the ball, escaped tacklers, and scored a touchdown.

Sentence Fluency

For fluent composition, writers must use a variety of sentence types and structures, and also ensure that they smoothly flow together when they are read. To accomplish this, they must first be able to identify fluent writing when they read it. This includes being able to distinguish among simple, compound, complex, and compound-complex sentences in text; to observe variations among sentence types, lengths, and beginnings; and to notice figurative language and understand how it augments sentence length and imparts musicality. Once students/writers recognize superior fluency, they should revise their own writing to be more readable and fluent. They must be able to apply acquired skills to revisions before being able to apply them to new drafts.

One strategy for revising writing to increase its sentence fluency is flipping sentences. This involves rearranging the word order in a sentence without deleting, changing, or adding any words. For example, the student or other writer who has written the sentence, "We went bicycling on Saturday" can revise it to, "On Saturday, we went bicycling." Another technique is using appositives. An appositive is a phrase or word that renames or identifies another adjacent word or phrase. Writers can revise for sentence fluency by inserting main phrases/words from one shorter sentence into another shorter sentence, combining them into one longer sentence, e.g. from "My cat Peanut is a gray and brown tabby. He loves hunting rats." to "My cat Peanut, a gray and brown tabby, loves hunting rats." Revisions can also connect shorter sentences by using conjunctions and commas and removing repeated words: "Scott likes eggs. Scott is allergic to eggs" becomes "Scott likes eggs, but he is allergic to them."

One technique for revising writing to increase sentence fluency is "padding" short, simple sentences by adding phrases that provide more details specifying why, how, when, and/or where something took place. For example, a writer might have these two simple sentences: "I went to the market. I purchased a cake." To revise these, the writer can add the following informative dependent and independent clauses and prepositional phrases, respectively: "Before my mother woke up, I sneaked out of the house and went to the supermarket. As a birthday surprise, I purchased a cake for her." When revising sentences to make them longer, writers must also punctuate them correctly to change them from simple sentences to compound, complex, or compound-complex sentences.

Skills Writers Can Employ to Increase Fluency

One way writers can increase fluency is by varying the beginnings of sentences. Writers do this by starting most of their sentences with different words and phrases rather than monotonously repeating the same ones across multiple sentences. Another way writers can increase fluency is by varying the lengths of sentences. Since run-on sentences are incorrect, writers make sentences longer by also converting them from simple to compound, complex, and compound-complex sentences. The coordination and subordination involved in these also give the text more variation and interest, hence more fluency. Here are a few more ways writers can increase fluency:

- Varying the transitional language and conjunctions used makes sentences more fluent.
- Writing sentences with a variety of rhythms by using prepositional phrases.
- Varying sentence structure adds fluency.

Writing Prompt

In response to the following prompt, write a 300- to 600-word essay.

> Substance abuse recovery centers in Florida have doubled in the past two years. Additionally, the centers that already existed are filled to the maximum occupancy. In order to accommodate the patients, some recovery centers are expanding their residencies and adding more staff. The reason for this rise in recovery centers speaks to the state of our nation with the abuse of drugs and alcohol. The substance abuse problem is worse than ever before and will only continue to grow if we allow the trafficking and consumption of drugs to go unpunished.

Write a response in which you identify your stance on the argument above. Once you've identified your stance, use concrete evidence to support your argument.

Greetings!

First, we would like to give a huge "thank you" for choosing us and this study guide for your CBEST exam. We hope that it will lead you to success on this exam and for your years to come.

Our team has tried to make your preparations as thorough as possible by covering all of the topics you should be expected to know. In addition, our writers attempted to create practice questions identical to what you will see on the day of your actual test. We have also included many test-taking strategies to help you learn the material, maintain the knowledge, and take the test with confidence.

We strive for excellence in our products, and if you have any comments or concerns over the quality of something in this study guide, please send us an email so that we may improve.

As you continue forward in life, we would like to remain alongside you with other books and study guides in our library. We are continually producing and updating study guides in several different subjects. If you are looking for something in particular, all of our products are available on Amazon. You may also send us an email!

Sincerely,
APEX Test Prep
info@apexprep.com

FREE

Free Study Tips DVD

In addition to the tips and content in this guide, we have created a FREE DVD with helpful study tips to further assist your exam preparation. **This FREE Study Tips DVD provides you with top-notch tips to conquer your exam and reach your goals.**

Our simple request in exchange for the strategy-packed DVD is that you email us your feedback about our study guide. We would love to hear what you thought about the guide, and we welcome any and all feedback—positive, negative, or neutral. It is our #1 goal to provide you with top quality products and customer service.

To receive your **FREE Study Tips DVD**, email freedvd@apexprep.com. Please put "FREE DVD" in the subject line and put the following in the email:

a. The name of the study guide you purchased.

b. Your rating of the study guide on a scale of 1-5, with 5 being the highest score.

c. Any thoughts or feedback about your study guide.

d. Your first and last name and your mailing address, so we know where to send your free DVD!

Thank you!

Made in the USA
Las Vegas, NV
21 October 2020

10207998R00096